MAKING THE BLACK ATLANTIC

Britain and the African Diaspora

JAMES WALVIN

CASSELL
London and New York

Cassell

Wellington House, 125 Strand, London, WC2R 0BB

370 Lexington Avenue, New York, NY 10017–6550

First published 2000

British Library Cataloguing-in-Publication Data
A catalogue record for this book is available from the British Library.

ISBN   0–304–70216–1 (hardback)
         0–304–70217–X (paperback)

Library of Congress Cataloging-in-Publication Data
Walvin, James.
   Making the Black Atlantic: Britain and the African diaspora/
James Walvin.
      p.   cm. — (The Black Atlantic)
   Includes bibliographical references and index.
   ISBN 0–304–70216–1 (hb.). — ISBN 0–304–70217–X (pbk.)
   1. Slave-trade—Great Britain. 2. Slave-trade—North Atlantic region.
3. Slave-trade—Africa, West. I. Title. II. Series.
HT1161.W355 2000
382'.44—dc21   99–27606
                                                              CIP

Designed and typeset by Ben Cracknell Studios

Printed and bound in Great Britain by Biddles Ltd, Guildford and King's Lynn

Making the Black Atlantic

THE BLACK ATLANTIC

General Editor: Polly Rewt, The Open University and University of Stirling

Series Advisers: Caryl Phillips, novelist; David Dabydeen, Centre for Caribbean Studies, University of Warwick; Vincent Carretta, Professor of English, University of Maryland; Angus Calder, writer.

The cultural and theoretical parameters of the Black Atlantic world are explored and treated critically in this timely series. It offers students, scholars and general readers essential texts which focus on the international black experience. The broad scope of the series is innovative and ambitious, treating literary, historical, biographical, musical and visual arts subjects from an interdisciplinary and cross-cultural perspective.

The books address current debates on what constitutes the Black Atlantic, both geographically and theoretically. They include anthologized primary material and collections of seminal critical value to courses on the African diaspora and related subjects. They will also appeal more widely to a readership interested in biographical and other material that presents scholarship accessibly.

Also in the series:
Nancy Priscilla Naro, *From Slavery to Farming: Fashioning Freedom in Brazil*
Alasdair Pettinger (editor), *Always Elsewhere: Travels of the Black Atlantic*
James Walvin, *An African's Life: The Life and Times of Olaudah Equiano, 1745–1797*

CONTENTS

ACKNOWLEDGEMENTS

The ideas which inform this book have been tried out in a number of academic gatherings. I am especially indebted to two York colleagues, Alan Forrest and Allen Warren, for permission to travel and work in distant locations. I am happy to thank Bernard Porter and his colleagues at the University of Newcastle for the invitation to give three lectures which form the core of this book. I wrote much of the text at the Australian National University in Canberra, where I was the guest of the History Programme in the Research School in the Social Sciences; I would like to thank Pat Jalland, Paul Bourke, Barry Higman and Bev Gallina in particular for their help. I am also immensely grateful to Iain McCalman, Director of the Humanities Research Centre at ANU, and to his colleagues for practical help and assistance (in addition to friendly companionship). Caryl Phillips kindly invited me to speak to the Barnard Forum on Migration at Barnard College, New York City, where I discussed some of the ideas in this book. Sandra Margolies has been an exemplary editor to work with and has greatly helped to improve the final text. I am grateful for her efforts.

I have also discussed some of the issues in this book at two meetings in the Liverpool Maritime Museum, and among my students in York. For many years, Gad Heuman has proved himself a marvellous colleague to work with and, better still, has remained a steadfast friend. Finally, and above all others, I dedicate this book to Arran Joshua Tate.

James Walvin
March 1999

INTRODUCTION

The story of Atlantic slavery has become well known in recent years. Not long ago, it was the preserve of academic scholars. Now the topic is familiar to millions of people via novels, TV and, more recently, major movies. However the story is told, Atlantic slavery remains an astonishing historical episode. Indeed it would be hard for even the most experienced and sensational film-maker or novelist to devise a more dramatic and terrible story than the reality which unfolded in the Atlantic between the early sixteenth and the mid-nineteenth centuries. Moreover the British were at the heart of this story.

It is now beyond question that Atlantic slavery was a critical element in the shaping of the Americas. What is more, it was a unique form of slavery. It consisted of Africans, and their descendants born in the Americas, who unlocked the economic potential of the tropical and semi-tropical Americas for the benefit of European, North and South American commercial interests.

In the course of Atlantic slavery, some 12 million Africans were forced into the slave ships bound for the Americas. The consequences of that vast enforced migration were profound and far-reaching across three continents. First and foremost, Africa suffered a massive haemorrhage of people, with manifold and as yet inadequately understood consequences. Secondly, large areas of the Americas came to be populated by African people and their offspring. Thirdly, African labour brought into being new economies, the benefits from which flowed back largely to Europe (and to a number of major commercial interests in North and South America).

The main objective here is to discuss the British involvement in this historical process. The British played a critical (if not pioneering) role:

British ships carried millions of Africans into slavery across the Atlantic; British colonies and settlements were made viable by absorbing large numbers of African slaves; British material well-being was greatly enhanced by the sweat of those same slaves. It is, however, tempting to imagine that the British – thousands of miles distant from the main stage of slavery – were effectively removed from this process. One purpose of this book is to show that, on the contrary, the role played by the British in the shaping of the enslaved Atlantic was crucial. Of course they were not alone; they were joined at various times (and preceded) in slaving enterprises by all the major European maritime powers. Yet at the height of the Atlantic slave system, the British shipped more Africans than any other nation; their slave colonies disgorged produce (and its associated prosperity) on an unparalleled scale, and Britain itself benefited from slavery to a degree which largely goes unrecognized.

The process of transporting enslaved African peoples, and the consequent reshaping of those peoples in their enforced exiles, has become known as the African diaspora, a concept which has gained widespread currency in the past 30 years thanks to the work of George Shepperson and others. It was a process which saw the development of new black populations – enslaved and freed – throughout the Americas. This book seeks to locate that diaspora as a central British concern in the Atlantic world. As an effort to describe the historical relationship between the British and their enslaved peoples in the Americas (in the West Indies and in North America), it is not merely an account of the history of slavery in the British Americas, for the African diaspora had profound effects on Britain itself. Much of Britain's Atlantic pre-eminence by the mid-eighteenth century was built on the backs of those enslaved African peoples. What lay behind the rise of Bristol and Liverpool? What underpinned a great slice of London's commercial successes in the American colonies? It was, of course, Africans. It is easy to overlook this fact, not least because Africa and the American slave colonies were thousands of miles away from the British metropolis. Despite periodic reminders – returning slave ships, planters coming 'home' awash with their slave-based wealth, the occasional black servant/slave in London or Bristol – the slave system was out of sight and, too often, out of mind.

It is generally true that historians of Britain have persistently overlooked or minimized the degree to which British life in the seventeenth and eighteenth centuries was integrated into the Atlantic slave system. What we have learned of slavery has come, by and large, from historians of

Africa, the Americas and, recently, from a team of outstanding economic historians concerned with details of maritime history. With a few striking exceptions British historians have tended to regard slavery as a distant (colonial, imperial, American, maritime) issue, of only marginal or passing interest to mainstream Britain.

There are dangers, however, in abstracting the British part of a historical process which was highly integrated and international. The African diaspora, and the creation of slavery in the Americas, formed a cohesive international system which drew together the economies and resources of all the major European maritime and colonial powers by integrating the economic and social interests of people on both sides of the Atlantic; from the indigenous peoples of the Americas making contact with European settlers, through to European peoples providing goods and services for the ships destined for Asia and the Americas. It was also a system which drew upon even more distant societies, for example, those of Asia, whose goods and commodities (textiles from India, for example) were transshipped through Europe, and were also used in the bargaining and exchange systems of Atlantic slavery. But the *key* to this integrated Atlantic system was the peoples of Africa – or rather those peoples who were ensnared, in ever larger numbers, in those webs of enslavement which centred on the European trading presence on the African coast.

In writing this book I have tried throughout to write a British history; to persuade the reader that here, in the world of Atlantic slavery, lies a major and formative area of the British historical experience.

James Walvin
March 1999

= 1 =

BEFORE THE BRITISH

Europeans used Africans as slaves long before they perfected the massive enforced migrations across the Atlantic. Moorish Spain, for example, made great use of enslaved labour, and the trade which developed between Christian Europe and the Muslim Mediterranean saw slaves move back and forth from one side to the other. For centuries trans-Sahara slave routes had brought black Africans via Timbuktu to Morocco, and thence into Spain. Slavery continued to thrive in Spain long after it was in decline in northern Europe, a fact confirmed in the legal code *Siete Partidas* of the 1260s. That code regulated slavery in the Spanish Americas until the nineteenth century, though often in transmuted form. However, slaves in Spain and in other parts of the Mediterranean were not solely African. Merchants in both Portugal and on Cadiz sold black slaves, and by the mid-fifteenth century there were noticeable pockets of blacks in Barcelona, Seville and Valencia. Slaves were similarly a common sight in the great Italian trading ports – Genoa, Florence and Venice. Indeed in the late fifteenth century there were an estimated 3000 slaves in Venice alone,[1] and the numbers of black slaves were even greater in the Muslim societies of the southern and eastern Mediterranean.

The Islamic Mediterranean acquired its slaves wherever convenient and available: from Europe (though this source had effectively dried up by the twelfth century), from Central Asia, but, above all, from black Africa. The Nile, the Red Sea and the trans-Saharan trade routes formed the basic trading and communication links with black Africa. This supply of African slaves to the Muslim world continued into the twentieth century.[2] Of course Africa provided many other commodities sought by outside traders besides slaves, notably gold – especially when a number of European states adopted gold currency. But in time black slaves were to become as sought-after as gold itself.

The European urge to make direct maritime contact with black Africa – or to circumnavigate the continent – faced serious navigational and cartographical problems. But the growing information about black Africa – and its apparent commercial potential, proved a powerful spur to European merchant adventurers and their backers. The Portuguese conquest of Ceuta in 1415 (the end of the line for a number of caravan routes to Africa) helped to persuade the Portuguese and their monarch, Henry the Navigator, of the need to seek direct sea routes to West Africa. With this in mind Henry established a base in the south-west of Portugal, close to the expanding port of Lagos, from which he could mastermind the maritime exploration of the West African coast, utilizing the latest improvements in map-making, ship construction and navigational expertise. Taking first the islands of Madeira and then the Azores, the Portuguese explorers pressed on and returned with local artefacts and produce (and black people) to offer their monarch. Each successive venture made it clear that trade, commodities and profits might be had in abundance along the coast. As were black slaves.

Portuguese sailors and merchants moved ever further south, returning with more and more Africans, often taken in surprise, piratical raids, which were all licensed by the Crown. For their part, coastal peoples began to resist these kidnappings. Gradually the Portuguese were forced to purchase Africans (who had normally been enslaved by warfare) from other Africans who realized there was a market to be had. By 1445 the Portuguese had built their first slave castle on Arguin Island, although its main role was to be an entrepôt for gold. From there and from other locations to the south, Africans were fed back to Madeira, the Azores and to Portugal. They came from a coast which stretched from the Senegal to the Gambia rivers (and from the interiors along those rivers). But compared to the vast and powerful interior states of the Mali and the Songhai, with their own extensive slaving systems which stretched south and north, the Portuguese coastal presence seemed puny and unimportant. It was, however, critical for what was to follow: it showed other Europeans that maritime trade to Africa was both possible and practical, and it established a pattern – however tentative – of maritime trade in black humanity.

These early Portuguese slaves were drawn from African Islamic peoples. In about 1471 the Portuguese reached the Akan peoples of the Gold Coast, and there they found other forms of slavery. They also encountered the main source of West African gold. It was there, in 1482, that they built the fortress El Mina (the mine), in the process engrossing perhaps one-half of the region's gold exports, to provide a substantial part of the Portuguese Crown's income. To pay for that gold they sold slaves from the north of Africa (upwards of 12,000 in the years between 1500 and 1535). They also made contact with the King of Kongo and his son, who converted to Christianity. In return for a variety of imported goods, Kongo began to provide slaves (some 2000 to 3000 a year by 1526) for the new Portuguese sugar plantations being developed on the island of São Tomé.[3]

From these small migratory beginnings, black communities began to take root and develop far from their native regions. It was all made possible by growing European maritime power and commercial daring in the eastern Atlantic, and by the willingness of Africans to sell slaves (although some communities refused to do so). The first batches of African slaves had been shipped to Portuguese settlements in the Atlantic islands and to Portugal. Though the numbers were small compared to the waves of Africans which followed, by 1505 some 151,000 had been taken to those destinations. Africans were auctioned publicly in Lisbon, and in 1550 there were an estimated 9500 African slaves in Lisbon itself, amounting perhaps to 10 per cent of the city's population. Both men and women were employed in a range of tasks and most were owned in small numbers. Black slaves attended their owners in public, as drivers, cabmen or general factotums. Even the royal court used Africans in the gardens and the kitchens – King Joao III, for example, had an enslaved black jester. It was very different from the gang slavery which was later to dominate the tropical Americas, but it was a striking black presence nonetheless. One man noted in 1535 that, 'In Evora, it was as if I had been carried off to a city in hell; everywhere I only meet blacks.'

A similar pattern unfolded in Spain (where there was an existing tradition of owning Moorish slaves). Families of means in Andalusia in the early sixteenth century normally had at least two slaves, and men returning from success in early American ventures inevitably made use of slaves.[4] In Seville there may have been a few thousand slaves as early as the 1470s. By 1565 there were 14,500 African slaves within the bishopric of Seville, and in the city itself they formed an estimated 7 per cent of the population. Though they were sold publicly on the streets, local authorities allowed them to meet and socialize in public. Between 1482 and 1516 some 2500 African slaves were imported through Valencia (possibly for work in the regional sugar industry). But in Spain – as in Lisbon – male and female slaves were generally owned and worked in small numbers, not in large slave gangs. They worked as servants and cooks, as escorts and as entertainers, as gardeners, porters, street vendors and shop workers – indeed in whatever capacity seemed appropriate. Though some inevitably found themselves in harsh occupations, they were generally not brutalized by their work as was to be the case in the Americas. Although they were sometimes ridiculed, slaves seem to have moved around easily in public. But their numbers, and the social importance of African slavery within the Iberian peninsular, declined when Africans became ever more important in the Americas in the late sixteenth century.[5]

More significantly, the Portuguese imported Africans into their Atlantic islands, for it was there that they had established sugar cultivation. It was the latest step westward in the slow spread of cane sugar cultivation, from the eastern Mediterranean to Cyprus, southern Italy and Sicily and on into Spain. In the fifteenth and sixteenth centuries, as Europeans broke out of the Mediterranean (thanks in the main to the 'maritime revolution' led by the Portuguese), they took with them crops and labour systems destined for new parts of the world.[6] In Madeira, for example, sugar production began to prosper following the importation of Africans; by 1500 some 2000 slaves worked there (out of a total population of between 15,000 and 18,000).[7] Sugar plantations were also established in the Canaries – granted to Castille after 1479 – and by the early sixteenth century African slaves were being imported there for plantation work, although they worked alongside local, Spanish and free labourers. Even in Atlantic settlements which were unsuitable for sugar cultivation (the Azores and the Cape Verde islands), Africans were imported for a number of local tasks: cotton growing, dye production and food cultivation.

The transformation which was to be most critical occurred in the islands of São Tomé and Príncipe, close to the Equator. Close enough to the African coast to be easily provided with African manpower, São Tomé was quickly converted to sugar production. By 1522 there were upwards of sixty sugar mills on the island. Bigger sugar planters owned as many as 300 slaves each. By the mid-sixteenth century, São Tomé produced more sugar than Madeira. Moreover, on São Tomé – unlike on other islands – a pattern was established which was to be replicated later on the far side of the Atlantic: plantations producing sugar with a labour force that consisted primarily of enslaved Africans. The island suffered, however, from the great disadvantage of distance from the European markets for its produce. The sugar ships took an eternity to battle their way against prevailing winds and current northwards to the Portuguese markets.

Thus, long before Europeans had planted those settlements in the Americas which turned, with ever greater hunger, to Africa for labour, Africans had found themselves scattered around the rim of European settlement and trade in the eastern Atlantic. Old Islamic trading and slaving routes had linked the Mediterranean with Christian Europe, and fashioned a connection – however tenuous – between black Africa and the Christian north. (They had also served to scatter numbers of Africans throughout the world of the early modern Mediterranean, and thence (admittedly in small numbers) to northern Europe – a fact reflected in a host of paintings and graphic imagery.) But it was the maritime and associated commercial changes of the fifteenth century which enabled Europeans, notably the Portuguese and the Spanish, to turn to the commercial potential of Africa with increasing interest (and success). From the earliest days Africans were shipped to Europe and to the Atlantic islands as slaves. They were not transported in vast numbers, but they travelled as a commodity; an item of trade which Europeans found commercially attractive. They could be seen in some numbers in Lisbon and Seville; they helped populate and make fertile the islands of the eastern Atlantic. They even began to make their presence felt in northern Europe.

Africans were also to be found in England and Scotland in the sixteenth century, many almost certainly having got there via Spain or Portugal. They were used as human items of decoration at Court and in fashionable society, acting as reflections of their owners' status and power, and sometimes employed as musicians – roles which were to be repeated time and again in the coming centuries. Such occasional examples were, however, few and far between compared to those major movements of Africans engineered by the Spanish and Portuguese. For the time being, most of this scattering of Africans had taken place in the eastern Atlantic; Africans shipped as slaves to Spain, to Portugal, to the Atlantic islands and even to Britain. In places they simply filled a vacuum, undertaking work where labour was scarce (or non-existent), elsewhere doing the hard, dangerous work free labour shied away from.

By the early sixteenth century, then, a distinct pattern had begun to emerge. Europeans had developed the habit of turning to parts of West Africa for enslaved African labour. They did not venture there *initially* in the hope of finding slaves, but rather to advance their general trading well-being, and to push ever further along and round the African coast. But Europeans quickly adopted local habits, first from Islamic Africans and later from dominant African nations and cultures, of acquiring African slaves, and selling them on, to other Africans for profit, or removing them to distant regions where labour was needed. All this happened *before* the labour demands of the New World made themselves felt.

More than that, Europeans – led by the Portuguese – had learned the remarkable material benefits to be derived from that distinctive mix of colonial trade and domination. Portugal's rise to power was linked to its expansive trade and settlements in Africa, South America, India and South-east Asia. Throughout the Crown was actively involved, deriving in return a substantial part of its income from overseas sources.[8] The mercantile community which emerged in Lisbon to mastermind and benefit from this trade was drawn from across Europe. Though Portugal led the way, commercial interests across the rest of western Europe quickly appreciated the way forward. Moreover, so many signs of maritime and commercial prosperity pointed to Africa. The 'commerce of Guinea', wrote a Portuguese royal advisor in 1530, 'yields us gold, ivory, wax, hides, sugar, pepper, and it would produce other returns if we sought to explore it further.'[9] It was also becoming clear that the trade in African humanity formed a profitable business.

The Portuguese involvement in African slavery was eased by a number of religious and moral provisions which lent a veneer of civility to the proceedings. The Portuguese Crown secured papal approval for the baptism of slaves in Lisbon (and in some cases at sea), and royal ordinances prescribed strict conditions for the treatment and baptism of slaves (they included the branding of Africans with a Christian cross). As we have seen in the case of Kongo, the Portuguese sought to win over their African trading partners and clients to Christianity. But such agreements meant little to the men on the ground – the tough and rapacious slave-traders and merchants, whose presence in Africa and their violent or seductive sweep for slaves generated mayhem and dislocation. The Portuguese needed African labour, especially for São Tomé, and could afford to turn a blind eye to the predatory activities of slave-traders, providing slaves were delivered to the thriving sugar plantations in the Atlantic islands.

There was, it is true, an objection to the rise of Portugal's slave-trading from Ferao Oliveria (1555), who denounced 'buying and selling peaceable free men, as one buys and sells animals'. This objection was later adopted by a Spanish cleric, and became part of the minority Catholic denunciation of slave-trading.[10] But such voices went largely unheeded in the abundance of maritime and material success flowing in and out of the Iberian peninsula from the Atlantic trade.

Material well-being, however, was only one way in which Africans, their descendants (and people who were a mix of Europeans and Africans) gradually made their presence felt. They were, as we have seen, a visible presence by the mid-sixteenth century. A new language – pidgin – emerged among the traders, settlers and sailors on the African coast, in the Atlantic islands, on the high seas and even in Portugal itself; a mix of the languages of Africa and Europe. This pattern was later repeated in the Americas, in all the European settlements which used African labour. Christianity itself began to be transmuted, especially in Africa where it mingled with African beliefs and musical forms. Even the decorative arts incorporated African (and Asian) themes and images, although this had long been true of western culture: the biblical gifts of gold, frankincense and myrrh are all African products. In all this and more, Portugal led the way, its global reach made possible by a maritime and military power which seemed out of all proportion to its population or natural resources. Portugal's potential, derived from its colonial toeholds and amazing maritime networks, seemed enormous, especially after the settlement of Brazil.

Initially, Brazil seemed a poor investment in men and effort. Settlement was restricted to a few outposts on the coast and local Indians proved less malleable, more elusive and less productive than the handful of Portuguese settlers wished. Indian peoples were culturally ill-equipped for the purposes and outlook (of industrious work for profit or surplus) demanded. The Portuguese settlers (and the Church) tried a variety of tactics to secure Indian labour: by uprooting them from their tribes and anchoring them to settler culture; by creating a wage labour culture; by enslaving them. All were unsuccessful.[11] The problem (for the Portuguese) was made worse by the introduction of sugar cane cultivation. Sugar production using African slave labour had already been successfully developed by the Portuguese in São Tomé, where proximity to Africa enabled local sugar plantations to use slaves on a scale never before seen in the Atlantic.[12] Once sugar had been successfully transplanted onto the Atlantic islands, it was perhaps inevitable that Europeans would try similar ventures when they settled in the Americas. Soon after the first European incursions into the Americas, sugar cane quickly followed.

Christopher Columbus had lived in Madeira and had worked for a Genoese company in the sugar business. On his second voyage in 1493, he took sugar cane for planting in the Americas. Sugar did not thrive in the new settlements until it took off in Santo Domingo early in the sixteenth century. Even then, its cultivation failed to develop in the Spanish settlements of the Caribbean, largely because the Spaniards were more attracted to the greater potential of settlement and prospects on the American mainland. But, after early experiments, sugar was firmly established in Brazil in the 1530s and 1540s, using expertise and skills imported from the Atlantic islands. Portuguese settlement henceforth thrived in those regions where the *fidaldos* (noblemen who were created estate proprietors by the monarch) turned to sugar cultivation, and where they were able to forge amicable relations with local Indians.[13]

Sugar began to prosper in the north-east of Brazil, through a potent mix of factors: royal Portuguese support, interested European capital and technical expertise acquired on plantations in the Atlantic islands. At first the Brazilian sugar plantations were generally small, and they operated without Africans. In the 1550s and 1560s 'there were virtually no African slaves at the Northeast sugar mills'. Thirty years later, however, there were an estimated 2000 African slaves working on 66 local sugar plantations. Wherever historical scrutiny has fallen on particular plantations or sugar regions, a similar pattern unfolds; the mid-sixteenth-century reliance on local Indian labour gave way to an ever-greater use of African slave labour. Thus the process of shipping Africans, which had already proved its commercial and social attractiveness in both the Iberian peninsula and the Atlantic, was effectively transplanted to the Americas. In retrospect, it seems inevitable that the labouring and artisan skills shaped in the Atlantic islands would be shifted across the Atlantic, especially when Brazilian sugars began to yield profits in European markets, and offered prospects of still more to come.

Africans were transported to Brazil for use as simple muscle power, but they were also employed as servants, as urban workers and for their sugar skills. Brazilian plantations first developed via Portuguese management and technicians, African sugar experience and skills, and local Indian labour. But by the last years of the sixteenth century the situation changed. As sugar production expanded, and as more and more Africans were introduced into Brazil, Indian workers on the plantations began to decline in numbers and importance. Indians were deemed less valuable, less durable and more difficult to replace than Africans, who had *already* proved their worth in the Atlantic islands, both as skilled workers and as labourers. Brazilian sugar planters came to think of the African, not the local Indian, as the natural worker in their sugar fields and factories. It was the African workers who yielded the best return on the planters' investment.[14]

This complex mix of forces lay behind the switch to African slave labour, which was driven forward by the profitability of Brazilian sugars in the European markets. Africans were also less prone to European ailments than the Indians (though they suffered horribly in the Atlantic crossing and its immediate aftermath). This pattern remained broadly true right across the Americas, from sixteenth-century Brazil to North America two centuries later, and formed one reason why Europeans consistently preferred Africans and their descendants to local Indian labour.

Few planters doubted that the African was a more profitable investment than the local Indian. But it is clear that the initial development of Brazilian sugar could not have taken place without the Indians. In the early days they formed a cheap source of readily available labour. Then, as the sugar industry expanded, and Indians were afforded some legal protection against enslavement, the cost of their labour rose. What ultimately determined the fate of both the Indians and the Africans was the nature of work and its organization in the sugar fields. By the last quarter of the sixteenth century a system was in place – the sugar industry of north-east Brazil – which, however small-scale and rudimentary, was to transform the face of the Atlantic world. European settlers, financiers and shippers had laid down the basis for sugar cultivation on plantations. But for this they needed the help of African slaves shipped across the Atlantic.

In 1570 there were perhaps only about 2000 to 3000 African slaves in Brazil. That had risen to 10,000 in 1590, and perhaps to 15,000 in 1600, though even then they remained outnumbered by Indians and matched by free Portuguese. Over the next half-century, the figures changed dramatically, as some 200,000 Africans were shipped to the buoyant sugar colony.[15] These figures show clearly that demand for African labour had become enormous. But it was a costly and complex business, made possible on such a scale only by crucial financial and mercantile connections in Europe. The Brazilians benefited from the relative decline in profitability of sugar from the Atlantic islands, and from the fact that they could build bigger, more efficient, water-powered sugar factories. They also had the advantages of geography. The journey time from north-east Brazil to Lisbon was shorter than for any other comparable route from the Americas to Europe. It was also faster than the routes from Africa. This served to cheapen the Brazilian slave/sugar system. Moreover, Lisbon provided access to a mercantile and financial community drawn from across Europe, which was already experienced (through trade to the Atlantic islands) in the peculiarities and benefits of the sugar business.

Portugal's Atlantic trade was, inevitably, periodically disrupted by warfare and privateering (especially by the efforts of the English and the Dutch to tap into the lucrative sugar trade). But Brazilian sugar continued to thrive, thanks in part to an Atlantic convoy system. By the end of the sixteenth century, Brazil was producing about 10,000 tons of sugar a year, a massive increase over all previous sugar producers. The signs of the Brazilian sugar boom were all around. Sugar and slave ships crowded the harbours of Recife, Bahia and Rio, Portugal's smaller ports joined in what had previously been a Lisbon monopoly, and Portuguese merchants linked up with other European partners for shipping and capital. The technology of sugar production was simplified and became cheaper, enabling men of humbler station to establish themselves as Brazilian sugar planters. In 1583 there were an estimated 115 sugar mills; by 1629 the 350 mills were disgorging upwards of 22,000 tons of sugar annually.[16]

There were some obvious beneficiaries from Brazilian sugar. The duties on it provided the Portuguese treasury with perhaps 40 per cent of its total income. Brazil began to attract migrants and Portuguese settlers poured across the Atlantic to join in the sugar boom. But their numbers – upwards of 4000 a year – pale into insignificance when we look at African arrivals. By 1630 there were 50,000 to 60,000 Africans in Brazil: Brazilian sugar had developed an appetite for African slave labour. Moreover, the Portuguese slave-traders were supplying *other* Europeans with African slaves, and were transporting perhaps 10,000 to 15,000 Africans annually. Portuguese, Brazilian and independent merchants fairly buzzed around the southern Atlantic, trading New World produce for Africans destined to work in the cultivation and production of those same products.

To recruit Africans in such numbers the Portuguese sought to enhance their presence and techniques of trading on the African coast itself. They faced growing competition there from a host of European rivals – mainly English and Dutch – who sought their own access to Africa's varied commodities, and who also wanted to establish a position in the slave trade. The Portuguese were more secure in their positions in south-west and central Africa. The origins of Portuguese involvement in Angola lie here. Everywhere, there and further north, the men who organized the recruitment, enslavement and shipment of Africans from Luanda to Brazil were men at ease with local African customs and languages; often they were the offspring of Africans and Europeans. By the late sixteenth century something like 10,000 Africans a year were leaving from the Angola region. The effect of this Portuguese presence on the African coast was that, by around 1600, they exercised an effective monopoly on the supply of African slaves. They had forged formal links with African states and kingdoms, penetrating ever further from the coast via their agents and freelance slave-traders, and had created an internal trade in humanity of enormous value to the Portuguese Crown and state. But they made even *more* money from supplying Africans to the *Spanish* settlements in the Americas.

The Spanish conquest of the Caribbean and Central America had brought a series of disasters for the native peoples throughout the region (though historians continue to argue about the levels of damage involved).[17] Imported European diseases swept through peoples who had little or no resistance, and European cavalry and firepower completed what invisible microbes began. Native populations everywhere collapsed before the advance of the Spanish. But the Spanish sought to put the Indians to work. Some were forced to work on Spanish *encomienda,* and in the mining of precious metals, many as slaves. The early settlements in Santo Domingo, Cuba and other islands were jeopardized when Spanish interest shifted firmly towards the Central and South American mainland, which had already yielded wealth in its traditional form of precious metals on a scale which dazzled all who saw or heard about it. By then, however, both the Church and royal officials had grown alarmed at the fate of the Indian peoples.

Africans filled the void left by the Indians in Spanish America. Some Africans had travelled on the early voyages of exploration, alongside the *conquistadores* (most were Spanish speakers from the Atlantic islands). Like those in the early Brazilian settlements, they were often skilled slaves and found their way into domestic occupations or trades. As demand for African labour grew, from 1518 the sale of slaves into Spanish America was licensed under *asiento* agreements.

The Church for its part was initially less concerned about African slaves (who seemed to thrive) than about the Indians (who did not). The early Spanish sugar plantations in the Caribbean islands had used both Indians and Africans though, again, Africans fared better than Indians. But the cost of establishing African-based sugar plantations was high, not least because they exported only small amounts of sugar back to Spain. Moreover, it was difficult to defend those isolated island plantations against the privateers who were lured into the Caribbean by the fabled wealth of the Indies. Spanish fleets were organized around the return to Spain of precious metals – not sugar – and plantation produce came a poor second in their transport arrangements.

Most serious of all, however, was the flight of Spanish settlers away from Cuba and Santo Domingo to Central America and Peru. For a long time the Spaniards effectively controlled only small pockets of settlements there. The hinterlands remained free territory for Indians and runaway Africans, and Spanish settlers were often harried by a mix of Indians and Africans close to hand, and by French and English privateers from the sea, and sometimes by both combined. Blacks who knew the terrain and the regimes of the Spanish transport system helped privateers lay siege to the invaluable mule trains hauling precious metals across the isthmus to the treasure and silver fleets destined for Spain. There were, then, good reasons for the Spanish to feel uncertain and to worry about further imports of Africans. Could they trust them to stay at their work and not to ally with the enemies of Spain? At times the Africans seemed more like an enemy within Spanish America than a necessary human tool for its development.

Not surprisingly, then, the import of slaves into Spanish America was small compared to Brazil: perhaps only 36,000 in the 40 years to 1595 (though many were imported 'illegally' and do not show in official Spanish records). But the numbers soon rose dramatically – as many perhaps as 268,000 – many obtained from Portuguese traders operating under the *asiento* system. By the early seventeenth century, more Africans were entering Spanish American lands than Spaniards. Africans helped to build the physical face of Spanish America and came to form a substantial proportion of the settler population. Half of Cuba's population of 20,000 in 1610 were slaves. There and elsewhere they formed the backbone of local labouring and skilled occupations.

The sale of Africans into the Americas became a major source of income for the Spanish Crown (which was united with Portugal in 1580). Between 1595 and 1640, the great bulk of Africans were shipped into Cartagena or Veracruz, with only a small proportion going to the Caribbean islands. Wherever we look, this African presence was reflected in local populations. Half the population of Lima was black in 1636. Mexico City's population in 1570 contained 8000 Spaniards and 8000 black slaves. Similar ratios could be found in towns and cities across the region.[18] They were highly urbanized people, but they also worked in mining (for silver – and panning for gold), in agriculture (both food and tropical export crops), in logging and in transport, by both land and water. They had in effect been infiltrated into most corners of the economy and society of Spanish America. Despite Spanish attempts to prevent it, it was inevitable that Africans, Indians and Europeans would mix, socially and sexually, creating new populations which bore the distinctive physical (and social) characteristics of their different parentage. Many Africans were able to secure their freedom, thus creating free black communities rather than just a self-sustaining slave community.

Spanish settlers in the Americas turned to Africans from the Atlantic islands, or, increasingly, from Africa itself, for solutions to their various labouring and settler difficulties in the Americas. In this they were encouraged by a Spanish Crown which saw the licensing of Atlantic slave-trading as a major source of income. Naturally enough, the Portuguese slave-traders were keen to oblige, though as demand from the Americas increased, they often had to sub-contract their slave licences to others better able to supply the Africans. There were plenty of other European traders and shippers willing and keen to involve themselves in what was clearly a lucrative and apparently endless trade. The result was that by the mid-seventeenth century, about a third of a million Africans had been imported as slaves into Spanish America. Though slavery within Spanish America never attained the levels of importance it was to reach in Brazil, the West Indies or in North America, it helped to prompt the expansion and refinement of the Atlantic slave trade. On the African coast, at sea, at the entrepôts in the Americas (and in the royal courts and counting-houses of Europe), the Atlantic slave trade established itself as a major and increasingly important area of international trade. There were some (clerics in the main) who were concerned about the attendant ethical and religious issues. On the whole, however, such worries were swamped by the obvious benefits which seemed to flow to everyone involved – excepting, of course, the wretched Africans.

Though sometimes forced to subcontract the work, the Portuguese slave-traders tried to keep other European maritime nations outside their lucrative slaving system and to insist on an effective slaving monopoly. But the expansion of the Atlantic trade in African humanity in the sixteenth and seventeenth centuries proved too great, too expansive, too diffuse and tempting for outsiders to resist. Traders, merchants and privateers (often with tacit backing from their governments at home) began to swarm into the slave zones, buying and selling Africans, raiding Spanish settlements, seizing Spanish treasure. They buzzed like flies over the decaying carcass of Spain's great imperial venture in the Americas, but they found even more attractive the trade in African slaves.

Privateers had been drawn to the Iberian slave system from its earliest days. After all, who was to say that nations should carve up whole regions of the globe, together with vast global trading systems, for themselves to the exclusion of others? French and English ships, often with government backing, were making periodic attacks on Spanish and Portuguese ships and settlements by the early sixteenth century. Trade to and from Africa, and on to the New World, was a tempting prospect to northern Europeans. Ships from Calais, Honfleur and La Rochelle, and later Bordeaux, traded to West Africa and on to the Americas. Inevitably the English were soon involved, led by William Hawkins in the 1530s. Thomas Wyndham sailed to the Gold Coast and Benin in 1553, returning with gold and pepper. When London merchants financed a voyage by John Lok to West Africa in 1554, he returned home with gold, ivory, pepper and 'certaine blacke slaves, whereof some were tall and strong men, and could wel agree with our meates and drinkes'. Not surprisingly, however, it was reported that, 'The colde and moyst aire doth somewhat offend them.'[19]

In the next three years William Towerson made two similar voyages, displaying a growing English interest which worried the Portuguese, who imagined the region to be theirs alone. But it was John Hawkins, under the new monarch Elizabeth I, who formally initiated the English slave trade with his voyage of 1562. He had already made various voyages to the Canaries where, among other things, he learned

> that Negros were very good merchandise in Hispaniola, and that store of Negros might easily bee had upon the coast of Guinea, resolved with himselfe to make triall thereof . . . .

With backing from friends and from commercial interests in London he sailed his small fleet of three ships and 100 men to Tenerife, and thence to Sierra Leone. There he

> got into his possession, partly by the sworde, and partly by other meanes, to the number of 300. Negros at the least, besides other merchandises which that countrey yeeldeth.

He sailed to Hispaniola, where he sold his English goods and some of his Africans, finally selling the remainder,

> for which he received in those 3. places by way of exchange such quantitie of mechandise, that hee did not onely lade his owne 3. shippes with hides, ginger, sugars, and some quantitie of pearles, but he fraighted also two other hulkes . . .

He arrived home in September 1563 'with prosperous success and much gaine to himselfe and the aforesayde adventurers'.[20] Despite the diplomatic repercussions, and notwithstanding Elizabeth's initial concern about the enslavement of Africans, such a commercial success was bound to generate further interest. Hawkins himself promptly embarked on another voyage (again with aristocratic and mercantile support), selling 400 Africans in the Caribbean and returning loaded with valuables and a reported profit of 60 per cent. When Hawkins was knighted, he appropriately used an African woman on his crest.[21] Hawkins's third voyage, on an even larger scale, ended in disaster and he (and the young Francis Drake) barely escaped with his life.

In the last years of the sixteenth century, English privateers made serious inroads into the Portuguese Atlantic trade, attacking and seizing slave ships and returning sugar ships, though a new Portuguese convoy system managed to repair some of the damage. Most ominous of all for the Portuguese, however, was the growing presence of the Dutch in the Atlantic from the mid-1590s onwards. Despite an initial domestic reluctance to engage in slave-trading, individual Dutch merchants and captains began to nibble away at the Iberian slave system, their profitable returns proving too great a temptation for other commercial interests in that remarkably commercially minded state. From the 1590s to the 1620s, however, Dutch slave-trading was sporadic and *ad hoc*. Thereafter, the Dutch West India Company (WIC) became more involved, though initially on a small scale. Not until the Dutch took Elmina in 1637 were they able to become serious Atlantic slave-traders. Before that date they had shipped only about 5000 Africans into American slavery.[22]

The Dutch became major players in the Atlantic system with their seizure of northern Brazil in 1630. Like the Portuguese before them, they found themselves with a plantation colony which needed African labour. The Dutch had long been involved in Brazilian commerce; their merchant ships had carried Brazilian sugar to the European refineries, and Dutch money had underpinned a great deal of Portuguese settlement and development in Brazil. Now, however, Dutch power waxed as Iberian power and empire waned. Indeed, the Dutch took over great swathes of the old Portuguese empire in Africa, South America and South-east Asia. By the mid-seventeenth century, the Netherlands was the world's greatest trading nation, its merchantmen the dominant force in the seas from 'Archangel to Cape Town and from New Amsterdam to Nagasaki'.[23] This global trade was masterminded by the two great Dutch joint-stock companies: the United East Indian Company (VOC) and the West India Company (WIC). The latter was to prove crucial in the Atlantic slave trade.

The Dutch in Brazil needed more Africans, to ensure adequate and regular supplies of which they had to secure reliable trading posts or forts on the African coast itself. They attacked the Portuguese posts and eventually drove them from Elmina, from São Tomé and Annabon, and from the coastal stations at São Paula and Benguela. When they took Axim in 1642, the Dutch had finally established themselves as the dominant presence on the West African coast. However, their grip on Brazil was always tenuous and unsure, and it reverted to the Portuguese in 1654. This uncertainty – which reflected the changing political troubles in Europe itself – prevented the Dutch from consolidating their entry to the Atlantic slave trade. Between 1630 and 1651 the Dutch took an average of 2500 Africans a year to Brazil, compared to the Portuguese, who shipped 3000 to 4000. Yet these years, the very apogee of Dutch power, saw them unable to maintain their toehold in Brazil. The West India Company had financial problems; it was fissured by policy splits and, in any case, could never get enough settlers to migrate to Brazil. The Dutch successes were in trade and commerce, not in colonization.[24]

Despite the upheavals in control – the switch from Portugal to Holland and back to Portugal – Brazilian slavery thrived on the back of local sugar. After 1650 the numbers of slaves increased (in the range of 60,000 to 100,000), but about a quarter of their number were employed *outside* the sugar industry. Black slavery, designed for sugar production, had slipped into all corners of the Brazilian rural and urban economy in a pattern which was to be repeated time and again across the Americas. The Dutch, looking for a role within the Atlantic system, had failed to make an impression as colonists. But they were to prove crucial in encouraging others to take up the same role. They helped the English make the transition from privateers, preying on the trade and shipping of others, to planters. With the help of Dutch money the English began to settle their own colonies in the Caribbean in the 1620s. They were destined to become the most powerful of all slave-based sugar colonies, but it would have seemed impossible to imagine, when looking at the deserted island of Barbados and the tiny island of St Kitts in the early 1620s, that these two islands would be the pacesetters in the transformation of the whole Caribbean. They did so under English control. However, even before the English entered the Atlantic slave system seriously, huge numbers of Africans had been uprooted from their homelands and scattered throughout the Atlantic world, from Lima to London.

Notes

1 Hugh Thomas, *The Slave Trade: The History of the Atlantic Slave Trade, 1440–1870* (London, 1997), Chapter 3.
2 See the essays, especially those of John Hunwick, 'Black Africans in the Mediterranean world: introduction to a neglected aspect of the African diaspora', and Ralph A. Austen, 'The Mediterranean Islamic slave trade out of Africa: a tentative census', in Elizabeth Savage (ed.), *The Human Commodity: Perspectives on the Trans-Saharan Slave Trade* (London, 1992).
3 John Iliffe, *Africans: The History of a Continent* (Cambridge, 1995), pp. 127–30.
4 Hugh Thomas, *Slave Trade*, p. 119.
5 Robin Blackburn, *The Making of New World Slavery: From the Baroque to the Modern, 1492–1800* (London, 1997), pp. 108–14.
6 Philip D. Curtin, *The Rise and Fall of the Plantation Complex* (Cambridge, 1990), Chapter 1.
7 Blackburn, *Slavery*, p. 109.
8 The best account still remains, C.R. Boxer, *The Portuguese Seaborne Empire* (London, 1969).
9 Blackburn, *Slavery*, p. 116.
10 *Ibid.*, pp. 120–1.
11 Stuart B. Schwartz, *Sugar Plantations in the Formation of Brazilian Society: Bahia 1550–1835* (Cambridge, 1985), p. 35.
12 *Ibid.*, pp. 12–14.
13 *Ibid.*, pp. 16–17.
14 *Ibid.*, pp. 65–8.
15 Blackburn, *Slavery*, p. 168.
16 *Ibid.*, pp. 170–3.
17 Francis Brooks, 'Revising the conquest of Mexico: smallpox, sources and populations', *Journal of Interdisciplinary History*, 24(1), 1993. But see the figures in D. E. Stannard, Section I.4 in K. F. Kiple (ed.), *The Cambridge World History of Human Disease* (Cambridge, 1993).
18 Blackburn, *Slavery*, pp. 142–4.
19 'The voyage of M. John Lok to Guinea, Anno 1554', in Richard Hakluyt, *The Principal Navigations of the English Nation* (London, 1926), 8 vols, vol. 4, p. 65.
20 'The first voyage of the right worshipfull and valiant knight sir John Hawkins . . . 1562', in Hakluyt, *Principal Navigations*, vol. 7, pp. 5–6.
21 Thomas, *Slave Trade*, pp. 156–7.

22 Johannes Menne Postma, *The Dutch in the Atlantic Slave Trade, 1600–1815* (Cambridge, 1990), p. 14.

23 C. R. Boxer, *The Dutch Seaborne Empire, 1600–1800* (London, 1973), p. 94.

24 Postma, *The Dutch in the Atlantic Slave Trade*, pp. 22–4.

= 2 =

THE COMING OF
THE BRITISH

The British came relatively late to the world of Atlantic slavery. In the century and a half *before* the British established themselves as major figures, something like 630,000 Africans had *already* been shipped out of Africa.[1] Historians have been tempted to describe such figures as small – tiny movements compared to what was to follow. But we always need to remind ourselves what lay behind the statistics: not merely the lives of the wretched victims coralled into the squalor of the Atlantic ships, but the dislocation, suffering and grief they left behind among kinsfolk, friends and communities. It is hard to see how historians can hope to capture this widespread and continuing process of devastation in Africa. Moreover, despite the huge numbers of Africans already uprooted, we need to recall that the arrival of the British – small scale at first – heralded a dramatic change in the history of Atlantic slavery. The British proceeded to transform the Atlantic world and in the process, they transformed themselves by their involvement in slavery.

The British were lucky with their timing, for the Spanish were desperately trying to fend off Dutch onslaughts in the 1620s and 1630s, and continental Europe was ravaged by the Thirty Years War (1618–48). The British were effectively free to pursue their own interests in the Western Atlantic. As we have seen, British privateers had already made tentative and profitable inroads into the Iberian slave trade and slave settlements, while at home the British had enjoyed the fruits of slave labour, notably sugar and tobacco, long before they began to establish their own American colonies. Such produce, however, had to come via Europe, normally Holland, and was inevitably subject to the caprice of foreign regulation and trade. British colonies, in the right place and with all the ingredients of successful settlement, could bypass this dependence on foreigners. A mere glance at the Spanish and Portuguese experience was enough to persuade the ambitious and the adventurous that settlement, as much as piratical maritime trade, was a proven route towards profitable business.

The men behind the impulse to colonize and settle were drawn from across the British social spectrum, from the gentry, the emergent bourgeoisie and from the land-owning, propertied classes. By the death of Elizabeth I, the New World had already yielded enough bounty (most of it from privateering) to attract the attention of Britons with money to invest. A substantial number of Members of Parliament invested in colonial and maritime ventures and they, like all others involved in the Atlantic trade, took black slavery for granted. The romance of the Atlantic ventures (in reality it was a brutal, sordid and violent world) was actively promoted by a number of early-seventeenth-century authors and publishers, most memorably by the compilations of Richard Hakluyt.[2] The fundamental lure, however, was financial. Ever more people were keen to tap into the world of Atlantic trade, which had by 1600 already been shown (with luck) to be profitable on a remarkable scale.

The British began with the unlikely (because remote and unfruitful) settlement of Bermuda – tentatively in 1609 and fully in 1612 – with finance coming from a group of nineteen London backers. The subsequent controlling company had 118 shareholders, the bulk of them city merchants. From the first it was intended to be a commercial venture which would bring profit to its backers and strategic advantage to the nation. Bermuda's economic potential remained untapped until it was developed as a provider of maritime services in the second half of the seventeenth century.[3] Barbados, however, claimed in 1625, was lush and fertile, and its land was quickly settled by smallholders backed by Dutch finance and London merchants. The initial cultivation of tobacco and cotton on smallholdings, often with indentured labour, was to give way to an utterly different system of sugar plantations worked by Africans. The number of landholdings subsequently fell from 5000 in 1650 to 3000 in 1680, with the number of large estates increasing as a result from 50 to 150. Large plantations began to dominate the landscape. At the same time the number of black slaves also increased from 50 per cent of the population to more than 70 per cent. The island's white population declined, migrating to other neighbouring islands, to North America and, most critically, to Jamaica (taken from the Spanish in 1655).

Barbados quickly became one of the world's most densely populated societies, with a rural labour force that was enslaved and African. The island's produce, primarily its sugar and rum, transformed tastes in Britain and created wealth 'beyond the dreams of avarice' for a fortunate few. By the mid-seventeenth century, thanks to Barbados, slave-grown sugar had entered the popular and mercantile imagination as the source of legendary wealth: a cornucopia which disgorged prosperity to all concerned (except for the slaves, of course). Inevitably the reality was more complex than it appeared at first sight.

Jamaica was taken by Cromwell's invading army in 1655, part of the 'Western Design' and a consolation prize for the British failure to secure Santo Domingo. Most of the troops, and the white settlers from Barbados who joined them later, lingered on the island's south coast before fanning out into the interior to settle on land allotted by the State. Using Barbados as the model, Jamaica was quickly settled and won over to the cultivation of a range of tropical commodities. By 1673 there were 17,000 people in the island (a quarter of the number in Barbados); 7500 were white and 9500 slaves. Though there were 500 estates, only about 150 were sugar plantations, but that began to change with the rise and rise of sugar. By 1700 the white population had fallen to 2000 (due partly to a series of natural disasters), but it began to increase again in the early years of the new century and had risen to 10,000 by 1740. By then, however, they were surrounded by a sea of Africans and their offspring – 100,000 slaves – the majority working on the island's 400 sugar plantations. At the top of this social pyramid rested a local plantocracy – the name itself indicative of their pretensions and ambitions to ape the style of their British superiors. Yet the planters had generally emerged from the humblest of settler origins; their links with British merchants and bankers (whose money and global mercantile connections kept the whole colonial edifice in place) securely placed them in the ranks of an emergent bourgeois class.[4]

In the early days of settlement the British colonies give little hint of the prosperity which was to follow. Smallholders experimented with a range of tropical crops, notably tobacco (the European taste for which had been initially cultivated by links to Spain and to the tobacco-growing Spanish colonies). Despite regular and official denunciation, tobacco consumption took hold in Europe, partly as an exotic commodity which, like many others, found its way into contemporary apothecary and medicinal use. West Indian tobacco was, however, rapidly demoted by the explosive rise of tobacco production in Virginia and Maryland, both 'founded as outposts of the English economy'. Financed by English money, with royal backing, the Chesapeake colonies survived their early years thanks to the help of local Indians. And it was on the Indians' former lands that the settlers planted the crop which transformed their lives, the very crop they had taken initially from the Indians – tobacco.

The first Africans were landed at Jamestown in 1619, but it took time before it became apparent that Africans held the key to local prosperity. In the 1620s and 1630s tobacco became the region's major export crop. About 65,000 pounds of tobacco were exported in the early 1630s. By the end of the next decade that had increased to one million pounds annually, and by the late 1670s it had grown to 20 million pounds.[5] At first the work was done by poor white settlers. In the 50 years to 1680, 75,000 whites had settled in the region, mainly poor young men from Britain. But there were rarely enough labourers for the tobacco planters' needs. High mortality rates, and the general desire among labourers for their own land (and families) once freed from their conditions of service, left permanent gaps in the planters' labouring ranks.

It was a region dominated by small planters up to the 1680s. Thereafter the social structure began to change. Planters turned increasingly to African labour, and began to gobble up neighbouring smallholdings and to develop large-scale tobacco plantations rooted in black slavery. By 1700 labour in the tobacco fields had become slave work. In 1660 there were only 1700 blacks in the Chesapeake, rising to 4000 in 1680 (most coming via the West Indies). Between 1695 and 1700 3000 more slaves arrived in the region, and over the course of the next century another 100,000 Africans were imported into the region.[6]

By the late seventeenth century, the British had become *the* major African slavers in the Atlantic. In the years 1660 to 1700 they shipped 329,600 slaves; the Portuguese, once the dominant force, carried another 263,700.[7] The British had risen to this position because they now possessed their own thriving slave colonies in the Americas. These colonies were shaped by migrating peoples, whose motives varied enormously: the founders (and metropolitan backers) of the various settlements sought profitable trade and business; labouring people wanted a better life for themselves; and the sponsoring government and Crown looked for an enhancement of their own power, with the added benefits of profit to all concerned. There were, of course, large numbers of losers in these ventures, the thousands whose lives were cut short by disease, sickness and violent death. The greatest losers of all were the cargoes of Africans whose potential labour was deemed increasingly important by successive generations of British settlers in the American colonies.

The Africans (initially at least) had no say in their fate. They were the one group who had the key decision made for them; someone else decided to have them shipped across the Atlantic into a lifetime's bondage. British indentured labourers (large numbers of them Irish and Scottish) could at least dream of freedom (and possibly some land) at the end of their service. The Africans had little to look forward to except a lifetime's labour in an alien land, under the control of equally alien people. As we shall see, they were able in the event to shape for themselves a much fuller, rounded, personal and communal life than we might expect. But at the moment of enslavement, during the ocean crossing and at the point of arrival in the Americas, the African's life seemed bleak beyond words.

There is a temptation to think about the American slave colonies in their mature form: when the slave plantations dominated the physical and economic landscape, when slaves were ubiquitous and when slave produce crowded the local dockside, waiting for loading and dispatch to Europe. However, there were interim phases to colonial settlement *before* the dominance of slavery when it remained unclear precisely how local economic and social life would evolve. It was not always as clear to contemporaries as it might seem in retrospect that slavery and slave-grown commodities would become *the* dominant local form (even after slavery had proved itself in other settlements in the Americas).

The sharp social distinctions forged by slavery were not always in evidence in the early pioneering days, when black and white lived cheek-by-jowl. The first settlers in all the colonies had simple, often stark, things on their minds. They needed to survive in a hostile situation, to resist the threats from native peoples (or from earlier settlers), to impose themselves on their new environment, to build shelter and begin the uncertain process of food cultivation. And everywhere they had to secure their lines of military and maritime communication with their distant homelands. In all this (and more), settlers needed all the help they could get. Their own efforts (frequently weakened and undermined by sickness in a new disease environment) were often inadequate. They required help and support from others around them. Whatever their rank back in their homeland, however vaunted their connections in the metropolis, they were reduced to a simple equality by the precarious hardship of settler life. It was difficult to maintain distinctions of rank and status, of background, money (or colour), when all fit people were needed to bend their backs to a common purpose.

The best-known example is perhaps the dependence of Virginia's pioneers on local Indians, to whom they turned for food and much else besides. They even adopted the Indian method of cultivation, 'including the system of field rotation the natives had perfected'.[8] The British settlers could not afford to drive away the Indians in the early years; had they done so, they would have starved.[9] Early settlers needed whatever labour was available, whatever its colour or origin – black, brown or white. All lived close to each other in conditions of crude settler discomfort. Whatever distinctions the British imported to the Americas with them, whatever attitudes they had towards Indians or Africans, towards black or white, were often qualified by the physical demands of settler life. It was hard, for example, to insist on demarcation lines between which tasks should be undertaken by which set of people. In various colonies, black and white could readily be found at work on the same task, at either end of the same saw. Large-scale African slavery put an end to all that.

Settlers in the Americas did not invent black slavery, but we need to recall that the mark of Cain had already been set on the Africans, in Europe and the Atlantic islands. Europeans already knew of the African as an enslaved object, to be bought and sought for European convenience and profit. Although slavery existed in all British colonies from the earliest days it was not yet the determining institution everywhere in the early years. Race relations (for want of a better phrase) were more fluid, more flexible, in those early days.[10] First, the legal system was ambiguous about slavery in British possessions, not least because slavery had effectively died out in England itself (though not in Scotland). Moreover, slavery had not become associated with particular work; blacks (and whites) were needed for whatever work came to hand. In the New England colonies, for example, slaves were few and far between (as little as 1 per cent of the population by 1680). A century later they had increased to a mere 14,000 (only 2 per cent of the regional population) and they tended to live in small clusters in towns in Massachusetts and Rhode Island. There they had greater equality before the law than their enslaved con-temporaries in other colonies. They could also buy their own freedom, and did so to the degree that, by 1790, the majority of blacks in New England were free. That itself was a sign of the marginality of slavery in the region.[11]

Slaves in New England worked as domestics (a job that was not without its own dangers and uncertainties) and as field labourers. Most unusual of all, blacks were allowed to marry whites (although that was outlawed in Massachusetts in 1705). In Bermuda in its first 50 years of existence, when slavery was unimportant, local blacks were also granted areas of freedom unknown in other colonies. And even Virginia, which became the pacemaker for North American slavery, was not initially attached to black slavery. It was a full century after the founding of Virginia before slaves in the Chesapeake formed 20 per cent of the local population. In the first 80 years or so, slaves were allowed a host of social freedoms which were denied to their descendants. There, as elsewhere, black and white worked side-by-side at the same tasks. There, too, black men formed sexual relations with, or married, white women in a way which was to become impossible (or dangerous) in later years.

It was, however, very different in Barbados. A mere 20 years passed between the initial settlement and the rapid and ubiquitous development of a slave society (i.e., one where slave-owning was *the* determining element).[12] The introduction of Africans was haphazard and *ad hoc*, though they were among the first people to settle in the island. Their numbers remained small in the first 20 years, with no more than 800 in the 1630s (a period when white indentured labour was available and cheap). Local Indians were also used as indentured servants. Sugar quickly put paid to these early economic and social relations in Barbados, and in this the Dutch played an important part.

Sugar cane was introduced into Barbados in the 1630s and was used initially merely to feed livestock. But in the 1640s, when war raged in Brazil between the Portuguese and the Dutch, Barbados switched to sugar as its main export crop. Unable to control Brazil (which supplied 80 per cent of Europe's sugar), the Dutch looked elsewhere. With their money, technology and slave shippers, they saw in Barbados an opportunity they had missed in Brazil. The benefits of turning to sugar cultivation were immediately obvious to Barbadian planters, and by 1645 sugar had become the obvious source of prosperity for them. In that same year George Downing wrote to John Winthrop Jr, telling him:

> if you go to Barbados you shal see a flourishing Iland, many able men. I believe they have bought this year no lesse than a thousand Negroes, and the more they buie, the better able they are to buye, for in a yeare and a halfe they will earn (with God's blessing) as much as they cost.[13]

Land quickly became more costly, small plantations began to give way to bigger sugar properties and year by year the island exported ever more sugar to England (where the appetite for sweetness increased accordingly). The 3750 tons shipped to England in 1651 had grown to 9525 in 1669, rising to 15,000 tons in the best years in the 1670s.[14] Barbados thus achieved the pioneers' aim of becoming a settlement designed for profit and was Britain's most valuable, and wealthy, colony in the Americas. It was 'the most prosperous 17th century insular colony on the globe',[15] and the source of that wealth was African labour.

At first, Dutch slave-traders, operating from Pernambuco in Brazil, provided Barbados with its cargoes of African slaves. But as indentured British labour became more costly (and from the mid-century, unobtainable), Barbados turned to Africa for its labourers. Between 1640 and 1700 about 134,000 Africans were imported, first from Dutch traders, then bought directly from the new Royal African Company, which was founded in 1672 as the way for the British to secure their own slave-trading monopoly to supply their slave colonies. All this was at a time when the white population of Barbados was in decline (dropping from 23,000 to 12,528 between 1655 and 1712).[16] Barbados established new laws to control and govern these new armies of African slaves, hoping to ensure a peaceable white dominance over their alien (and overwelmingly hostile) black labour force. Driven into racial isolation (even when numerically dominant), the slaves – those 'dangerous kind of people' – were controlled not simply by the terrifying weaponry of a worried plantocracy, but by a punitive and fierce legal system acting in the slave-owning interests. The legal code governing Barbadian slaves effectively 'legitimised a state of war between blacks and whites, [and] sanctioned rigid segregation'.[17] It also provided a model for other British colonies which subsequently turned to slavery.

The transformation of Barbados was also an indication of changing and complex international forces. It was, first and foremost, a reflection of changing patterns of European power and trade. The initial trading and settler empires of the Spanish and Portuguese had given way to the emergent global reach of the Dutch Republic. By the 1620s British power was on the rise, her mercantile and political classes anxious to secure both their own profitable settlements overseas and a niche in the Atlantic slave-trading markets. British financiers and merchants (and their political and Court supporters) did not need to see the book-keeping details of their European rivals and enemies – the prosperity spawned by the Atlantic trades was very visible. What they desired was an arrangement similar to that forged by the Spanish and the Portuguese in the previous century: a system which brought together the financial and mercantile interests of Europe (which reached out to Asia), the export potential of Africa (especially its enslaved manpower), and the productive potential of tropical and semi-tropical American colonies. What had happened in Barbados was confirmation of that process.

The impetus behind the colonization of the Americas lay, obviously, in Europe. Both the Dutch and the British began to attack and unravel the fabric of Iberian power in the Atlantic and the Americas in the 1620s. The British had learned a great deal from the Iberian pioneers in the Americas about the value of European settlement there and of the African trade to sustain key parts of it. To more and more Britons, the Americas offered a solution to manifold problems at home. Colonies would, for instance, 'solve' the problem of domestic poverty and overpopulation, in addition to the economic benefits which might flow back and forth across the Atlantic.

Though early efforts were directed to colonize New England, it was the southern colonies which began to lure ever more British emigrants; by 1640 52,000 had settled in the sugar and tobacco colonies, compared to 22,550 in New England.[18] The numbers of migrants were astonishing – a reflection as much of desperation at home as prospects in the Americas. Somewhere between 170,000 and 225,000 people left for the Americas between 1610 and 1660, the largest group heading for the Caribbean.[19] Beginning with St Kitts in 1623, by 1660 the British had put down roots in six West Indian islands.

There was, from the first, a desire to cultivate tropical produce and to circumvent the earlier reliance on Iberian competitors. Behind this lay groups of financial interests in London, acting in syndicates, in pursuit of the kind of colonial and maritime wealth which they had seen flow back to Lisbon, Seville and, more recently, to Amsterdam. Men with mercantile and shipping experience in older European, African, East Asian and American trades now put their money into speculative ventures in the West Indies. At first, their investments did not seem secure in the face of natural disasters and attacks by native peoples and Spanish forces. But once secure, the settlements in St Kitts and Barbados provided a base for subsequent British settlement and development in the region.[20]

At the centre of the financial support for West Indian settlement lay a consistent *political* commitment; a substantial number of direct financial backers were MPs, for example. Though they often had formal royal backing, these financial speculators in the Caribbean were expected to look after themselves. In time, of course, their efforts were to bring enormous material benefit to both Crown and government.

It was the success of Virginian tobacco which showed how an appropriate local export crop could generate returns which only the most imaginative of investors could dream of. The risks, however, often deterred bigger, more traditional investors, and thus it was that the new colonies attracted the money and efforts of smaller men with less to lose – but much more to gain.[21] The trade to the Americas attracted and shaped this new breed of merchants: groups of men funnelling their money, goods (even their skills) into ships of the Atlantic trade. Goods and commodities were shipped back and forth on credit, the return trip underwriting the other. Merchants, captains and planters developed into a major Atlantic force, shipping goods into the plantation societies and returning with tropical produce to repay their British backers. The Dutch could offer all of these services, and they could also, of course, offer African slaves.

In addition to the capital, expertise and equipment needed to set up such pioneering ventures, the early planters needed labour. With the switch to local export crops – sugar in Barbados, tobacco in Virginia – they also needed slaves, and the Dutch (unable, in 1646–48, to sell to Brazil) were happy to oblige. But the British began to organize their own slave-trading forays to West Africa, officially through the Guinea Company but, more effectively, by interloping merchants able, from the 1640s, to sell Africans in the expanding slave markets of Barbados.

During and after the English Civil War there was a growing concern in Britain that British interests would best be served by the *exclusion* of Dutch slaving interests: that the supply of slaves ought to be in English hands. This process was first effectively asserted under the Commonwealth by the early Navigation Acts, which subsequently orchestrated the emergence of the British Atlantic trade. These Acts specified that trade to and from the colonies should be restricted to British ships. It was in effect the origins of a mercantilist system, supervised by Vice-Admiralty Courts, which sought to advance British trade and settlement to the exclusion of all other European rivals.[22] The obvious trade in which to secure a monopoly was that supply of Africans which had been so lucrative a business for earlier nations and hordes of interlopers. It was, however, a system which could only be secured by an increasingly powerful Royal Navy, able to enforce the law against foreign (and domestic) intruders on the high seas. State power, mercantile interests and colonial settlement all were, by the mid-seventeenth century, fused together in mutual interdependence, and the lubricant of the entire system was the African slave.

In 1663 the Company of Royal Adventurers into Africa, with royal and mercantile patronage, was given a monopoly in West Africa 'for the buying and selling bartering and exchanging of for or with any negroes, slaves, goods, wares and merchandises'. By the late 1660s the Company had secured a string of posts and forts from Senegambia to Benin, but financial problems led to a re-formation of the Company as the Royal African Company, in 1672. It was an attractive proposition for London money. Demand for Africans in the Caribbean was buoyant and shares in the new company were oversubscribed. Trading between Senegal and Angola, company ships (most hired from traders) poured ever more Africans into the slave colonies, mainly Barbados and Jamaica. The African Company shipped an annual average of 5250 Africans – a total of 89,000 between 1673 and 1689 (the great majority in the 1680s). By 1713 when the monopoly was ended, the Company had exported 120,000 Africans.[23]

Yet, even such numbers did not satisfy the West Indian planters. They wanted still more Africans and they felt that the Company's prices were too high and it did not always provide what they wanted. They complained that the Company took care 'that the Planters shall never be furnished with Negroes sufficient to follow their Business with Satisfaction'.[24] Despite governmental prohibitions, and the financial risks, interlopers were always ready to pierce the Company's monopoly, knowing that ready sales were to be had among planters anxious for still more African slaves. As a result, even as early as 1700 most of the slaves landed in the British islands came from interlopers. Free trade was, in effect, winning the battle against monopoly. A rising chorus of voices was raised against the slave-trading monopoly; more and more were convinced that the 'national interest' was best served by a free and open trade in Africans. Few felt that such trade was wrong, fewer still that it was uneconomic. The British slave trade was fully opened up in 1713 (though the Company monopoly had effectively ended in 1698). It is easy to minimize the importance of the African Company, but by the time its power was ended it had shipped 120,000 Africans, dispatched 500 ships to Africa, and had imported 30,000 pounds of sugar.[25]

Even at this date, the slave trade had done more than just create the slave colonies. It had also served to transform the metropolis. The most obvious, daily and ubiquitous social change was the massive domestic consumption of slave-grown produce.[26] But the impact of slavery could also be seen in a host of other ways. London had begun to outstrip Amsterdam both as a financial centre and as the entrepôt for imported tropical goods. Sugar and tobacco formed a rising proportion of the capital's imports, many of which were re-exported to other parts of Europe. London itself, far and away the nation's biggest city, was a major market for imported goods. By the mid-seventeenth century, the capital was forcing its way towards the centre of the Atlantic system, its finances supporting the trade, shipping and insurance, its quayside warehouses receiving and transshipping an increasing share of produce from the Americas, its mercantile class an obvious beneficiary of the trade.

Other ports looked at London, hoping to enjoy similar fortunes. By 1700 Bristol, England's second largest city, was keen to destroy the monopoly of the Royal African Company, and was poised with well-tried shipping routes and a buoyant economic hinterland to enter the Atlantic trades.[27] Groups of powerful Bristol merchants began to pressurize State and parliamentary bodies to open up the trade to their city. From the 1690s onwards Bristol had a succession of powerful political voices (Merchant Adventurers, MPs and merchants) advocating, then defending, that city's access to the Atlantic trades. The slave trade, said the Bristol merchant John Cary in 1695, 'is indeed the best Traffick the Kingdom hath'.[28] Bristol's entry to the Africa trade was slow and hesitant (compounded by war between 1702 and 1713), but peace saw the city make massive strides towards taking a major share in the African slave trade. By 1728–29, half of the British tonnage clearing for Africa came from Bristol. London's trade declined as Bristol's rose, and by the end of the 1730s Bristol had become the nation's greatest slave-trading city. From the very first, Bristol merchants were interested not so much in Africa's other varied exports – ivory, timber, gum, wax – but in slaves, and Bristol capital was poured into the slave trade (by 1730 the average cost of a slave voyage involved an investment of about £4000). In the early 1730s Bristol merchants were sinking £50,000 to £60,000 a year into the slave trade. Two decades later it had risen to £150,000 a year. By then, merchants in Liverpool had also begun to make their own initial incursions into the Africa trade.[29]

The Africa trades (which meant, increasingly, the maritime trade in African humanity) had begun to seduce all sorts and conditions of British people. By the 1730s, the open slave trade was in full flow – a massive enforced surge of Africans across the Atlantic in the misery of hundreds of British ships. Over the century, between 1700 and 1810, the British transported almost three million Africans across the Atlantic.[30] Even at this remove, these are stunning figures. But they also provide statistical indicators of just how important the African had become to the British; to slave-traders, to planters, to British mercantile and commercial interests clean across the country, and to British consumers.

First and foremost, of course, Africans formed an army of uprooted and transported people, cast to the far side of the Atlantic, in unspeakable conditions, for the economic betterment of their captors and tormentors. In all this, the British were central. They had not been the first, and they were not alone. But the British had brought the Atlantic system to a degree of economic perfection which profited themselves and their colonies in proportion to the plundering of Africa and the violation of their African captives. As if the horrors of the British slave ships were not bad enough, the lives of most Africans who survived the Atlantic crossing were promptly damaged even further by what happened to them on the plantations of the Americas.

Notes

1 David Richardson, 'Slave trade. Volume of trade', in Seymour Drescher and Stanley L. Engerman (eds), *A Historical Guide to World Slavery* (Oxford, 1997), pp. 385–8.
2 P. J. Marshall and Glyndwr Williams, *The Great Map of Mankind* (London, 1982).
3 Michael Craton, 'Property and propriety: land tenure and slave property in the creation of a British West Indian plantocracy, 1712–1740', in *Empire, Enslavement and Freedom in the Caribbean* (Kingston, 1997), pp. 73–5.
4 *Ibid.*, pp. 88–92.
5 Allan Kulikoff, *Tobacco and Slaves: The Development of Southern Cultures in the Chesapeake, 1680–1800* (Chapel Hill, 1986), pp. 31–2.
6 *Ibid.*, pp. 40–4; James Walvin, *Questioning Slavery* (London, 1996), pp. 74–5.
7 Richardson, 'Slave trade', p. 387.
8 Allan Kulikoff, *Tobacco and Slaves*, pp. 28–9.
9 Edmund S. Morgan, *American Slavery, American Freedom* (New York, 1975), pp. 72–4.
10 Philip D. Morgan, 'Encounters with Africans and African-Americans', in Bernard Bailyn and Philip D. Morgan (eds), *Strangers within the Realm: Cultural Margins of the First British Empire* (Chapel Hill, 1991), p. 163.
11 *Ibid.*, pp. 167–8.
12 *Ibid.*, p. 163.
13 Elizabeth Donnan, *Documents Illustrative of the Slave Trade to America*, 4 vols (Washington, DC, 1930–35), vol. 3, p. 8.
14 Hilary McD. Beckles, *A History of Barbados* (Cambridge, 1990), p. 22.
15 Jack P. Greene, *Pursuits of Happiness: The Social Development of Early Modern British Colonies and the Formation of American Culture* (Chapel Hill, 1988), pp. 43–5.
16 Hilary Beckles, *Barbados*, pp. 31–3.
17 Richard S. Dunn, *Sugar and Slaves: The Rise of the Planter Class in the English West Indies, 1624–1713* (London, 1973), p. 246.
18 Richard B. Sheridan, *Sugar and Slavery: The Economic History of the British West Indies* (Kingston, 1994), p. 77.

19 Robin Blackburn, *The Making of New World Slavery: From the Baroque to the Modern, 1492–1800* (London, 1997), p. 228.
20 *Ibid.*, Chapter 5.
21 *Ibid.*, p. 227.
22 Michael Craton, 'Caribbean Vice Admiralty Courts and British imperialism', in Michael Craton, *Empire*, Chapter 5.
23 James A. Rawley, *The Transatlantic Slave Trade* (London, 1981), pp. 153–8.
24 William Wilkinson, *Systema Africanum* (1690), in Michael Craton, James Walvin and David Wright (eds), *Slavery, Abolition and Emancipation* (London, 1976), p. 20.
25 Rawley, *The Transatlantic Slave Trade*, pp. 159–63.
26 See below, Chapter 8.
27 K. Morgan, *Bristol and the Atlantic Trade in the 18th Century* (Oxford, 1993).
28 Rawley, *Slave Trade*, pp. 173–4.
29 David Richardson (ed.), *Bristol, Africa and the Eighteenth-Century Slave Trade to America* (Bristol Records Society), 4 vols, 1986–1996; vol. 1, *The Years of Expansion, 1698–1729* (1986), pp. vii–xxviii.
30 Richardson, 'Slave trade', p. 387.

=== 3 ===

ORIGINS AND DESTINATIONS

African origins

The British were prompted to pay serious attention to the potential of trade and settlement in the distant Atlantic by the success of others. They came into a world whose human and economic contours were already shaped by the pioneering example of the Spanish, the Portuguese and the Dutch. The structure of the Atlantic system was in place. But the British were to perfect and hone that system to levels of unparalleled profitability and importance, thanks to millions of African slaves shipped across the Atlantic. The basic outlines of the British Atlantic resembled the older Iberian version: labour from Africa, shipped to the Americas, to cultivate produce destined for European markets. Beneath that outline gloss, however, there lay a remarkably complex geographical and human system. This was especially striking in the case of the slaves. Africans were drawn from a vast expanse of coastal and interior Africa, and found themselves scattered across huge swathes of the Americas and (in smaller numbers) Europe.

Europeans trawled for slaves along an African coastline of 3000 miles. The first two-thirds, east to west, Europeans knew as Guinea; the rest, north to south, they called Angola. Beneath this simplicity lay a mosaic of cultures, languages and polities into which the Portuguese intruded from the 1440s. The British remained relatively uninterested in the region for a further century, deferring to the Portuguese claims to the region. Even the initial British slave voyages were exceptional. By the early seventeenth century, however, the British were emerging as the greatest rivals to Dutch power in the Atlantic, searching for access to Africa's varied export crops – notably gold, woods and hides. The Company of Adventurers, given the monopoly to trade to Africa in 1618, established a string of factories and forts on the Gold Coast from its initial base in Sierra Leone, and traded onwards to Benin and the Atlantic islands. But the Company faded in the teeth of growing numbers of interlopers, foreign traders and companies.

Trading interests on the African coast, organized by a new monopoly company, began to shift to slaves, with a base on James Island and a takeover of the Gold Coast factories. In search of still more slaves, the British began to trade further east, at Allada and to New and Old Calabar, though gold remained more important than slaves. After the formation in 1672 of the new Royal African Company, British interests in West Africa henceforth concentrated on the trade in African slaves. The Company promised to deliver 5000 to 6000 Africans a year to the Americas (though never managing those levels), from its bases in Gambia, Sierra Leone and the Gold Coast, though some of its ships traded as far south as Angola. So attractive was the trade in African humanity that the coast attracted more and more interlopers, who threatened the Company's position. Moreover the African Company's debts were compounded by warfare (between 1689 and 1697) and political upheavals in Britain (in 1688). The consequent political and economic debate in Britain about how best to organize trade to and from Africa saw victory go to a freer, more open, trade in slaves. And as that trade opened up, Bristol began to replace London as England's main slave port.[1]

By 1670 British merchants had established their dominance of the Atlantic slave trade. Thereafter, until Parliament abolished the trade in 1807, they remained the major shippers of African slaves to the Americas. In the 150 years before 1807, 'the British shipped as many slaves to America as all other slave-carrying nations put together'.[2] The overall figures are stunning, though they often serve to deflect attention from the individual and collective misery which lies behind them. In the years of British dominance, British (or British colonial) ships carried more than 3.4 million Africans, about half the total carried in those years. This was all within a roughly triangular system: from Britain to Africa, then to America, and back to Britain. Year after year, more and more Africans were herded into British slave ships. Numbers ran at about 6700 a year between 1662 and 1670, and a century later they had risen to 42,000 a year. When the Dutch and

French effectively dropped out of Atlantic slave-trading in 1793, the British share of the trade rose to unprecedented levels. Yet there is an historical curiosity which continues to puzzle historians and to which we will need to return. At the very moment when the British seriously began to challenge the slave trade, during the last years of the eighteenth century – when moral and ethical doubts were hurled at slavery as never before – those involved (investors, slave-traders, planters and others) continued to view the trade in Africans as a major, viable and promising branch of maritime trade.

The massive expansion in British slave-trading came in three major waves; between 1650 and 1683, 1708 and 1725 and 1746 to 1771. There were, inevitably, dips and reductions in the trading patterns (usually caused by warfare), but, overall, the trade in African slaves remained an expansive, buoyant branch of Britain's maritime trade. More striking were the changes in the ways the trade was organized, notably, of course, the shift from monopoly company to free trade. Yet so voracious was the demand for slaves in the Americas that, even when the 'monopoly' theoretically ruled, perhaps one African in four was landed 'illegally' (i.e., by interloping free-traders). In the changing patterns of British slave-trading, the centre of mercantile (and maritime) gravity shifted, first from London to Bristol, and then to Liverpool. A string of other British ports joined in, but Liverpool became pre-eminent after 1750. Until the early eighteenth century London merchants financed about 63 per cent of British slave voyages; by 1750–80, Liverpool sources financed a majority of slave voyages (upwards of 75 per cent in the last generation of British slave-trading).[3] Throughout, however, London remained crucial – its merchants and financiers guaranteeing and remitting bills of exchange used by West Indians, Americans and Liverpudlians. Moreover, London merchants also supplied slave-traders in other ports with cargoes to be shipped to Africa and the Americas. Even when most ships sailed from Bristol and Liverpool, London's financial and mercantile system was vital to British Atlantic slaving.

This massive area of maritime trade all hinged on the supply of Africans on the African coast, and we need to know more precisely where those millions of Africans came from and how they got there. Most Africans bought by Europeans came not from coastal societies but from the interior, though the great majority of slaves shipped to America by the British were acquired on the Atlantic coast. In sharp contrast to the slave patterns of other nations, they took more from the Bight of Biafra, and fewer from the Bight of Benin and Central Africa. Though the British bought slaves from a vast stretch of coastline, from Senegambia to the south of Angola, it was an uneven process, and unlike the French, for example, the British took few slaves from beyond the Cape of Good Hope. The six major slave-trading coastal regions are easily described. Senegambia, stretching south to the Gambia River, yielded 246,800 slaves; Sierra Leone provided 483,100, and the Gold Coast (from the Volta to the Niger) another 509,200. Something like 359,600 slaves came from the Bight of Benin. But it was the Bight of Biafra which disgorged the greatest number of slaves to the British, some 1,172,800 in all. Furthest south of all was West-Central Africa, where the British collected 634,000 slaves.[4]

The British traded for slaves in these regions on the African coast at different periods – slave-trading in one region declined when the trade increased elsewhere. Most slaves came from the Bight of Biafra in the 1660s, from Benin in the 1680s, and after 1700 they came from Central Africa, the Bight of Biafra, the Gold Coast and Senegambia. By the mid-eighteenth century, trade had declined from Senegambia, the Gold Coast and Central Africa. The years 1748 to 1776 were dominated by trade from the Bight of Biafra and Sierra Leone, though that too declined from the 1770s. Thereafter the British turned again to the Bight of Biafra, the Gold Coast and Central Africa. With the exception of the Bight of Biafra, the British throughout had to face the competition of other European slave-traders, notably the French and Portuguese.[5] Many of these coastal trading patterns were dictated by changing conditions. It was, for example, quicker to acquire and load slaves in one region rather than another; and the ratio of men to women differed greatly between the different slave-trading regions. It is clear that these and other patterns need to be explained not in terms of what happened on the coast, but in terms of upheavals and events occurring within particular African societies in the interior, far from the view and comprehension of the Europeans.

We need to remember that the European presence on the coast was, in most places, no more than a precarious toehold for much of the era of slave-trading. It did clearly reflect an apparently insatiable appetite for Africans, but European slave-traders could not dictate, still less control, the supply of Africans *arriving* at the point of purchase. The supply of African slaves remained firmly in the hands of *African* dealers and middlemen, who organized the movement of slaves from the initial point of enslavement in the interior to the European traders on the coast. There were, quite simply, important trading and governing elites in West and Central Africa making profitable trade from the supply of Africans to the

Europeans. With a few exceptions (notably in the very early days of European slave-trading) the supply of Africans from the hinterland (near or far) to the coast was organized by Africans.

Slavery was commonplace in a host of African societies long before European maritime trading had an impact on the coast. Indeed, it was the *existence* of African slavery (in law, social structures and in trading systems) which pre-disposed Europeans to accept African slaves as one element of their trading relationship with Africans. John Thornton even claims that 'This pre-existing social arrangement was thus as much responsible as any external force for the development of the Atlantic slave trade.'[6] However, European trading had a transforming impact on Africa. Europeans poured into Africa enormous volumes of commerce – the whole range of European manufactured goods and hardware, notably firearms, luxury goods (especially alcohol) and transshipped items from Asia (particularly textiles). This stimulated a widespread taste for imported goods, which was satisfied in part by the exchange and transfer of slaves. Warfare between African states (which were, a few empires excepted, much smaller than traditional European states) yielded prisoners, and those prisoners were fed into the maws of the Atlantic trade.[7] Slaves who could be sold on, especially male slaves (and Europeans generally preferred male to female slaves), provided a form of wealth and income to the enslavers. This process, which already existed before the Europeans arrived on the coast, was greatly accelerated by the European demands for ever more Africans. It is also clear that some African states consciously chose not to involve themselves in the slave export trade.

The growth in slave-trading after about 1650 was explosive, and it coincided with the British settlement of the American colonies and the switch to slave labour in those colonies. The consequences for Africa thereafter were enormous, most crucially in terms of demography. The Atlantic slave trade may have retarded the population growth of the regions concerned (this was especially so in Angola), in addition to the damaging intrusion into the region of outside diseases brought by Europeans on the coast.[8] It is easier to assess the political upheavals prompted by the European demand for slaves. Three major states of West Africa collapsed: the Greater Jolof in Senegal, the Kongo kingdom and the Yoruba Oyo kingdom in south-west Nigeria. But by the same token, new states arose on the back of slaving: the Asante empire of the Akan people on the Gold Coast, and the kingdom of Dahomey. Other mercantile states were created elsewhere, notably in Angola.[9] Furthermore, the European slaving presence stimulated a growth of slavery *within* West Africa, especially for female slaves, and it prompted an ever-more-brutal acquisitiveness among African slaving societies. In brief, the European slaving presence had a seismic impact throughout vast reaches of West and Central Africa, though in places there was a striking 'capacity of privileged Africans to create or adapt institutions in order to survive the slave trade'.[10]

Africans who were driven down to the coast had been enslaved at some earlier (and distant) point; they were normally deprived of their freedom by kidnapping, or had been captured in war or convicted of a crime. Often they travelled – like Olaudah Equiano – for months and over great distances by land and water (repeatedly sold *en route*), before finally being sold to the European slave-traders on the coast. This final sale, to the Europeans, was normally by middlemen (Africans or Afro-Europeans) operating in the coastal region, men who were keen to restrict white traders to the coast (though in fact disease was the prime factor keeping Europeans out of the interior). On the coast itself, Europeans bought and processed Africans in various ways. Best-remembered perhaps (because the buildings survive) was the gathering of Africans into the slave forts and factories. This was, however, a costly way of handling slaves, and really dates from the seventeenth-century monopoly companies. More common was trading direct to the slave ships, which cruised up and down the coast and up the bigger rivers, buying coffles of slaves here and there, until they were ready for departure into the Atlantic trade winds. In both forms of slaving, the Africans had ultimate control due to prolonged and skilful haggling, 'lubricated by hospitality, bribery, political alliance, copious alcohol and personal relations between two commercial groups with much in common'.

British and other slave-traders enticed the African middlemen with a range of goods and luxuries from throughout Britain and from Britain's global markets and settlements. Whatever their social or military purpose, those goods were attractive enough to persuade African rulers and others to 'sell other Africans towards whom they felt no obligation, much as medieval Venetians and Genoese sold other Europeans to Muslims'.[11] Once the deal had been finally done, in the latest of a string of upheavals which served to traumatize millions of slaves, Africans were handed over to Europeans on the slave ships, transferred from forts and from beaches, from stations on river banks, from coastal barracoons and from small boats plying from shore to ship. And all this before the most horrible of all enslaved experiences: the transatlantic crossing.

Destinations

Landfall for the miserable African arrivals did not herald their final destination. But for many of the sick, their ailments contracted on the long route-march to the African coast or, more likely, from within the pestilential holds of the slave ships, landfall was all too often their final resting-place. Sick and dying Africans were of little interest to potential purchasers, who wanted strong, healthy slaves for local work.

The precise landing points of these human cargoes followed the patterns of economic expansion and buoyancy of local societies in the Americas. Where a particular crop was in the ascendancy, the Africans were poured in by the boatload. Barbados, the pioneering British sugar island, attracted almost one-half of all the slaves shipped by the British in the 1680s (most of the others going to Jamaica and the Leewards). Sizeable numbers were also shipped into the Chesapeake at much the same time, making possible the switch from white indentured workers to African enslaved labour in tobacco cultivation. Between 1680 and 1725, however, the British began to ship a higher proportion of Africans to Jamaica and to the Leewards (especially to Antigua and St Kitts), to feed the demand from local sugar fields, and to the tobacco colonies of Virginia and Maryland. The early development of rice cultivation in South Carolina also saw more Africans imported into Charleston in the same period, a pattern that continued until the 1770s. By mid-century, the development of Georgia had begun to attract imports of African slaves.[12] In Virginia, African imports peaked after 1725, trailing away when the local slave population began to reproduce itself, thus saving slave owners the cost of buying new Africans from the Atlantic ships. The islands won from the French in the peace of 1763 (Dominica, Grenada, St Vincent and Tobago) absorbed large numbers of Africans and were taking perhaps as many as Jamaica by the early 1770s.

The American War of Independence (1776–83) disrupted the slave trade, but was followed by a remarkable revival in the numbers of Africans imported into Jamaica and into the islands acquired in 1763. Jamaica continued to buy Africans in large numbers right up to the abolition of the slave trade by Parliament in 1807. Between 1795 and 1804, 101,000 Africans were landed in Jamaica. The British also directed African arrivals to newly captured slave colonies (notably Demerara and Martinique), in the hope of capitalizing on their new possessions, though not all of these colonies were retained after the peace settlements. Something like 75 per cent of the Africans transported across the Atlantic in British ships were landed in British colonies, but perhaps around 675,000 were supplied to other nations' colonies. Of course, warfare intervened periodically, but the British supplied both Spanish and French colonies with large numbers of African slaves in the eighteenth century. Moreover, in the eastern Caribbean, large numbers of Africans were re-exported from their arrival point in a British island to a foreign colony in the region. Large numbers of Africans, imported into Jamaica in the eighteenth century, were shipped on to Spanish America. Altogether, it has been calculated that of all the Africans transported in British ships between the years 1700 and 1807, one in three (850,000) were sold on to other colonies.

Knowing where the Africans were landed tells us only one small part of the story. For most Africans, landfall did not mean an end to their travels, nor an end to their physical miseries. Accounts are legion of their miserable condition on arrival, despite the efforts of slave captains to make them look more presentable, healthier and therefore more valuable. The arrival of a slave ship was heralded by its characteristic stink of crowded, sick humanity which had been wallowing in stable-like squalor for weeks past. Sometimes the slaves were sold on board their ship. Often they were herded on shore into holding pens and barracoons, where they were prepared for inspection and sale, the event being announced in the local press. Once cleaned and ready for sale – or inspection – the Africans, invariably terrified by the latest twist in their miserable fortunes, were paraded or displayed before potential vendors, eagerly gathering for the slave sales.

Long before the British developed their own slaving system, this sale process had been pioneered and perfected by the Portuguese and Spaniards in their own colonies. In Rio – the main entry point for most Africans shipped to Brazil between the seventeenth and nineteenth centuries – a visiting Frenchman was horrified to see 'shops full of these wretches, who are exposed there entirely naked, and bought like cattle'.[13] In fact, this imagery – the shocked realization that slaves were treated like animals – was a recurring theme in outsiders' accounts of the arrival and sale of African slaves in the Americas.

The main slave entrepôt for Spanish America was Cartagena, which evolved an elaborate ritual for slave arrivals. The sick were separated from the healthy and held outside the city walls, in barracoons described as 'veritable cemeteries'. The survivors, fit and ready for sale, were branded to show they had been imported legally (and the duty paid). Potential purchasers came from the far edges of the Spanish empire, from Mexico and Lima, and many Africans thus embarked on yet another epic trek, across the Isthmus, down the Pacific coast, or deep into Mexico. Even then, they might be sold once more on arrival. Elsewhere in Spanish America, Africans were landed in Buenos Aires for onward transport to the slave markets of Cordoba, and thence even to Chile, Bolivia and Peru. For these Africans, the cold of high-altitude South America was the latest physical horror in the continuing saga of their enforced migration, which must, for the survivors, have seemed unending.[14]

Each European slaving nation had its own toehold in the Americas where its Africans were landed, spruced up, inspected and then sold on, either to local slave holders or to yet another slave merchant, who dragooned them onto another leg of their enforced migration. The Dutch used the two small Caribbean islands of St Eustatius and Curaçao, which naturally attracted all sorts and conditions of slave-traders, slave merchants or slave-owners from across the Caribbean and the Spanish mainland.[15]

Though they came late to this Atlantic world of trading in Africans, by the early eighteenth century, the British dominated it. In Bridgetown, Kingston and Charleston, and a string of smaller towns and ports, the British disembarked millions of Africans. Some of the sales took place on board ship, in the Chesapeake for example, where urban facilities for slave sales were rare. Tobacco planters or their agents came on board to inspect the cargo, sometimes leaving with their choice. The Africans 'were bought one by one, in pairs, or in larger groups over several afternoons'. Some, especially the weaker, sicker ones, remained unsold and were returned to their chains below decks to wait for another purchaser. In this way, many suffered the gross indignities of enduring several slave sales before finally being purchased. Slave ships to Virginia sometimes took two and a half months to sell off their entire African cargo. Throughout, the miserable Africans were hauled back and forth before a parade of likely purchasers.[16] Writing of Jamaica in 1680, Richard Blome wrote that the planters bought slaves 'on Ship-board, as men Buy Horses in a Fayr, and according as they are handsome, lusty, well-shapen, and young'.[17]

In the West Indies, auctions – scrambles – were common and are best described in Equiano's account of his own experiences. Slaves were prepared for sale on board ship or in their new prison, the slave barracoon. Sometimes attempts were made to cheer them up before would-be purchasers arrived to prod and poke and to test their condition. Few captains could sell all their slaves in one session. More common was a gradual whittling down of the slave numbers, the healthier, younger ones being selected ahead of the older and weaker. There then remained the 'refuse' slaves, already consigned by the slaver's vernacular to worthlessness, people for whom enslavement and shipping had been a process of withering away to ailing uselessness. They were the most abject of all in a world where suffering and pain were commonplace, unexceptional even.

Slave sales organized through the 'scramble', where buyers rushed among the slaves to grab the best ones, were a mayhem of noise and terror. Purchasers grabbed their targets as best they could, roping them together, determined to keep rivals at bay, and generally terrorizing the enfeebled Africans. What were they to make of such organized chaos?

> The poor astonished negroes were so much terrified by these proceedings, that several of them, through fear, climbed over the walls of the court yard, and ran wild about the town; but were soon hunted down and retaken.[18]

New arrivals were sometimes sold to agents in the islands who had already submitted an advance order for fresh Africans. Many were bought by local merchants, men based in colonial cities and ports who sold them on to planters and others in the interior, or simply acquired them as investments for future sale and profit, much as they would any other item of trade and commerce.[19] The process was often supervised by other, acclimatized slaves – Africans already settled in the colony and able to speak to the new arrivals, to explain what was happening to them and to reassure them about their fate (and, presumably, able to advise their masters/owners about any problems among the Africans). Historians often cite the example of Equiano's arrival at Barbados and his prompt onward sale to Virginia, but less attention has been paid to his role as a middleman among newly arrived Africans in St Eustatius, Jamaica and the Mosquito Coast. Because of his skills he was often used as the first contact point with newly arrived African slaves, people he described as 'my own countrymen', i.e., fellow Igbo whose language he spoke.[20]

Though the Africans may have longed for an escape from the filth of the slave ships, landfall did not bring an end to their painful migrations. They simply exchanged one owner (the slave captain, his company or merchants) for another (the colonial-based merchant or planter), keen to move the Africans on closer to their point of final settlement and labour. In the smaller islands it was usually no great distance to the final destination, but even that might entail a hazardous journey, by smaller vessel, or by foot into the interior, across the mountainous terrain. In South Carolina, Africans were shipped along the complex river system leading from the Charleston slave sales to the rice plantations. In the Chesapeake, Africans were similarly sailed up the tortuous riverine system which feeds into the Bay, before they were led off by land to their new home. On the bigger islands, where the frontier of eighteenth-century settlement had moved deep inland, the Africans had an even more arduous trek, often through lush and agriculturally rich lands, to remote places. Penetrating the fastness of Jamaica, or St Domingue, or Cuba was no easy task for Africans whose physical strength had been comprehensively sapped by the voyage. For that reason alone, their new owners appreciated the need to keep them in their urban barracoons and pens close to their point of disembarkation, allowing them time to recover and replenish their strength before marching them off to inland plantations and settlements. Slaves who were turned over to heavy work too quickly – too soon after their arrival – were often incapable of useful labour. When the owner of Worthy Park, a sugar plantation in the centre of Jamaica, bought a large number of new African slaves in 1792–93, the death rate on his estate increased dramatically. In desperation, he removed the survivors to his provisioning grounds 'for a change of air' and the problem receded.[21] Even the less-taxing work of tobacco cultivation proved too much for the new African slave Ayuba Suleiman Diallo in Maryland in 1730. He 'grew sick, being no way able to bear it; so that his Master was obliged to find easier work for him and therefore put him to tend cattle'.[22]

In 1776, with the breakaway of the North American colonies, about half a million blacks were removed from formal British control. By 1810 the black population of North America had risen to 1.4 million. To get some idea of the dramatic rise of the black population within the British empire we need to cast our mind back. In the mid-seventeenth century it had been restricted to a few islands in the Caribbean. By the time of American Independence, blacks were to be found scattered across the eastern Americas, 'from Maryland to East Florida on the mainland and from the Bahamas to Tobago'. (They were also to be found in small but significant numbers in the British homeland itself.) In terms of migrants, the British Americas were more black than white.[23]

The British (and others of course) had scattered Africans and their descendants across the face of the newly settled Americas, and to Europe. They had done so to advance their economic interests, primarily through the cultivation of sugar and tobacco. But as the American colonies emerged from precarious pioneer settlements into complex and sophisticated societies, black life was itself transformed. Slaves – and free blacks – broke away from the early roles created for them by white owners and masters. Destined to be the beasts of burden in the varied physical tasks of colonial development, Africans emerged as key players in a varied range of economic and social occupations. No Jamaican planter, surveying his sugar plantation in, say, the 1680s, could have imagined that a literate, devout African shopkeeper (Ignatius Sancho) would emerge from slavery to be lionized by polite London society a century later, his published letters becoming a lasting memorial to contemporary black life.[24]

Two factors lay behind this dispersal of African peoples. First, the Atlantic slave trade, and second, the varied demographic experience of slave society in the Americas. The obvious question arises (one which puzzled slave-owners and traders for years); why (with exceptions) did slaves not reproduce themselves in the slave colonies? Why were the plantations of the Americas permanently in thrall to the Atlantic slave-traders for continuing supplies of new Africans to replenish their labouring gangs in the fields? The glaring exception to this rule was North America. From the 1720s onwards, the natural increase of the North American black population outstripped the importations of Africans, and was even greater than the rate of population growth in Europe. It was an entirely different story in the Caribbean, however, where the slave population would have declined without African imports. Though 800,000 Africans had been shipped into the region by 1750, the slave population was only 300,000. There were exceptions to this general rule of course (notably in the Bahamas and, just, in Barbados), but the simple point remains. The sugar islands were 'a graveyard for slaves', but in North America demographically they flourished.[25]

Fertility among Caribbean slaves was low. It was, for instance, 80 per cent higher among North American slaves. In the mid-eighteenth century, about one-half of *all* female slaves in the West Indies never bore a child, and those women who did have children seemed to become infertile in their mid-thirties. The figures change when we move away from the sugar plantations. Slave women not working in sugar stood a better chance of bearing children, so clearly the problem was sugar. The sugar plantations created a set of physical and social determinants which militated against healthy conception, pregnancy, childbirth and infant survival. The work and the physical environment suited to sugar were corrosive of slave health and reproduction. And it was on the sugar plantations that we find the highest concentration of African (as opposed to Creole, i.e., local-born) slaves.

All the criteria of sickness, premature death and debility were at their worst among African slaves. In part this was a continuing consequence of the disruption and damage of enslavement and transportation. The wonder is that *anyone* emerged from the slave ships capable of a normal, healthy (and sane) existence. Moreover, Africans often had trouble finding partners, and seem to have been reluctant to have children. Those who did bear children tended to breast-feed their babies for long periods, helping to depress their fertility still further. Such detailed demographic data serve to confirm what had been obvious for a long time: life for sugar slaves was harsh, and that harshness bred a continuing need for African imports. Yet the more Africans we find on the plantations, the higher the levels of mortality, and the lower the levels of fertility. Work was harder in sugar than in any other agricultural work. Diet was also poor because, in the drive to get the most from their lands and to cultivate as much sugar as possible for export, planters often left slaves short of good cultivatable food land. On top of this, the slave nuclear family seems to have been weaker in the Caribbean than in North America.[26]

All these indications of the miserable experience of West Indian slaves lead back to sugar. There, in the fields and factories, labour was marshalled and dragooned as never before in the modern world; outsiders were fond of using military metaphors when looking at how the sugar slaves were organized. Sugar plantations found a way of extracting labour from all slaves, from the very young to the very old. Moreover, sugar production came to dominate some of the slave societies to the exclusion of most other activities. On smaller islands, nine in ten slaves worked in sugar. Even in Jamaica – the largest and geographically most varied of British islands – where different crops found a suitable home in different locales and altitudes, sugar continued to dominate life for 60 per cent of the slaves by the end of the eighteenth century. Across the British slave islands, sugar was king. It was maintained in its regal position by annual waves of Africans, stumbling from the slave ships to fill the depleted slave ranks in the sugar fields.

However, this concentration on sugar can deceive. Even where sugar dominated the local economy, slaves were used in a host of other occupations. Slaves laboured as domestics on the plantations and in towns (which, by the end of the eighteenth century, hosted small but noticeable slave communities). They worked as traders and hawkers in markets and on street-corners. On the plantations they worked as cultivators and as skilled men and women, from distillers and refiners to carpenters, masons and coopers. They cared for the livestock and managed the transport of goods (and people) to and from the plantations. There was a large range of crops, both foodstuffs and export goods, which were cultivated by slaves in all of the islands. By the end of the eighteenth century, the emergence of coffee cultivation on a string of islands where conditions were right was made possible, again, by slave labour. The coffee shops of London came to depend for both their coffee and its inevitable companion, sugar, on slaves in the Caribbean. Slaves cultivated the tropical produce the wider world craved and manhandled the finished produce on and off the ships bound for Europe. Slaves worked at the quaysides, loading and unloading the Atlantic ships, and manning the coastal and riverine vessels. They fished the waters of the Caribbean and the Atlantic, to feed themselves and for sale. A striking proportion of sailors in Atlantic shipping were black, both free and enslaved.[27]

In all the slave colonies of British America, slaves (generally women) cared for the sick and the young (both black and white). They fed, clothed and generally cared for their owners and employers. They often shared their owners' beds, bearing and rearing their children. In North America, where slave labour was rarely as harsh as in the islands (a result primarily of geography and local crops), most slaves worked in farming and domestic work; by the 1760s about half worked in rice, tobacco and indigo production. Slaves worked in the forests of central America, felling the logs, notably mahogany, which provided British craftsmen with the basic materials for those pieces of eighteenth-century furniture which are now costly antiques.

Skilled slaves were vital in all slave societies, and were important even in the British slave-trading toeholds on the African coast. Wherever we look, however, skilled slaves, though crucial to local operations, were only ever a small proportion of the overall slave population, the very great majority of which remained manual labourers. Wherever we find slaves, there we also see people who turned from working for their owners to working for themselves. Independent labour, on plots and gardens, or at whatever skill and aptitude they possessed, enhanced the slaves' material lives. It yielded foodstuffs and animals, goods to barter and sell, and generally helped to improve the slaves' material well-being, although all this came from the sweat of their own brow.

The brutal dispersal of millions of Africans across the Atlantic had, in effect, ushered in an utterly new world in the British American colonies. It had, first and foremost, transformed the human face of the slaving societies, making them, as many contemporaries recorded, an 'image of Africa'. In time, as the colonies matured, Africans and their descendants moved (or were moved) into most corners of the inhabited Americas. They even formed runaway communities, in the distant mountains and forests, safe from the control and punishments of local white society and living in effect independently, beyond the pale of settled empire.[28] The black presence was inescapable in the world of the late-eighteenth-century British Atlantic empire. They had even found a home in London.

Notes

1 For the most recent account of the initial British involvement with West Africa, see P. E. H. Hair and Robin Law, 'The English in western Africa to 1700', in Nicholas Canny (ed.), *Oxford History of the British Empire*, vol. I, *Origins*, Chapter 11.

2 David Richardson, 'The British Empire and the Atlantic slave trade, 1660–1807', in P. J. Marshall (ed.), *The Oxford History of the British Empire*, vol. II, *Eighteenth Century*, Chapter 20, p. 440.

3 *Ibid.*, pp. 444–7.

4 *Ibid.*, pp. 443, 450–1.

5 *Ibid.*, pp. 452–3.

6 John Thornton, *Africa and Africans in the Making of the Atlantic World, 1400–1680* (Cambridge, 1993), p. 97. This fact needs to be set against the transforming impact of the sugar revolution in the Americas.

7 *Ibid.*, pp. 103–5.

8 John Iliffe, *Africa: The History of a Continent* (Cambridge, 1996), pp. 137–9.

9 *Ibid.*, pp. 142–5.

10 *Ibid.*, p. 147.

11 *Ibid.*, pp. 134–5.

12 Betty Wood, *Slavery in Colonial Georgia* (Athens, Georgia, 1984).

13 Quoted in Hugh Thomas, *The Slave Trade: The History of the Atlantic Slave Trade, 1440–1870* (London, 1997), p. 431.

14 *Ibid.*, pp. 433–4.

15 For the details of the slave trade to and from these islands, see Johannes Menne Postma, *The Dutch in the Atlantic Slave Trade, 1600–1815* (Cambridge, 1990), pp. 223–4.

16 Allan Kulikoff, *Tobacco and Slaves: The Development of Southern Cultures in the Chesapeake, 1680–1800* (Chapel Hill, 1986), pp. 322–3.

17 Richard Blome, *A Description of the Island of Jamaica* (London, 1680), p. 37.

18 Alexander Falconbridge, *An Account of the Slave Trade on the Coast of Africa* (London, 1788), p. 34.

19 Trevor Burnard and Kenneth Morgan, '"To separate one from another": the dynamics of the slave market in mid-eighteenth century Jamaica'. Paper given at conference on The African Diaspora, Australian National University, April 1998.

20 Olaudah Equiano, *The Interesting Narrative* (1794), edited by Vincent Carretta (Penguin, 1995 edn), p. 205.

21 Michael Craton and James Walvin, *A Jamaican Plantation: Worthy Park: 1670–1970* (London, 1970), p. 131.

22 Quoted in P. D. Curtin (ed.), *Africa Remembered* (Madison, WI, 1967), p. 41.

23 Philip D. Morgan, 'The black experience in the British Empire, 1680–1810', in P. J. Marshall, *Eighteenth Century*, p. 465.

24 Reyahn King (ed.), *Ignatius Sancho: An African Man of Letters* (National Portrait Gallery, London, 1997).

25 Philip D. Morgan, 'The black experience', pp. 467–9.

26 *Ibid.*, pp. 469–70.

27 W. Jeffrey Bolster, *Black Jacks: African American Seamen in the Age of Sail* (Cambridge, MA, 1997).

28 Michael Craton, *Testing the Chains: Resistance to Slavery in the British West Indies* (Ithaca, NY, 1982), Chapters 5–7; Richard Price (ed.), *Maroon Societies: Rebel Slave Communities in the Americas* (Baltimore, 1972).

4

PLANTATIONS

The majority of Africans shipped across the Atlantic were destined, initially at least, to work in sugar. To work in sugar meant to work on a plantation. Like sugar and slavery, the plantation was an alien import into the Americas and had proved its economic value (to its owners if not to the labour force) much earlier. Plantations had been a tool of colonization in a host of different settings, most recently in the British settlement of Ireland. The British settlements in North America were known from the first as 'plantations' and the government body which oversaw these various projects after 1660 was the Council of Trade and Plantations.[1] However, long before British involvement, the plantation had been a traditional form of settlement and cultivation, and had long been associated with the cultivation of sugar cane.

Europeans first encountered sugar cane on plantations in the eastern Mediterranean at the time of the Crusades. An account of the First Crusade had described how Crusaders came across 'certain ripe plants which the common folk called "honey cane" and which were very much like reeds . . . In our hunger we chewed them all day because of the taste of honey.'[2] Cane sugar found its way from these plantations to northern Europe, establishing a taste for sweetness among European elites – the only people who could afford such costly imported fare. By the fifteenth century, cane sugar had become an ingredient in the kitchens of the rich, and was displayed in its most elaborate forms and shapes to impress guests and visitors at the dining table.[3]

Sugar-cane cultivation moved slowly westwards across the Mediterranean, finally breaking out into the Atlantic with the colonial settlements of the Atlantic islands of Madeira and the Canaries, and later São Tomé and Príncipe in the sixteenth century. There, as we have seen, sugar was cultivated with African slave labour. As more sugar became available, more and more Europeans were able to afford to consume it, a process greatly accelerated by the dramatic changes in the Americas.

The British had already established a plantation system closer to home; in the Cromwellian conquest and settlement of Ireland. The plantation seemed an ideal way of subduing and controlling the resistant Irish, and imposing on them an alien settler class. It was, of course, a very different plantation system from anything subsequently developed in the Americas. But early British settlers in both Bermuda and Virginia were aware of the Irish plantation experiments and were conscious of the lessons to be learned from them.[4] They hoped that the American variant would provide a secure garrison, an urban and agricultural base for economic growth and a means of maintaining links to the homeland. The Atlantic versions were in utterly different settings and were to veer away from the original Irish pattern dramatically. But what happened in the Americas needs to be seen more as a continuation of an old plantation tradition, rather than the invention of something new.[5]

The sugar plantation grew in size and sophistication with each new step of expansive European colonization. Even before crossing the Atlantic, the plantation had grown in size and complexity, and had forged vital links to the main centres of European finance and trade. It was clear enough to those men interested in colonization, in government, finance and business, that the plantation offered great potential for their commercial and colonial ambitions. It seems inevitable that the plantation, like the Africans and the sugar cane, would cross the Atlantic with the migrating Europeans.

The Spanish planted cane in 1517 in Santo Domingo, and then in other Caribbean islands, but the centre of their colonial interests quickly switched to the mainland and to the unimaginable riches apparently available in Mexico and Peru. Even so, by the time of the union of the Spanish and Portuguese crowns (in 1580) there were some 150 Spanish plantations in the West Indies and on the mainland, cultivating 7500 tons of sugar, thanks to the efforts of some 10,000 slaves.[6] It was, however, the Portuguese who firmly established the importance of sugar plantations in their Brazilian settlements, exporting their first sugar in the 1520s, and expanding their plantations (*engenhos*) using both Indian and African slaves in the 1540s. By 1600 Brazilian planters were producing perhaps 16,000 tons of sugar, thanks to a technology already used in the Atlantic islands and with finance from Antwerp (and later Amsterdam).

There remained a labour problem: Indians died off, or simply melted away from European contact. Moreover, opinion – led by the Jesuits – turned against Indian slavery, and legislation was introduced against it from 1570. Brazilian settlers therefore turned to one source of labour *already* in use in the Atlantic islands and in Portugal and Spain, African slave labour. This shift to African slave labour in Brazilian sugar production was not completed until the 1630s, but it proved a successful combination: European management, finance and markets, American lands, and African labour. In effect, the Brazilian sugar plantations pointed the way to subsequent American settlers – any labour-intensive tropical or semi-tropical crop might be best handled (i.e., most profitably for the Europeans) by the use of African slaves.

When the British began to settle in the tropical Americas, the tried-and-tested plantation proved irresistible, but only when the colonists turned to sugar cultivation *after* other unsuccessful agricultural experiments. The settlements and smallholdings of the pioneers gave way to plantations devoted to sugar cultivation. The drive to sugar production became contagious, with plantations proliferating across the landscape. In Barbados in 1650 there were perhaps 300 plantations. Twenty years later, the number had increased to 900. An early Jamaican map named 146 plantations; 13 years later that had grown to 690. By the time of American independence, there were some 1800 sugar plantations in the British West Indies.[7] This whole colonial plantation edifice was supervised from Whitehall by the Council of Trade and Plantations.

The plantation was not simply a means of bringing land into fruitful and profitable cultivation; it became an instrument for transforming the landscape. The natural habitat was chopped and burned into submission, alien flora and fauna were introduced (along with alien peoples) and man-made systems of roads, fields, buildings and walls were put in place. Planting food for survival, building shelter for protection, and then cultivating crops for export, settlers (white, black and mixtures of both) slowly imposed a manageable physical shape and an orderly regime of work and life on what had recently been virgin land.

Not all planters were successful. Many failed, especially in the early, dangerous days of settlement. Disease, starvation, natural disaster, attacks from native peoples – sometimes even a totally mysterious disappearance – all (and more) took their toll of people whose grip on the New World was always precarious. Some failed in their first endeavours before trying their hand elsewhere, moving to different colonies with different work and different crops. But some, a tiny minority – the best-remembered because they were so successful, so prosperous – thrived as others faded. Successful plantations gobbled up less successful neighbours. Worthy Park in Jamaica was founded in 1670 with an initial land grant of a mere 840 acres. For a generation, the numbers of local slaves remained small, but a century later, at the height of its slave-based fortunes, its cane fields were worked by some 560 slaves.[8]

Looking back from the surviving splendours of plantations, especially those planters' Great Houses which have been preserved as tourist sites, it is tempting to imagine them at their most splendid: architectural monuments to the wealth and style of their white owners (although mention is rarely made in the tourist literature of the black *helots* who made it all possible).[9] But most plantations were quite different, particularly in their early phases, when the priorities (for both black and white) were simple: secure shelter, cultivation of food and bringing the land into profitable use. But surviving Great Houses, and contemporary pictures of plantation houses, have created a firm impression of a prosperity built on the back of local slaves. In one slave society after another, a planter elite emerged as the arbiters of local taste and style, though often couching their social pretensions in terms of distant, metropolitan taste.

More important perhaps, the planters emerged as the brokers of political power, dominating local colonial political systems and controlling legislation and its implementation. Local colonial assemblies were their power base (although these were sometimes brought to heel by representatives from London); they were forums where the planters ensured that legislation was enacted, and political influence exercised, in the pursuit of slave-owning interests. Slaves – the very sinews and muscle of the whole system – were mere noises off-stage; their interests were heeded only to the extent that they coincided with the planters'. Planters also exercised influence in the distant capital, sometimes directly (when they absented themselves from the colonies to take up residence in Britain), or indirectly through agents and paid lobbyists. They had come to form a distinctive socio-economic group: the 'plantocracy'. Planters (in league with their commercial and maritime backers) formed cabals and pressure groups to influence metropolitan opinion and policy towards their own colony and towards the Atlantic slave system as a whole.

The elite of the planters – the wealthiest of all the West Indians – had become by the mid-eighteenth century almost a caricature of themselves, aping the fads and customs of their British peers and anxious to flaunt their wealth, often to a vulgar degree, in London and the fashionable spas. In the slave colonies, planters sought to impress friends, neighbours and, above all, visitors by lavish displays of consumption. West Indians were notorious for the abundance of their food, and especially of their drink. Often they managed to get things out of kilter. They sometimes filled their relatively humble homes with the most costly of imported items. In the words of Bryan Edwards, it was not uncommon

> to find, at the country inhabitations of the planters, a splendid sideboard loaded with plate, and the choicest of wines, a table covered with the finest damask, and a dinner of perhaps sixteen or twenty covers; and all this in a hovel not superior to an English barn.[10]

When Thomas Thistlewood arrived unannounced at an acquaintance's Jamaican estate in 1761, he was invited to lunch:

> Had duck stewed in claret, a roast turkey & hamms & greens, fryed ortolans, cheese & bread, oranges & a very fine shaddock, punch, madeira wine and claret.[11]

In the company of other white friends and neighbours, surrounded by hostile slaves and in a naturally threatening environment, planters drifted from lavish meals to protracted and excessive drinking bouts.[12] Special occasions or distinguished visitors prompted elaborate meals. Thistlewood again (this time in 1775) gave a lunch party (which lasted till 9 p.m.) consisting of:

> mutton broth, roast mutton & broccoli, carrots and asparagus, stewed mudfish, roast goose and paw-paw, apple sauce, stewed giblets, some fine lettuce . . . crabs, cheese, mush melon, etc. Punch, porter, ale, cyder, madeira wine & brandy etc. . .

Not surprisingly, he had a thick head the following day.[13]

As sugar prospered, West Indian plantations got bigger, nowhere more obviously so than in Jamaica, the island which, by the mid-eighteenth century, had become the most valuable of British slave colonies. The process first began in Barbados: in 1650 there were an estimated 300 plantations there; 20 years later there were perhaps 900. As early as the 1650s a group of major sugar magnates had emerged from humble beginnings and amalgamated smaller holdings into bigger plantations. Some of the more successful plantations, however, emerged from a different process – the division of truly massive land-holdings into more manageable units. It seems that the basic formation of the plantocratic elite in Barbados was established in the early years of settlement, though the process was consolidated from the mid-seventeenth century onwards. In 1673 a contemporary estimate showed how 74 of the island's 'most eminent' planters owned 29,050 out of 92,000 acres of farm land, ranging from 200 to 1000 acres each. By 1680, 175 of the biggest planters (only 7 per cent of all the property owners) controlled 54 per cent of the land, and 60 per cent of the slaves. They formed a powerful group, their political position firmly rooted in the wealth disgorged by their sugar properties. Though there were inevitable upheavals in the island during the English Civil War and Commonwealth, the Restoration settlement confirmed the plantocracy's domination of island politics and society. Unsuccessful settlers left the island; in the 1660s and 1670s something like 8000 whites quit Barbados, mainly for other islands. It was also in these years that Barbados's sugar dominance gave way to Jamaica.[14]

Large or small, wealthy or not, the plantation dominated the physical and social landscape of Barbados. The same process unfolded in Jamaica (where large numbers of people from Barbados had settled after 1655). A map of 1671 showed 146 plantations on Jamaica. A new map 13 years later named 690.[15] A century later, when Jamaica had firmly established itself as the most profitable of the British colonies, more than half of the island's planters owned more than 500 acres. By then, the classic Jamaican plantation employed 200 slaves. Indeed, by the same period, the average slave-holding in the British islands was 240 slaves. What had sustained this massive expansion of the plantations was the continuing flow of Africans across the Atlantic. On the eve of the American Revolution, some 1.5 million Africans had been imported into the British islands. We only have to glance back to the early days of pioneering settlement to see what had been wrought by the potent mix of sugar cultivation and African slavery. The slave plantations had brought forth tropical bounty on an unimaginable scale. Wherever plantations grew and increased, local exports multiplied. In 1620 Brazil had produced only 15,000 tons of sugar annually. Barbados alone managed to produce that figure 50 years later. And the figures became even more remarkable with the emergence of Jamaica and then the French sugar island of St Domingue. Between them, the French and British sugar islands were producing 150,000 tons of sugar annually by 1760. Thirty years later, the figure had risen to 290,000 tons.[16]

The plantation did more than facilitate the emergence of massive sugar production. It had become *the* social organization for land settlement and cultivation in a host of other crops and industries. Tobacco cultivation was similarly transformed by the plantation, and by enslaved African labour. In 1700, for example, the Chesapeake exported 20 million pounds of tobacco; by 1775 that figure had increased tenfold. The tobacco plantation system was, however, very different from the West Indian sugar version. For a start, tobacco plantations had been shaped by pioneering white owners who worked alongside their indentured labourers and the occasional slave. From the first, tobacco plantations tended to be small, and rarely approached the vast acreage of West Indian sugar plantations. Even in 1775, about 63 per cent of Virginia's slaves were owned and managed in groups of five, and not in the great gangs which dominated the West Indian plantations. Most tobacco slaves lived on small plantations, and this had enormous consequences for the nature and development of local slave society.[17] This network of small-scale tobacco plantations was nonetheless responsible for the massive increase in tobacco production and export to satisfy the European craving for smoking.

Plantations in South Carolina came closest to their West Indian counterparts. There were close connections between what became South Carolina and the West Indies, especially Barbados. Many of the early settlers had come from the West Indies with their slaves, and the region had, from an early date, a higher proportion of slaves than other mainland colonies. But the early population struggled in coastal South Carolina. Life changed, however, following the introduction of rice in 1690 and the development of rice plantations, where slaves outnumbered whites, between 1690 and 1720. Complex irrigation schemes and the scale of rice cultivation edged the planters towards plantations not unlike the West Indian versions. To expand the slave ranks, planters imported about 600 slaves each year in the 1720s, rising to 2000 in the 1730s. They came mainly through Charleston, their large presence affecting local language and customs – they even gave Charleston a black majority. By 1740 there were about 40,000 slaves in the region, and though some were part of large slave-holdings, most were owned in small groups.

What made the lives of South Carolina slaves different from their counterparts in the Caribbean was the use of the task system on the rice plantations; slaves were given a particular task or target and their work was finished when that task was completed. Many slave-owners disliked the task system for allowing the slaves too much latitude, too much room and time for independent activity. Nonetheless, it was African slaves who opened a hostile environment to profitable cultivation. The dangerous swamplands of the South Carolina coastal region were transformed into fruitful plantations, which supplied the growing rice export trade (much of which was used not as food but to produce starch) and the rewards of which enabled the wealthier planters to retire to stylish homes in Charleston.[18]

Thus, from the Chesapeake to north-east Brazil, the plantation had become essential, though there were enormous differences between plantations. The sugar plantations especially were massive operations, their gangs of slaves often striking visitors more like a regimented military force, with the strongest and youngest thrown at the toughest, most demanding work. But other plantations were very small, and saw black and white working close together in the same endeavour. Sugar and rice plantations were the most physically demanding, largely because their respective crops thrived best in the harshest of physical environments. During the sugar and rice harvests and at planting times, slave life was arduous in the extreme; hours were long – as long as natural light would allow – and breaks were few. But this was true only for *part* of the agricultural year. Elsewhere, slave work was less demanding. However, wherever we look, it was the slaves on and around the plantations who tapped the land for its material benefits. It was slave labour which enabled planters to amass their wealth, to retreat to their local or European fashionable homes. And it was these same slaves who made possible the emergence of new tastes and pleasures in distant lands, among people who scarcely recognized the debt they owed to Africans and their descendants.

The plantations of the Americas stood on the very edge of empire and settlement. Indeed, the concept of a 'plantation' was partly seen as a means of establishing a Christian and civilized outpost in an alien and unknown environment.[19] They were, in effect, beachheads for securing a new region for European (in this case British) domination. It was ironic that this political (and economic) ideal could only be achieved with hordes of African slaves. In time, those same slaves were to create massive problems of a different kind for their owners. Even today, it is possible to gain a sense of the isolation, the feeling of insecure frontier life, which pervaded the planters' minds and dreams. Stand on the veranda at Good Hope in Jamaica, south of Falmouth on the island's north coast, and look south to the wild and uninviting 'cockpit' country of the interior. Here was a world which beckoned the runaway slave, which harboured independent, free black communities and which threatened whites through its sinister impenetrability and its raw wildness. That sense of precariousness, the feeling of clinging to the slippery edge of civilization, helped to shape the mentality of plantation whites. Their friends were distant, military assistance might be days away, and there could be no guarantee that unrest might not rattle their doors without the least warning.

The plantations were in many respects outposts, garrisons, where an enslaved labouring force was kept hard at the task of turning the wilderness to profit. They were also instruments for the disciplining and control of the labour force. They were peculiar institutions. Europeans needed them for their own economic well-being and for their own protection (though, when they looked at the slave quarters, they saw an enemy there within the plantation). Equally, the plantations needed the outside world. They needed the metropolis for their own survival. Plantations thrived on the profit of trade to distant ports and capitals, but they could only survive on what they, in their turn, imported from abroad. Having cultivated and then satisfied the distant taste for tropical goods and produce, the plantations of colonial America, in their turn, required a range of imported goods from Europe. Quite simply, the plantations could not survive without massive and continuing imports from across the Atlantic. Indeed, the hope that plantations would stimulate British manufacture and employment had been an important issue from the start. As early as 1686, the colonists' produce enabled them to purchase about £1 million worth of goods in London. It also enabled them, of course, to buy slaves. Over the centuries, the value of goods imported into the plantation colonies was enormous, with all the consequent benefits flowing into Britain and her economy.[20]

The most critical import was the labour force itself; plantations owed their existence to the Africans. In the 50 years to 1700, the slave population of the British Caribbean rose from 15,000 to 115,000.[21] In North America, where the slave birth-rate soon enabled planters to dispense with the import of African slaves, the plantations needed, not Africans, but the descendants of Africans. But throughout the British American slave colonies, plantations devoured other imports to maintain the existence of both black and white.

Much of the maritime trade which flowed into the slave islands and the slave colonies of the north was the lifeline of the plantations. And it is here, in the apparently simple facts of everyday plantation life, that we begin to encounter the complex economic ramifications of the Black Atlantic. Slave food, slave clothing, slaves' implements; planters' clothing and furnishings; the everyday items of domestic life – all and more were imported. Moreover, the imported Africans were *themselves* purchased on the back of British goods. The plantation was the hub around which this mighty wheel of Atlantic activity moved.

Plantation accounts record the varied cargoes received each year from Britain. The papers of Worthy Park Estate in Jamaica illustrate the point. In 1789 the plantation took delivery of mosquito nets, thread, copper boilers, strainers and other metal goods, furniture, glass, slaves' hats and blankets, coal and foodstuffs for both the slaves and the whites, gunpowder, stationery, tools and medicines. Looking at the ledgers of imports it becomes immediately apparent that here was an organization which was inextricably and intimately linked to the British heartland. Worthy Park Estate had risen to commercial viability thanks to its African slaves. But those slaves could not do their work (and nor could their white masters) without the regular arrival of goods from Britain.

Slaves wore imported clothes and hats. The salt-fish they ate was imported. The tools they used to hack at the sugar cane and to till the ground were imported. And, of course, the slaves themselves were imported. The machinery, equipment and chains in the sugar factories were either imported or fashioned from imported metals. The story is much the same for the whites. They dined off imported crockery and tableware; some of their foodstuffs came from England and Ireland. They rode on British saddles, restored their health with imported medicines (though many also turned to their slaves for African herbal treatments). They washed down their elaborate meals with imported wines. Whites maintained their security against the slaves with firearms and powder from abroad (in addition to the omnipresent colonial forces, especially the Royal Navy). Between 1768 and 1770 Thomas Thistlewood imported more than 200 different kinds of trees and seeds to plant on his property in western Jamaica. He recorded regular deliveries of crates and boxes containing clothes, foods and books from his agent in London.[22]

Colonial and slave societies also developed their own complex and sophisticated skills in manufacturing and production. Both black and white made the most of the range of local products which came to hand, or which could be cultivated or refashioned and crafted in their own region. But imports were ubiquitous and vital. Imported goods formed the lubricant of plantation life; planters, like slaves, could not survive without British imports (and the same was true, of course, for other European slave colonies). In some respects the level of importation was more obvious and striking among the whites than the slaves, for the material of their social and private lives was fashioned more directly on life on the far side of the Atlantic. Much of their clothing, furniture and luxuries (such as the tea-urn and the chinaware in the planter's house at Rooksby Park, Jamaica) were imported. As with propertied peoples everywhere, some of the planters' material possessions eventually found their way into slave hands. Clothing, shoes, tableware – essentials and luxuries – all passed into the slave quarters. Bryan Edwards noticed, when looking into slave homes, especially those of the better-off slaves (i.e., those closest to local whites), that some had mosquito nets and even 'display a shelf or two of plates and dishes of Queen's or Staffordshire ware'.[23] Though such evidence has problems (by the late eighteenth century, planters were keen to let the outside world know that their slaves enjoyed better than basic conditions), it is consistent with other data. Slaves acquired (and seemed to want) goods, especially if they were exotic and had a social cachet. We know, for example, of one slave stealing a clock from another slave in St Ann, Jamaica, in 1788.[24] Such incidents, small and unimportant in themselves, provide a key to a much broader issue – the degree to which imported goods affected all levels of people within plantation society.

As we have seen, the plantations absorbed enormous volumes of imported British material. Similarly, imports flowed back and forth between the plantations of North America and the West Indies. The consumption by plantations was a major element in the growth of British export trade. In 1689 alone, 329 ships exported 598 different kinds of goods (most of them manufactured) to the American colonies.[25] Within the wider world of British overseas trade the West Indies emerged to a position of major importance. From the early eighteenth century, some 45 per cent of English exports to the Atlantic empire went to the West Indies. The ramifications of this West India trade went far beyond the simple trade to and from England; it yielded trade to Scotland, to North America, to Africa, to other parts of the Caribbean and to the Atlantic islands. Imports to the Caribbean grew from about £500,000 in 1682 to £5 million in 1774. The West Indies imported more than £263,000 worth of commodities in 1682–83; by 1773–74 that had increased to £1,652,000.[26]

As the eighteenth century advanced, the plantation colonies bought ever more goods from England, from Ireland (Irish textiles and foods were especially important), and from the colonies in North America. Initially, trade from North America was more valuable to the Americans, but that changed as the islands absorbed more imports from the northern colonies. It was said that the whole region – northern and Caribbean colonies – had become in effect 'one great plantation'.[27] And the region, like the individual plantations which formed the small parts of the greater whole, generated trade (and profit) in a host of directions. The slave colonies generated trade to and from North America and Ireland, helping those regions in their turn to trade with England. The slave colonies, of course, also prompted a remarkable trade to and from Africa. And all helped promote trade to and from Asia. In short, the plantations, and the broader colonial economies of which they formed the central part, were a powerful economic engine whose global reach and importance brought to the metropolis enhanced commerce and profit from all corners of the world.

From the pioneering days of the plantations through to 1807 (when the slave trade was abolished), the most obvious and enduring plantation import was African slaves. To describe this particular trade in the language of the eighteenth-century account books is to run the danger of over-looking the human beings involved. Nonetheless, Africans *were* bought and sold, traded and exchanged, like all other items of commerce. When we examine the details of the transactions which brought Africans to the plantations, we find further proof of the critical role played by plantations in the broader world of the Atlantic economy. Africans were bought and bartered by a trade which further enhanced British material well-being. Planters paid the slave-traders and merchants who brought the Africans across the Atlantic in a variety of ways. Those same Africans had been purchased initially, on the West African coast, by the exchange and barter of British goods. Again, a key – *the* key – element in the shaping of the plantation (i.e., the slave) was made possible by British manufacture and trade. It would be wrong, of course, to claim that slaves were the *only* trade between Europe and West Africa. But this transfer of Africans into the hands of British shippers was effected by British industry and global trade. It also lured a growing fleet of ships from a range of British ports to the African coast. All of those ships were filled with goods and produce destined for African merchants and middlemen, and thence to wider African markets. This whole complex trade was to secure slaves destined for labour in the Americas.

Slave-traders on the African coast wanted a range of goods in exchange for Africans. The main complaint from traders on the coast in the late seventeenth century was that not enough goods were imported to satisfy African demand, and as the trade expanded in the eighteenth century, goods flowed to Africa in even greater volumes. Any single cargo could illustrate the general point. When the *Hope* left Lancaster for Africa in 1792, its holds brimmed with goods from that city and from industries and producers throughout the north-west of England. Liverpool merchants provided beads, earthenware, knives and rice; salt and metal goods came from Cheshire; cotton goods from Manchester; flagons, food and chests from Lancaster; sails from Kirkham; weapons and iron goods from Liverpool; and pots from Preston. This one single vessel headed for the African coast with a variety of goods drawn from a broad northern hinterland.

It is clear that the trade in African humanity involved many more than the obvious participants – traders, sailors, merchants and planters. There was an extraordinary web of British economic and social involvement which drew all sorts and conditions of British people – small-scale operators, merchants, even shopkeepers and craftsmen – into the trade in slaves. The links, in the case of the *Hope* between north-country merchants, Atlantic traders and West Indian planters, were direct and unbroken and formed a series of connections joining the heartlands of Britain to the very edge of colonial settlement and trade on the plantations.

The plantations transformed much more than the physical face of their own regions. They transformed black life itself. Slaves came to be deemed essential to plantation success. Slaves (and only slaves) were thought appropriate for labouring in sugar, rice and tobacco. And those slaves were African, or descended from Africans. Plantation slavery was *racial* and, to justify the peculiar bondage of the Americas, there evolved a language of race. Arguments in favour of slavery *tout court* were not sufficient, for these were not merely slaves; they were *black* slaves. Plantations were the occasion and cause of the emergence of a new language of race: of society and status, rank and position, humanity and inhumanity, all shaped by a complexity of racial definitions. Plantations ushered in a new categorization of mankind, designed to justify and secure the use of slavery for the economic advancement of all concerned – except the slaves, of course.

The plantation story did not end with the ending of British slavery in 1834–38. It had proved itself too valuable an economic tool to be abandoned in a fit of moral outrage. Plantations struggled to stay in place in the ex-slave colonies, though often the labour force slipped away, unwilling to linger as free people in the house of bondage. Sometimes other forms of unfree labour had to be invented or imported to fill the vacuum left by the departing ex-slaves. Especially striking was the British shipping of more than half a million indentured 'Indian servants' to the former British slave colonies (and elsewhere). Sometimes, when the local crop declined and faded, plantations disappeared; others were maintained or revived as handsome properties, later to become tourist sites, with visitors lured by the architectural and rural beauties. The slaves, however, generally remained 'noises off-stage', unremarked, unnoticed and even ignored, an ugly reminder of the historical and human suffering which brought the plantation into being in the first place.

In places the plantation enjoyed a revival of fortunes. As the United States spread southward and westward, and as cotton took hold, the plantation (often on a massive scale) again proved its economic worth to owners, management and capital. Much the same was true, even later, with tobacco-growing in Cuba, and coffee in Brazil. As long as slavery seemed to make economic sense (and it lasted in Cuba and Brazil into the 1880s), the plantation thrived; it might be different in size and scale from one place and crop to another, but was recognizably the same institution which had fashioned slavery into the key form of labour across whole swathes of the Americas, and had become the source and occasion of manifold black miseries.

Even the ending of slavery did not see off the plantation. It had proved its economic worth throughout the tropical and semi-tropical Americas. In the nineteenth and twentieth centuries, it was transplanted into a host of societies in order to bring new land into profitable cultivation, on the back of a labour force which needed to be regulated and disciplined. New plantation systems thrived (with free and sometimes less-than-free labour) in West Africa (palm oil and cocoa), East Africa (tea), India and Ceylon (tea), Hawaii (fruit), Central and South America (coffee, fruit), Australia (sugar), and Malaya (rubber). The plantations differed one from another, but the fact that the system survived, however transmuted its shape and nature, is proof enough of its remarkable success and value to its owners and backers. It brought little to its labour force, however, except sweat and toil.

The plantation had been first brought to a peak of modern perfection, shaped into an efficient tool of management and control, in the slave colonies of the Americas. It was instrumental in rendering work on tropical staples more efficient and profitable, and also in the subjugation and control of millions of imported Africans. In this the British played a critical part. As with the Atlantic slave trade itself, the British did not invent or pioneer the plantation. Indeed they came relatively late to both systems. But it was the British who effectively perfected the plantation complex – the rapid spread of plantations across a whole society, and the emergence of what came to be known as 'plantation societies'. It was the British who perfected the Atlantic system – maritime trade, African labour, tropical produce, domestic consumption and manufacture – which hinged on the plantations. The plantation continued the process first begun on the slave ships, of hammering millions of African slaves into a disciplined submission. Of course it did not always work exactly as the British (or other Europeans) wanted. Slaves did not automatically follow their owners' wishes or instructions. But it was on the plantation that the British and other settler peoples took the sick and distressed African arrivals from the slave ships, and shaped them into the labouring instruments of tropical profitability.

Plantations were a key element in the evolution of very different societies. The pioneering, early settlements in the Americas (many of them largely urban, though admittedly on a small scale) gave way to huge rural economies.[28] They became societies where great tracts of land had been won over to fruitful and profitable cultivation, the produce from which was dispatched in convoys of British vessels to quaysides around Britain. None of this was possible without African labour. To provide that labour, the British alone embarked on 12,000 slave voyages.[29] Something like 70 per cent of all African slaves were destined (initially at least) for the sugar fields. But so expansive were the slave societies, so buoyant the economies created by the millions of Africans, that slavery quickly slipped its moorings and slaves were to be found everywhere across the Americas, and in Europe and on the high seas. The Atlantic economy, with its massive movement of shipping, commodities and peoples, all criss-crossing the Atlantic, saw the movement of Africans and their descendants to all corners of the Atlantic world. This enslaved Atlantic system saw a massive dispersal of African peoples from Lima to Liverpool, from Bahia to Bath, from the American frontier to the most fashionable of European homes. And in this scattered diasporic exile, black culture was transformed.

Notes

1 Nicholas Canny, 'The origins of empire: an introduction', in *The Origins of Empire: The Oxford History of the British Empire* (Oxford, 1998), p. 8.
2 H. S. Fink, trans., *A History of the Expedition to Jerusalem* (Knoxville, 1969), p. 130.
3 Sidney Mintz, *Sweetness and Power* (London, 1985).
4 Nicholas Canny, 'Origins', p. 9.
5 Michael Craton, 'The historical roots of the plantation model', in Michael Craton, *Empire, Enslavement and Freedom in the Caribbean* (Kingston, 1997), Chapter 1.
6 *Ibid.*, p. 27.
7 Richard B. Sheridan, *Sugar and Slavery* (Baltimore, 1973), p. 262.
8 Michael Craton and James Walvin, *A Jamaican Plantation: Worthy Park, 1670–1970* (London, 1970).
9 See, for example, the plantations on the James River in Virginia, in Bruce Roberts, *Plantation Homes of the James River* (Chapel Hill, NC, 1990).
10 Bryan Edwards, *The History, Civil and Commercial, of the West Indies*, 2 vols (London, 1790), vol. II, p. 10.
11 Douglas Hall (ed.), *In Miserable Slavery: Thomas Thistlewood in Jamaica, 1750–1786* (London, 1989), p. 123.
12 *Ibid.*, p. 216.
13 *Ibid.*, pp. 236–7.
14 Hilary McD. Beckles, *A History of Barbados* (Cambridge, 1990), pp. 23–8; Richard S. Dunn, *Sugar and Slaves: The Rise of the Planter Class in the English West Indies, 1624–1713* (London, 1973), pp. 96–103.
15 James Walvin, *Black Ivory: A History of British Slavery* (London, 1993), pp. 69–70.
16 Robin Blackburn, *The Overthrow of Colonial Slavery, 1776–1848* (London, 1988), p. 12.
17 Allan Kulikoff, *Tobacco and Slaves: The Development of Southern Cultures in the Chesapeake, 1680–1800* (Chapel Hill, NC, 1986), pp. 319–34.
18 P. D. Morgan, *Slave Counterpoint* (Chapel Hill, NC, 1998); Charles W. Joyner, *Down by the Riverside* (Urbana, IL, 1984).
19 Nicholas Canny, *Origins*, p. 10.
20 Nuala Zahedieh, 'Overseas trade in the seventeenth century', in Nicholas Canny, *Origins*, pp. 410–18.
21 *Ibid.*, p. 414.
22 Douglas Hall, *Thistlewood*, pp. 115, 293, 303, 305.
23 Bryan Edwards, *History*, Vol. II, p. 165.
24 *Slave Trials*, St Ann, Jamaica, 19 August 1788. National Library of Jamaica.
25 Nuala Zahedieh, in Nicholas Canny, *Origins*, pp. 414–15.
26 Richard Sheridan, *Sugar*, pp. 308–10.
27 *Ibid.*, p. 314.
28 Ira Berlin, *Many Thousands Gone* (Cambridge, MA, 1998).
29 Hugh Thomas, *The Slave Trade* (London, 1997), p. 805.

= 5 =

SLAVE CULTURE

When the British freed their slaves (partially in August 1834, completely in 1838[1]) the local celebrations were led by colonial officials. Governors and their formal retinues attended church throughout the colonies to give thanks for the blessing of black freedom. Large numbers of slaves also celebrated by attending church, crowding the recently built chapels with a noisy but peaceable presence. Their behaviour formed a sharp contrast to the worst fears of their former owners and managers, who had predicted 'blood and destruction on the 1st of August; in this they were wrong'.[2] Black freedom was ushered in peaceably. A Methodist missionary writing from Abaco in the Bahamas on 1 August 1834 ('that memorable day in the annals of British history') remarked that it had passed quietly. 'I walked from one end of the place to the other end . . . not a disorderly person was to be seen nor a voice heard.'[3] Tranquillity marked the subsequent anniversaries, celebrated each 1 August. The first anniversary was marked, according to another Methodist (again in the Bahamas), by 'the coloured people'

in a manner highly creditable to themselves and satisfactory to all who had the pleasure to witness their orderly upright and religious proceedings as well as the joy and gladness they manifested on that memorable and never to be forgotten day.[4]

This is, surely, a curious situation: people of African descent, thrust into or born into slavery of the most brutal form, celebrating the return of their long-denied freedom by giving thanks to the God of their white masters. It had not always been so. For centuries, Europeans had invoked their deity to bless and succour their slave-trading ventures.

When embarking on his 1564 slaving ventures in Africa and the Caribbean, the English privateer John Hawkins had ordered his men to, 'Serve God daily.'[5] Slave-traders regularly recruited God to what later generations came to think of as their godless endeavours. Two centuries on, another British slave-trader, John Newton, following a similar Atlantic route to Hawkins, from Africa to the West Indies, hoped that threats of rebellion among his shipboard African slaves would be overcome with the help of 'Divine Assistance'. With his vessel finally loaded with sugar in the Caribbean, Newton weighed anchor in Antigua on the final leg of his voyage, 'bound (by God's permission) for Liverpool'.[6] This same deity once invoked to bless and assist British slave-traders was thanked, in 1834, by Africans and their children for the blessings of their new-found freedom. Clean across the British colonies in 1834 and 1838, blacks celebrated their freedom with thanks to a Christian God. Something, clearly, had changed.

African slaves stepped ashore in the Americas sick, near naked and with no material possessions. They had been as thoroughly deracinated as could be imagined. Though they had forged friendships and bonds with other slaves while on route to the coast, and especially in the holds of their wooden prisons, they landed in the Americas alone. The varied societies from which they had been plucked in Africa were, henceforth, distant memories which inevitably got dimmer with the passage of time (though periodically refreshed by the arrival of African slaves with recent news from their homelands). Africans did not see themselves as 'Africans'; they belonged to much more specific groups of peoples and cultures, and saw their identities and loyalties in terms of those origins, of kinship ties, of language, region and beliefs. It was outsiders – Europeans and American settlers – who tended to see them simply as Africans. It is an irony that this belief in an African identity was forged initially by outsiders looking at Africa and its inhabitants, and was then adopted by slaves in the Americas when they found themselves immersed in slave societies which demarcated black from white in the simplest and most brutal of fashions. Time and again, throughout the *Narrative* of his life, the ex-slave Olaudah Equiano referred to 'fellow countrymen'; he meant, not other Africans, but fellow Igbo people from his native region.

Landing and settling in the Americas involved a process of massive cultural change (and for whites too, of course). Africans, and their local-born children, were changed by the new circumstances of their lives in the Americas – by their relationships with other slaves (many from different parts of Africa), by the physical locations they lived in, by their relations with local white people, by the work they were forced to do. This process of cultural change was shaped, however, not simply by impersonal and haphazard events over which people had little or no control. Slaves were instrumental in shaping for themselves key areas of their personal and communal life. Yet they did this from the unrewarding social and material conditions confronting them in all slave colonies.

Newly arrived Africans, whatever their African origins, were united by the experience of the slave ships. The enslaved oceanic crossing was (and remains) perhaps *the* emblem of the Atlantic slave experience, even though millions of slaves, born in the Americas, learned of it only at their parents' and grandparents' knee. The traumas of the Middle Passage were endured by all eleven million survivors, and they were not easily remedied. Most obviously, the physical damage of the seaborne experience was embedded in black life, in the form of horrific statistics of death and illness among all African survivors, who suffered the consequences for years afterwards. Though New World slave-owners made efforts to restore Africans to good health (if only for economic reasons), Africans remained afflicted by the range of illnesses and miseries contracted in the filth of the slave decks. This was, of course, in addition to whatever mental distress the process of enslavement and transportation had caused. Even landfall did not bring these agonies to an end, for many Africans were, as we have seen, sold on – by ship and by foot – to other, distant, destinations. The simple point is this: for years after leaving their shipboard imprisonment, Africans continued to be troubled by its consequences. Many simply faded away and died from the effects of their enslavement and crossing. Millions died, first in Africa, in the process of enslavement and travel to the coast, and while waiting on the Atlantic coast for purchase by Europeans, and then in transit across the Atlantic and in that difficult period of initial adjustment to the Americas ('seasoning' in the harsh vernacular of the slave-owners).[7] One African in four died within the first year of landing in the Chesapeake, for instance.[8] There was, however, something uniquely appalling about the sufferings on the Atlantic crossing. The slaves' shipborne sufferings were experienced – and witnessed – publicly, normally under the most distressing of circumstances. All surviving Africans emerged in the Americas from a foul, almost unimaginable, experience. There was no place to hide in the communal squalor of the slave decks, no escape from the physical decline of the sick and the dying, no refuge from the noise and the stench, from the cries of pain and from the shrieks of the mad. European commentators (sailors, traders, merchants, doctors) were united in accounts of their physical revulsion at the sights and smells when they peered below into the slave decks. But what was it like on the other side? What did it mean to be on the inside – to be chained to a heaving mass of sick and afflicted humanity, pitching and rolling in their own communal filth for weeks on end? It is easy to sensationalize this seaborne experience, but no historical reconstruction or commentary can do full justice to the lived (and dying) experience endured by every single African on the slave ships. The memories – nightmares really – of the time on the slave ships united survivors, however different their African origins. It was also the first and formative element in shaping relations between black and white. For the very great bulk of African slaves, their initial dealings with white people before they landed in the Americas was the process of re-enslavement on the Atlantic coast and the sufferings of the slave ships. Here was an experience conceived in violence, tempered by maritime imprisonment and misery, and forged by sickness and dying. And all this *before* the slaves stepped ashore in the Americas.

It is tempting, in the teeth of this terrible set of conditions, to imagine that the slaves were denuded of their cultural *persona* by the trauma of their transit to the Americas. In fact, they brought to the New World a myriad personal and social characteristics from their varied African backgrounds which, in turn, helped to shape slave culture in the Americas. Many carried their physical markings, facial and body scars which denoted ethnic, tribal or local origins, and which Europeans tended to regard as signs of African ugliness or primitivism.[9] When Thomas Thistlewood bought a batch of new slaves in 1765, most sported African markings. He described them variously:

> . . . several rows of punctures across the belly, & thus on the face.
> . . . 3 perpendicular scars down each cheek.
> . . . several perpendicular small & one diagonal scar on each cheek.
> . . . her belly full of her country marks.
> . . . holes through her nose.
> . . . her face all over Champherred . . .
> . . . on her face 3 long strokes down each cheek, 2 small oblique, etc. Her belly full of country marks and an arch between her breasts.[10]

(A white man, whose face and body had been permanently scarred by slashes from slaves in the Jamaican rebellion of 1760, was known thereafter by the nickname 'Coromantee Gordon'.[11])

Africans in the Americas naturally gravitated towards their own people, to Africans from similar backgrounds, whose languages and customs they recognized and understood. This was easier where large numbers came from similar regions. In the eighteenth century, the British transported vast numbers of Igbo people. Indeed, as many as 80 per cent of the African arrivals in British colonies in the years 1700 to 1807 may have been Igbo-speakers.[12] Not surprisingly, when Equiano (himself an Igbo) worked the Caribbean and Atlantic shipping routes as an enslaved, and later a free, sailor he regularly bumped into fellow Igbo in St Eustatius, Barbados, Jamaica and London – and almost certainly elsewhere.[13]

When Equiano sailed to Kingston in 1771–72, he expressed himself surprised

> to see the number of Africans, who were assembled together on Sundays; particularly at a large commodious place called Spring Path. Here each different nation of Africa meet and dance, after the manner of their own country.

By a quite remarkable coincidence, the young Englishman Thomas Thistlewood, landing in Jamaica 21 years earlier, had made an almost identical observation in his diary for 29 April 1750:

> In the evening, Mr Fowler and I walked to Spring Path, to the westward of the Town, to see Negro Diversion – odd Music. Motions, etc. The Negroes of each Nation by themselves.[14]

Africans had to understand, and make themselves understood, in this new world. Surrounded by slaves who spoke their own African language, they had no problems. But most slave quarters contained a mix of African cultures and languages. It has been calculated that some 1000 languages were spoken among the African peoples shipped into the British colonies. As long as Africans poured from the slave ships, African languages dominated the slave quarters. But this inevitably changed with the rise of a local-born slave population and with the imperatives of comprehending instructions from white owners and bosses. The key to understanding was to master the rudiments of their owners' language – whichever European language was the *lingua franca* in that colony. Failure to understand was to invite a cuff or a beating. Slave incomprehension laid the basis for the pervasive white belief in black stupidity and, in general, it simply made life difficult and (often) dangerous for the African slaves.

Language was one obvious point of contact. So slaves learned their masters' languages; their children spoke those languages as their own. Thus we find slaves speaking Dutch (in New York as well as the Dutch islands), German in Pennsylvania, French in Quebec, and on the French islands, Portuguese in Brazil, Spanish in Spain's colonies and, of course, English in the British slave colonies. Some, in the North Carolina Highlands, even spoke Gaelic.[15] But the process was much more complex than merely learning to speak a master's language.

In addition, a local *patois* emerged everywhere; this was a language whose roots, inflexions and vocabulary lay in an African – and native Indian – past and which melded with English and other European languages to produce a hybrid which made sense to the slaves. These Creole languages were to be found across the slave colonies, from Trinidad to the Sea Islands off South Carolina, and they have provided rich pickings for students keen to trace the various ethnic origins of New World languages.[16] Many Africans became bilingual, working as English-speaking middlemen with local whites, but reverting to their native language when dealing with newly arrived slaves. Equiano is just the best-known of many such slaves who were employed to negotiate between newly arrived Africans and their white masters.

The Europeans, especially the slave-traders, always needed interpreters. Slave captains employed 'natives and freemen of the Country' on the African coast

> who we hire on account of their speaking good English, during our time on the coast; and they are likewise brokers between us and the black merchants.

Slave-traders used African interpreters to explain to the terrified slaves on their ships precisely what was about to happen to them. Captain Snelgrave gave instructions that, while on board the slave ship, should anyone abuse the slaves, 'they are to complain to the linguist, who is to inform me of it, and I will do them justice'. On an earlier crossing, William Smith, involved in suppressing a shipboard slave rebellion, 'called for the linguist and bid him ask the negroes ... "Who had killed the white man?"'[17]

Some Africans were already multilingual in African languages, even before they were enslaved. Others, especially those working at sea, became proficient in a host of standard languages, though few could have been as impressive as the slave runaway advertised in Jamaica in 1790. He was a man 'of the Coromantee nation' with experience of the Windwards and of North America and spoke 'the English, French, Dutch, Danish and Portuguese languages'.[18]

Most Africans were doubtless happy to operate at a less-exalted level; it was enough simply to make themselves understood in the confusion of new cultures they were plunged into. This simple proficiency was provided by the local *patois*. In fact, this *patois* (though they were many and varied) emerged initially among Africans and Europeans working on the African coast, in the ports, in the barracoons and slave forts, and then on the Atlantic ships themselves. In the slave colonies there were bewildering confusions of languages, especially when those colonies were exchanged back and forth between warring Europeans, with slaves evolving a new or parallel *patois*. In Trinidad, for example, both French and English Creole flourished, each of them drawn from 'the linguistic systems of the Niger-Congo' (Yoruba) and from French and then English, as the island passed from one European power to another.[19] There was, in effect, a web of Creole languages which spanned the whole Atlantic world, from the edge of European involvement in Africa (and even, via Afro-European traders, much deeper into Africa than the coastal or riverine settlements), on the slave ships plying the Atlantic, and in the various slave colonies of the Americas, enabling vastly different peoples from Europe, Africa and the Americas to understand each other. It was the linguistic lubricant vital to the functioning of this vast Atlantic slave system.

In the British colonies, slaves came to speak English Creole (though that broke down into different distinctive types).[20] In these languages Africa was ubiquitous; the words, inflexions and syntax of West Africa were a linguistic reminder of the world that had disappeared over the horizon as the slave ships ploughed westward. The durability and persistence of these African forms varied greatly. Where the white (European) presence was strong (i.e., where whites outnumbered blacks) – especially in North America – the influence was more muted than in those slave colonies where the Africans greatly outnumbered whites.

When slaves and freed blacks sought to speak 'standard' English, when they managed to master their owners' language, they were often mocked for their pretensions. When they dressed in European fashions, adopted the social styles of whites and when they spoke as close to whites as possible, they incurred a vengeful mockery – especially from cartoonists and graphic caricaturists who found the idea of black Europeans or Americans too ludicrous to contemplate.

A series of early-nineteenth-century cartoons, 'Life in Philadelphia', portrayed gross images of black pretensions, images which were accompanied by quotes from contemporary blacks designed to ridicule the way they spoke. One black woman, trying on a large hat, asked a friend:

Question: What you tink of my new poke Bonnet Frederick Augustus?
Answer: I don't like him no how, case dey hide you Lubly Face, so you can't tell one She Nigger from another.

Dismissed as stupid when they could not understand English, slaves and ex-slaves were decried as pretentious when they did. Mocked when they sought respectability – in dress, social engagements and manners – blacks were a target for the most rancid of ridicule which traced its roots back to the worst accusations of planters and their supporters. Images of prospering blacks simply walking in the streets, of black women taking formal dancing lessons, of others turning their back on former black friends – all these and more provided ample scope for caricatured dismissals of black social pretensions.[21]

If observers agreed about one feature of slave culture across the Americas, it was on the importance of slave music. Music clearly had a special place among slaves throughout the Americas. Indeed, musicality had been encouraged among Africans in Europe even before the development of slavery in the Americas. Europeans had returned from the Crusades with black musicians. In the mid-sixteenth century black drummers, flute players and black dancers (at royal weddings) were established figures in Lisbon. Black musicians had also begun to appear in royal and courtly circles in England and Scotland, a fashion which gained in popularity, and spread down the social scale with the increased contact with Africa in the seventeenth and eighteenth centuries. British military bands employed black musicians – a fad which reached its height in the late eighteenth century. Black trumpeters and drummers were especially common both in Britain and in Europe, and by the late eighteenth century, no British regiment with any social pretensions could be without black musicians, often 'procured' from the West Indies.[22]

Black drummers were widely used on eighteenth-century warships, where the drum beat out the rhythm of the maritime day and dispatched instructions around the ship, especially in battle. It was also assumed that competent fiddlers could be recruited from among the black sailors, to entertain the crew. The Europeans' direct involvement with African music began, like much else besides, on the coast of Africa. There, European sailors picked up local habits of singing at rhythmic work, on land and on board the ships. Where black and white sailors worked alongside each other, whites quickly acquired what was thought to be the 'black style' of singing.[23] Europeans assumed that Africans found pleasure and comfort in music and music-making, to the extent that slave-traders sometimes went through the absurd ritual of forcing slaves to dance on deck. They thought it might afford them pleasure in the midst of their misery.

The roots of this white interest in black musicality reached back, then, to Africa, to the role of music and music-making in a broad range of African cultures. Europeans came to accept as a matter of fact that Africans, and their New World descendants, were 'naturally' musical and took every opportunity to encourage them. In Europe this took the form of fashionable music (there was a fad for instructing blacks, like Equiano, to play the French horn). In the slave colonies, slave music was ubiquitous, and slave dancing was inescapable. They have, wrote Richard Blome in 1680,

> antick actions, their hands having more of motion than their feet; and their head, than either; nor do the men and women *Dance* together, but apart; the *Musique* to which they *Dance*, being a sort of *Kittle-drums*, one bigger than another, which makes a strange and various noise.[24]

Though Africans entered the New World with no material possessions, they soon fashioned for themselves musical instruments they remembered from their African pasts. They manufactured them from whatever local materials came to hand – horns and shells, bones, string and rope, wood, calabashes and skins. At high days and holidays, at the end of harvest, at weddings and funerals, and, increasingly, at Christian festivals (Christmas, Easter, Shrove Tuesday), slaves played their music – and crowds of slaves danced to it. Time and again, from one slave society to another, visitors and resident whites marvelled at (and often distrusted) the mass enjoyment of musical pleasures. It was the first aspect of slave life noticed both by Equiano and by Thomas Thistlewood when they landed in Jamaica.

Here was a world which seemed to owe little to the whites. It was a communal pleasure, fashioned from memories of the past, which led back to Africa. Though Europeans needed to maintain and exercise their dominance over the slaves, this aspect of slave life – musical culture – seemed beyond their ken and control. In the words of one observer of the West Indies in the early nineteenth century, 'a spectator would require only a slight aid from fancy to transport him to the savage wilds of Africa'.[25] Whites saw in slave music an enthusiasm and a sensuality that was Africa transplanted into the Americas. It was to become one of the most enduring legacies of slavery to the New World, and thence to the Old.

There were, however, aspects of black musicality, notably drumming, which worried whites in all slave colonies. Drums were played at most slave ceremonials and pleasures. Funerals, for example, were night-long vigils accompanied by drumming (and drinking) which did not fit European ideas of appropriate mourning ceremonials. Even when slaves were won over to Christianity, they invested Christian festivities (celebrated by Europeans in a more sedate fashion) with a throbbing musical pleasure, the sound of drumming being inescapable, which often made whites uneasy. Drumming and blowing on a conch-shell were widely thought to be means whereby slaves communicated with each other, especially in times of unrest and rebellion. They were, accordingly, often restricted or banned.

What is abundantly clear is that, despite the manifold obstacles put in their way, a great deal of African aesthetics were brought to the Americas. How could it be otherwise when those aesthetics were so deeply rooted in the individual and collective make-up of the people driven into the enslaved diaspora, who had to re-invent themselves in the slave quarters? The story is the same wherever we look, from early Brazil to the mature slave quarters of Jamaica and North America, from the French slave islands to the slave quarters of South America. Slaves played music – drums especially – and contemporary white observers assumed that their instruments, though locally made, were in effect African ones. Indeed, slave social life was so often *described* as African that the point is made time and again. For much of the era of slavery, slaves were described as 'African', their villages were 'African', their music, instruments, pleasures and pastimes, their passions and their playthings, all were 'African'. Yet, to repeat an obvious point, the great majority of those slaves who *were* indeed African had stepped ashore with no material artefacts whatsoever. It was the 'Africanness' of slaves which whites disliked most and which white society sought, everywhere in the Americas, to contain, to restrict and to modify.[26] They needed African strength, but they sought to limit and suppress other features of African life which had crossed the Atlantic alongside that muscle power.

For whites, perhaps the most troublesome feature of the 'African' cultures transplanted into the Americas was religion. Often they simply refused to accept African belief systems as being religions at all. For much of the history of black slavery in the Americas, slaves adhered to African beliefs, sometimes blended with particular features of Christianity. The continuing arrival of Africans ensured that African beliefs were regularly infused into the slave communities. There were, of course, enormous variations in the religions among Africans landed in the Americas, ranging from followers of Islam[27] to some who had already been exposed to Christianity on the African coast. Obviously, most African arrivals were not Christian. Indeed (with the exception of Islam) African 'paganism' offered Europeans a justification for slavery itself. Whites tended to see most African slaves as locked into African 'superstitions' which fell beyond the pale of acceptable religions.

These African religious beliefs were, however, able to accommodate ideas and practices from other religions, a factor which enabled early Catholic missionaries to win over African slaves in Spanish and French America. The result was the emergence in those regions of slave religions which looked African under a guise of Catholic procedures. Slaves could practise their remembered African faiths and still be proclaimed Catholic. The syncretic mixes of different faiths were more obvious in Catholic colonies. It was different in British Protestant slave societies (in so far as slave colonies, which often seemed particularly godless and where local clergy was both sparse and inadequate, could be called Protestant). One religious characteristic which emerged in most slave societies was the relegation of *benevolent* spirits (so common in African faiths) and the emergence of *malevolent* spirits, which were able to harm or damage people by a secretive process. This feature was clearly a reflection of the harsh world inhabited by the slaves. It also reflected their need to turn to magical, supernatural forces to harm those people who seemed beyond the bounds of normal control and reprimand. Sorcery, under various names and guises and with a variety of African origins, most notably *obeah* (African spiritual practices), was a potent force in slave quarters. It was attacked, outlawed and severely punished, but it was never eradicated.[28]

It is easy to see why Europeans felt uneasy about slave religions. After all, Britain itself had only recently moved beyond an acceptance of magic as part of the natural cosmos. Magic and all its practitioners were consigned to the realms of ancient superstitions, unworthy of a modern society, and certainly not to be compared with devotion to formal religion. Yet here, in the New World, whites found themselves surrounded by armies of slaves who seemed more influenced by a world of magic, by soothsayers and by forms of witchcraft, than by formal religion. Of course, whites sometimes accepted that there *were* benefits (for example herbal and natural medicines) to be found in slave religions. Although whites sometimes heeded slave practices, especially herbal medicine which sometimes seemed more effective than western medicine,[29] they remained uneasy with those aspects of slave religion which seemed most blatantly 'African'. The problem was that many slave-owners (especially in the British West Indies, along with their Anglican church) remained unwilling to convert slaves to Christianity until relatively late, though this was much less true in North America.

There was no one in the British islands comparable to the Jesuit Fray Pedro Claver, who greeted African slaves arriving at Cartegena. He entered the stinking slave ships to meet the slaves, to dress their wounds, to carry out the sick, and to baptize them into the church. Between 1616 and 1654 he baptized tens of thousands of Africans.[30] In the British islands, slave conversion was generally resisted by the planters. They feared that baptism would lead to black freedom, and worried that preachers and churches (which operated beyond plantocratic control) would create a forum for slave independence and give slaves access to an alternative voice and ideals. Whites sought to restrict slave life as much as they could, and were unhappy with slave autonomy (even though, in economic matters, they clearly needed independent slave activity).[31] Slave-owners were often bemused by the way slaves adapted Christianity, investing it with myriad cultural forms – African, European and American – which outsiders could barely recognize as Christian. This was especially striking at Christmas and at slave burials. The rituals of slave death, interment and bereavement struck whites as purely African. They were as far removed as possible from the quiet, restrained grief of most white funerals. Instead they were marked by music (drumming again), by drinking, by noisy corpse-side vigils and by placing a range of artefacts and foodstuffs alongside the deceased. For many slaves it was the point of departure back to Africa.[32] White observers tended to see it as yet another reminder of African primitive cultures.

In the course of the eighteenth century, Christianity gradually began to intrude itself into the slave quarters. The process tended to begin via the efforts of individual slave-owners (and their wives), keen to win over their wards to 'civilized' life. Formal church efforts (led from 1701 by the Society for the Propagation of the Gospel in Foreign Parts) faced a host of problems, led by the slave-owners. It was, however, the emergent dissenting groups and sects which made the most effective inroads among the slaves, beginning with John Wesley and George Whitefield, and later the Presbyterians, then the Baptists and Moravians. The evangelical surge of the late eighteenth century swept along large numbers of slaves in the islands and in North America. Slaves were seduced by a message of 'universal salvation through divine grace, an intensity of feeling and physical expressiveness, and a church structure that was quite egalitarian'.[33] The most notable example of a former slave won over in this way was, of course, Equiano, whose autobiography was in many respects the diary of a soul, an account of his own discovery of Christian truth and light.

Though converted late, slaves in the islands worshipped in ways which, again, were quite unlike traditional white practices. Black congregations – notably Baptists and Methodists – were noisy, musical, enthusiastic, with communal responses in ecstatic form (and often with black preachers). Sometimes convulsive, black Christianity became a form of slave expression and community in ways which planters had feared but had not been able to predict or prevent. Moreover, the Bible – and its associated literacy – provided a potent tool for slave interpretation of the world and the hereafter. Black Christianity quickly became a means of collective expression and improvement. Preachers rose from the ranks of ordinary slaves; powerful speakers and black leaders emerged via the churches (some of them associated with the great slave upheavals in the West Indies in the early nineteenth century). Thus black Christianity (in the West Indies at least) became a powerful social force which planters found impossible to control.

Chapels and churches gave slaves a place to meet, to congregate and to exchange ideas away from the overpowering presence of their place of work. There were, not surprisingly, important links between black Christianity and the slave revolts in Barbados (1816), Demerera (1823) and Jamaica (known as the 'Baptist War' of 1831–32) and the Denmark Vesey upheaval in South Carolina (1822). In all of them, powerful Christian leaders, the language of Christian egalitarianism and the networks provided by chapel membership served to ferment black unrest. When, in 1831, Nat Turner led his own resistance in Virginia, he couched his claims in Christian terms; 'I was ordained for some great purpose in the hands of the Almighty.'[34]

From the earliest days of African slavery in the Americas, slave-owners had feared their slaves *as Africans*. Now they worried about their Christianity. However, it would be wrong to claim that upheaval and discord were Christianity's sole contribution to the slaves. It enabled them to fashion key areas of black culture which, though developed in the years of slavery, became powerful forces in the years of freedom. In many respects Christianity formed the bedrock for a much broader black culture and aesthetics in the English-speaking Americas.

The Christian churches among slaves and their descendants were varied, distinctive, often unusual and self-created. They became the social and cultural points around which a great deal of black culture evolved. Black Christianity focused on the Bible and hymnals, on the words and efforts of local (black) preachers, and was forged by the powerful imagery and vocabulary of the Old Testament, so many elements of which seemed to speak for and to the slaves. Christianity came to fill a major proportion of the free time granted by all slave systems, notably the Sabbath. Here is another illustration of how slave culture emerged from a peculiar mix of black and white. Christianity was the whites' religion after all, and yet everywhere across the enslaved Americas it became the strength and the solace of black slaves. In so many ways, slave Christianity seemed far removed from the religion of the whites. It had, in effect, been transmuted into a new phenomenon by slaves who adopted it for their own ends and needs and incorporated their own cultural memories. Put simply, those whites who encouraged slaves to become Christian could never have imagined what *kind* of Christians those slaves and their descendants would become. In slave hands, Christianity became an instrument of communal black expression. As such it was difficult for slave-owners to manage and shape. Once the enslaved Christian genie was out of the bottle, it was impossible to control.

Christianity confirmed what had been taking place in the slave quarters from the earliest days of settlement: the emergence of family life among the slaves. Despite the destructiveness of slavery, despite the tensions militating against family life, slaves created family structures which became the bedrock of social life. Through the consequent networks of family, kin and friends, the slave quarters developed into organic social institutions, no longer merely an aggregation of labouring people imported to work for their owners. Of course the prospects for family life varied enormously. For African males in pioneering settlements, the chances were remote. As long as the Atlantic trade continued to ferry a preponderance of men into the slave quarters, many of those men would be denied access to permanent female partners and family life. Yet nuclear families *did* emerge among the slaves, though partners were often separated across properties. Family life emerged among North American slaves earlier than among slaves in the West Indies, but in North America family break-up and separation were also more common, especially in the nineteenth century, when the advancing cotton frontier in the south and west saw the transfer of armies of slaves from the slave communities in the 'old South'. This was in effect an *internal* US slave trade. Despite these enormous difficulties and disruptions, the slave family became the norm. It was the crucible from which new generations of slaves emerged, drilled by parents and older relatives in the lessons and cautions of the hostile world at large. Moreover, slave-owners came to recognize that the slave family was critical not merely to the slaves' overall happiness but also for the planters' own well-being.

Slave families and slave Christianity were two of the more striking of the myriad changes which went to make up slave culture in the Americas. Much of that culture was a process of pulling away from white domination, of creating a separate cultural identity. Yet, however powerful the urge to pull away, slave life remained permanently fixed in the gravitational field of local white society. Slave independence flourished in social and economic terms, but could never fully escape from local whites. Although slaves were granted or seized areas of independent existence which they made use of for their own good and benefit, this often helped their owners. This was strikingly so on the plots and gardens granted by their owners, where slaves cultivated foodstuffs and reared animals in their free time at weekends and evenings. From the fruits of their independent efforts they sold, bartered and traded, often at local markets, acquiring money, material goods and small luxuries which enhanced their lives. They dressed and decorated themselves and improved their homes with the rewards from their independent work.

Accounts of slave dwellings in the pioneering stage of settlement compared to a century later give some idea of the material progress slaves had made. A report in 1680 told how West Indian slaves 'must be contented to lye hard, on nothing but a *board*, without any *Coverlet*, in their *Hutts*, or rather *Hogsties*'.[35] A century later, slave homes had improved, largely through the slaves' own efforts.[36] By the late eighteenth century British West Indian slaves were renowned for the attention they paid to their non-working appearance: the elaborate dresses, personal fineries and expense generally lavished at festivals and high days. Jewellery and refinements, costly clothing and entertainments – all went hand-in-hand with a ragged daily existence. Many slaves had clearly been able to acquire a degree of material well-being which staggered visitors – and sometimes their owners (though we should not exaggerate its extent). This was an achievement wrought by their own individual efforts, initiative and enterprise, on their plots and gardens, capitalizing on whatever skills they possessed. Outsiders found it hard to grasp how slaves could afford such 'luxuries', how people who had stepped ashore from the slave ships with no material goods *whatsoever* could, a few years on, flaunt such worldly goods. The artefacts were normally quite simple; pipes for men, home-made jewellery for women, a decent set of clothes for celebrations and holidays.[37] But, compared to the filthy rags and nakedness of their arrival, it is a stunning contrast, representing a triumph of individual will and effort over the most savage of adversities.

Though the effort which went into improvement was individual and familial, it took its most expressive form in communal activities. Slave communities formed a web of family and kinship ties which spread from one slave property to another. They created a network of self-help and sustenance which was especially important for slaves on the move; slaves travelling (often great distances) to see loved ones and friends, slaves running away (though often running *to* someone), slaves lurking on the edge of slave-owning society, all could be sure, normally, of help and succour from these slave networks. These local communities were the forum for those ceremonies of birth, marriage and death, of child-rearing and communal care which, though mundane and ubiquitous in some ways, were vital elements in the shaping, bequeathing and acquisition of slave culture.

Slave culture evolved in the workplace (especially in the fields through the particular rhythms of agricultural work) and in the free time afforded to local slaves by their owners. This may at first sight seem to fly in the teeth of all we know of slavery, an institution which seemed to take pleasure in visiting regular pain and suffering on the heads of its victims. Yet slaves *did* have free time; they *did* have customary (in some cases legal) days of rest (Sundays) and holidays. Slaves used that free time to pursue their own interests (though often that involved yet more work) and to enjoy themselves as they saw fit, with friends and family, with neighbours and workmates, at home or with neighbours, quietly or in the most explosively noisy of fashions. Here was a culture which varied enormously from one slave colony to another and which, obviously, changed fundamentally with the passage of time. Slave life in the early days of settlement was quite different from life in the mature slave societies, especially when the flow of Africans had ceased and Africa was receding in the communal mind – receding but rarely forgotten.

Slave culture may have lacked many of the aesthetic features which white society recognized as cultural attainments, although we need to recall that slave-owners themselves were rarely famed for their culture. The latters' achievements were more material and economic, their excessive flamboyance an object of snobbish ridicule among 'old money' in Britain. Despite the dismissiveness of white observers, the evidence of African aesthetics surfaced throughout the enslaved Americas, in ceramics and textiles, in music and in culinary traditions.[38] But slave culture was much more than simply the transfer of African traits and skills into the Americas. It was a process, not a static object, an evolutionary system which developed and which drew sustenance and inspiration from a host of cultural roots, among them local European settlers in the Americas. After all, slaves eventually came to speak their masters' languages and to accept their masters' religions. But they adapted and transformed these cultural roots, shaping them to their own particular needs and interests, taking what they wanted, what they found consonant with their own experience and what suited their present condition. It was a lived experience, and thus was bequeathed to those who came after slavery. Slave culture survived (again, in transmuted form) into the world of late-nineteenth-century freedom – and then beyond to the twentieth century. Black culture in the world of the modern Atlantic could not have evolved as it has without its slave past.

Notes

1 The first date marked the introduction of 'Apprenticeship' to replace slavery. Apprenticeship itself was abolished fully in 1838.
2 Dispatch of Lord Sligo, December 1834, in Michael Craton, James Walvin and David Wright (eds), *Slavery, Abolition and Emancipation* (London, 1976), p. 330.
3 Michael Craton and Gail Saunders, *Islanders in the Stream: A History of the Bahamian People*, Vol. 1 (Athens, GA, 1992), pp. 392–3.
4 *Ibid.*
5 'The Voyage made by M. John Hawkins Esq . . . 1564', in Richard Hakluyt, *The Principal Navigations of the English Nation* (London, 1926), 8 vols, vol. 7, p. 7.
6 B. Martin and M. Spurrell (eds), *Journal of a Slave Trader* (1788) (London, 1962), p. 43.
7 Johannes Menne Postma, *The Dutch in the Atlantic Slave Trade, 1600–1815* (Cambridge, 1990), Chapter 10.

8 Allan Kulikoff, *Tobacco and Slaves: The Development of Southern Cultures in the Chesapeake, 1680–1800* (Chapel Hill, NC, 1986), pp. 326–7.

9 For some good examples, see Mary Karasch, *Slave Life in Rio de Janeiro* (Princeton, 1987), pp. 11, 190.

10 Douglas Hall (ed.), *In Miserable Slavery: Thomas Thistlewood in Jamaica, 1750–1786* (London, 1989), p. 135.

11 Manuscript 968.F.20.a.21, *Du Simitiere Collection*, Historical Society of Pennsylvania, Philadelphia.

12 Douglas B. Chambers, '"My own nation": Igbo exiles in the diaspora', in David Eltis and David Richardson (eds), *Routes to Slavery* (London, 1997).

13 James Walvin, *An African's Life: The Life and Times of Olaudah Equiano, 1745–1797* (London, 1998).

14 Olaudah Equiano, *The Interesting Narrative* (1794), edited by Vincent Carretta (Penguin, 1995 edn), p. 172; Douglas Hall, *Thistlewood*, p.12.

15 Philip D. Morgan, 'The black experience in the British Empire, 1680–1810', in P.J. Marshall (ed.), *The Oxford History of the British Empire*, Vol. 2, *The Eighteenth Century* (Oxford, 1998), p. 479.

16 R. B. Le Page and Andree Tabouret-Keller, *Acts of Identity: Creole-Based Approaches to Languages and Ethnicity* (Cambridge, 1985).

17 Quoted in Hugh Thomas, *The Slave Trade* (London, 1997), pp. 402, 405, 424.

18 *Daily Advertiser*, Kingston, 7 June 1790.

19 Maureen Warner-Lewis, *Guinea's Other Suns: The African Dynamic in Trinidad Culture* (Dover, MA, 1991), p. 159.

20 Philip D. Morgan, 'Black experience', p. 480.

21 'Life in Philadelphia', and see Tregear's *Black Jokes, Being a Series of Laughable Caricatures on the March of Manners amongst the Blacks* (London, 1834). Set of prints, Library Company of Philadelphia. These cartoons, first published in Philadelphia, were reprinted in London as part of the pro-slavery, anti-black campaign in the campaign against slavery in the early 1830s.

22 Peter Fryer, *Staying Power: A History of Black People in Britain* (London, 1984), pp. 79–88.

23 W. Jeffrey Bolster, *Black Jacks: African American Seamen in the Age of Sail* (Cambridge, MA, 1997), pp. 32–4, 120–2.

24 Richard Blome, *A Description of the Island of Jamaica* (London, 1680), p. 39.

25 George Pinckard, *Notes on the West Indies*, vol. I (London, 1806), pp. 263–8.

26 For an interesting discussion of the African aesthetic see John Thornton, *Africa and Africans in the Making of the Atlantic World, 1400–1680* (Cambridge, 1992), pp. 221–34.

27 In 1773 a European observer, travelling in St Domingue, witnessed an African slave write out a line from the Koran. His copy of the inscription contains his comment; 'the above was written in my presence by a Negro Mondinga at Leoganne in January 1773'. *Du Simitiere Collection* (961.f.), Library Company of Philadelphia.

28 Philip D. Morgan, 'Black experience', pp. 481–2. For examples of *obeah* in Jamaica, see Douglas Hall, *Thistlewood*, p. 279.

29 Richard Sheridan, *Doctors and Slaves: A Medical and Demographic History of Slavery in the British West Indies, 1680–1834* (Cambridge, 1985), Chapter 3.

30 Hugh Thomas, *Slave Trade*, p. 433.

31 James Walvin, *Questioning Slavery* (London, 1996), Chapter 8.

32 For accounts of slave funerals, see extracts in Roger D. Abrahams and John F. Szwed, *After Africa* (New Haven, 1983), pp. 163–79.

33 Philip D. Morgan, 'Black experience', p. 483. For the latest study, see Sylvia Frey and Betty Wood, *Come Shouting to Zion: African American Protestantism in the American South and the British Caribbean to 1830* (Chapel Hill, NC, 1998).

34 Confession of Nat Turner, in Willie Lee Rose (ed.), *A Documentary History of Slavery in North America* (New York, 1976), pp. 123–33.
35 Richard Blome, *Jamaica*, pp. 38–9.
36 Bryan Edwards, *The History of the British Colonies in the West Indies*, 3 vols, 3rd edn, 1801, Vol. III, p. 165.
37 B. W. Higman, *Montpelier, Jamaica: A Plantation Community in Slavery and Freedom, 1739–1912* (Kingston, Jamaica, 1998).
38 John Thornton, *Africans*, pp. 221–34.

= 6 =

PROFITING FROM SLAVERY

In common with much of Britain's seventeenth- and eighteenth-century global empire, the British Atlantic slave empire was driven forward by financial imperatives. The emergence of British power and the rise of domestic British well-being (although not dispersed evenly throughout the population, of course) were so closely linked to the growth of global trade and dominion that it is hard to disentangle empire from the transformations in British life itself. Key aspects of British social behaviour (the massive consumption of tobacco and of sweetened tea, for example) flowed directly from empire and long-distance trade. Few doubted in, say, 1750 that empire was profitable. Indeed, some of the most elaborate displays of contemporary wealth in Britain were flaunted by men returning from distant corners of empire: nabobs from India and planters from the West Indies. The Atlantic slave system seemed an especially fruitful source of business and trade, and its prospects seemed boundless.

It was, however, all dependent on the Africans. The Africa trade was 'the main spring of the machine, which sets each wheel in motion'. African slaves were the vital lubricant of the plantation system, 'without whom our plantations could not be improved or carried on'.[1] Was it so *obviously* lucrative though, when the first British investors, merchants and settlers embarked on empire in the late sixteenth and early seventeenth centuries?

The British urge to build an empire was prompted in large part by the example of others, by looking at the global successes of Portugal, Spain and

Holland and coming to realize that empire and trade had created formidable worldly wealth and business in Seville, Lisbon, Antwerp and Amsterdam. To repeat a point which recurs like a refrain through this book: the British came late to the realization that African slaves offered a distinctive kind of lucrative empire. The remarkable riches of empire could be seen reflected in the lavish wealth of the more successful Spanish, Portuguese and Dutch imperial agents and adventurers. Both Lisbon and Seville (the latter growing from 49,000 to 100,000 people between 1530 and 1594) had been transformed by wealth from long-distance maritime trade and settlement. Both cities had attracted cosmopolitan mercantile communities to join in, promote (and benefit from) trade and empire. The new banking system in Seville, with Genoese money prominent, was linked closely to oceanic trade. Closer to home, Antwerp, the financial centre of a complex global trading system, displayed similar signs of trans-oceanic prosperity, until it was ruined by the rise of Dutch state in the late sixteenth century.[2]

Many of Antwerp's services transferred themselves to Amsterdam, which, in turn, established itself as Europe's financial centre. Though that city's fiscal and trading roots were in the Baltic trades, it was increasingly able to dominate the economies of Spain and Portugal. By the late sixteenth century, Amsterdam had become the main European entrepôt (and beneficiary) for the flow of goods and bullion from Europe and the wider world. When excluded from Iberian ports by revolt and war, the Dutch squared the circle. Instead of relying on the imperial adventures of others, they embarked on their own colonial empire in Asia, Africa and the Americas. The result was not simply the rise of the Dutch empire, orchestrated by the East and West India companies, but the glorious confirmation, centred on Amsterdam, of the fruits of trade and empire. The Dutch Golden Age was the age of Dutch supremacy in Asian, African and American waters after 1590. It was a trade built on old foundations, on the experience, structures and profits from European trade – but it was colonial trade which served to transform the Republic into Europe's dominant financial, commercial and maritime power.[3] It was, of course, the associated wealth which shaped the civilization immortalized by the creative genius of its great painters.[4]

The Dutch ability to make money from the wider world derived from a complexity of factors, all of which came together after 1590. Most critical of all was the emergence of the Dutch 'rich trades' in lucrative exotic commodities. To penetrate to the point of production – to by-pass obstructive Iberian powers – groups of Dutch merchants came together to pool investments and to launch speculative long-distant trading raids to Asia. Initial success led to massive and prompt investment in further missions by merchants in Dutch seaports. From the need to control the massive Dutch scramble for oceanic trade there emerged the unique joint-stock companies, their monopoly backed by the state but organized in a federal system, such as the East India Company (founded in 1602). This was a company armed with full military and plenipotentiary powers, able to conquer distant polities and impose a Dutch imperial presence on them, and was designed to tap the region for its sought-after produce. The centre of Dutch interest was in Asia, where forts, factories and large Dutch communities thrived from Goa through Malacca to Batavia (Jakarta).

Dutch settlements in Africa and America were altogether more modest. By 1598, however, the Dutch had replaced the Portuguese in the West Africa gold and ivory trades, though they left the Portuguese to trade in slaves across the Atlantic. After a string of trading and colonial efforts in the Americas, Dutch trade and settlement in the Americas were eventually assigned to the West Indian Company (1621), itself modelled on the earlier East India Company. However, it was unable to make a serious impact in the region until it took Recife in 1630 and Curaçao in 1634.[5] By then British interest in global trade and settlement had begun to develop. The British looked to the Dutch both for inspiration and for more practical assistance with finance and technical know-how. Although they were just the latest European people to appreciate the commercial benefits of overseas trade, the British were more directly influenced by what they had seen of Dutch progress in the previous half-century.

The British had nibbled at the edges of this remarkable explosion in global trade in the sixteenth century; interlopers, fishermen, raiders of one kind or another had all periodically invaded the preserve of other dominant European powers. That began to change in the early seventeenth century. The English East India Company (1600), and the first effective settlements in America, created an entirely new situation. A massive change in the *nature* of British overseas trade followed, with a notable switch to trade to and from American and Asian markets. Europe became less important, and the wider world more important, to Britain. From mid-century, the British immersed themselves in oceanic trade more directly; trade with the plantation societies and with India accounted for 30 per cent of imports and 15 per cent of exports. At the heart of those figures lay produce created by slaves in the Americas, and goods drawn into the Atlantic trades for onward sale or barter in the Atlantic system.

The first great British commercial success was, as with the Dutch, the burgeoning trade to Asia, modelled like theirs on a joint-stock company backed by the State's authority. The opening of the Atlantic, however, followed a different commercial route. London monopolized the East India trade, but the Atlantic trade was developed first by the capital and later by other ports – notably Bristol and Liverpool. Efforts to develop American settlement by joint-stock companies did not work, for the simple reason that the Atlantic trade involved not merely trade. It was a complicated process of *settlement* – spearheaded by plantations – of provisioning, of transporting labour vast distances and of cultivation. Though Indian peoples provided traders with local produce (notably the furs, pelts and skins of North America), the British Atlantic system involved cultivating commodities which Europeans introduced into the region (notably sugar and coffee), or crops which were transformed by new systems of cultivation (tobacco, rice and cacao).

After a number of early failures and disasters, the British sank successful roots along the eastern seaboard and across the chain of West Indian islands. It was a slow, laborious process which yielded little profit initially and was best managed by men supervising their own investment in the land (and the labour), not by investors on the other side of the Atlantic. Its ultimate success could be measured by the flow of people across the Atlantic. By about 1700 some 350,000 British people had migrated (much to the satisfaction of theorists who thought the motherland overpopulated). These settlers, however, had to find ways of paying for the range of imports that kept them alive. In the Caribbean they tried a range of tropical produce, until sugar became *the* money-spinning commodity of the region from the 1640s onwards. Tobacco had the same effect in Virginia and Maryland, rapidly transforming precarious settlements into lucrative investments. The northern colonies helped these plantation colonies to survive, and then thrive, by supplying wood, foodstuffs and shipping.[6]

With the development of the main staples, planters sold their produce on commission in Britain, or to merchants in colonial ports. The system was not suited to monopoly or restrictions (hence the problems of the Royal African Company). The Atlantic trade thrived not via joint-stock companies (though they played a role) but on open trade. And with the opening of the Atlantic trade, men (and women) from a range of propertied backgrounds sank money into it. It attracted 'manufacturers, retailers, gentlemen, and widows: an opportunity for all'.[7] Hundreds of London merchants invested in the West Indian import and export trades, though most only on a small scale. A majority of those merchants exported or imported goods valued at less than £50 from the West Indies in the late seventeenth century. It was a trade whose attractions were diffused across a wide spectrum of metropolitan interests. Men with small amounts of money to invest were willing to run the commercial gauntlet of trans-oceanic trade to the slave colonies, knowing that the prospects of high profits outweighed the risks of war, weather and market fluctuations. The one group who avoided the universal risks of poor or dishonest agents were the Quakers, and they managed that by relying on the honest trading practices of other Quakers in North America and the West Indies.[8]

The Atlantic trade *was* high risk and, understandably, a high proportion of it came to be concentrated in the hands of a small number of wealthy merchants. Something like 50 per cent of the value of the West Indian import trade came the way of a mere 28 merchants in 1686. Seven merchants dominated almost 30 per cent of the imports from North America. Groups of merchants tried to create monopolies in various branches of the Atlantic trade, but their only real success (and then only for a limited period) was in the slave trade. Politicians were involved too. Successive generations of British politicians and statesmen encouraged the import of ever-more colonial produce, for the duties levied on sugar, tea and tobacco (and other consumer goods) were a crucial financial support for the expansive military state in the seventeenth and eighteenth centuries, especially as indirect taxation became more important than direct.[9]

By the end of the seventeenth century, the Atlantic trade had revealed the weaknesses of monopoly. Curiously, however, there was one area where the State could effectively insist on a form of monopoly: in the vital sphere of shipping itself. The development of each European nation's maritime power in the Atlantic had been at the expense of other nations' faltering ability to keep hostile traders at arm's length. Having intruded into the maritime trades of others, the British had no intention of allowing outsiders to muscle in on their own. With an eye on the Dutch, the British aimed to ensure that their maritime trade was routed, uniquely, through British ports and that colonial life was serviced by, and in its turn would feed into, British ships and *only* British ships. This system was given shape by a series of Navigation Acts from 1651 onwards, each new one refining the others. It was moderated by the Vice-Admiralty Courts in North America and the West Indies, and enforced by the growing reach and power of the Royal Navy.[10] For all its flaws, evasions and blind-eye turning (in the Americas), it worked, and yielded remarkable results. By the end of the seventeenth century, the signs of economic benefit derived from the Atlantic trades (and from oceanic trade in general) were there for all to see: in the expansion of ports and shipping, in the proliferation of facilities to refine and process imported produce (e.g., sugar refineries and tea warehouses), the expansion of industries to feed the Atlantic trades, and in the range of financial services which underpinned the whole system.[11]

The most obvious area of economic growth in the Atlantic system was the massive increase in shipping, which more than doubled in tonnage between 1640 and 1686. This expansion created employment for an army of skilled men, both in the construction and in refitting the ships. A great deal of maritime material was North American. Partnerships of merchants invested upwards of £3000 in each vessel, and the whole enterprise was topped off by the employment of the most crucial man of all: the captain, who served as navigator, manager of men and negotiator in Africa and the Americas. The Atlantic ships also needed ordinary crew members; some 10,000 men as early as 1680, in work which was regarded as a vital training school for the Royal Navy (though abolitionists, a century later, were to show that sailors' mortality levels on the slave ships rather undermined this argument).

Dockside facilities mushroomed in London and Bristol – quaysides, warehouses, small boats and armies of dockside labour. Ships and their crews bound for the Americas devoured huge quantities of goods. The 300 ships which left London in 1686 for America 'needed provisions for over 9,000 men (larger than the population of all but six or seven towns in England)'. Foodstuffs bound for the plantations stimulated the growth and commercialization of English food production and distribution.[12]

The maritime trade which concentrated on Atlantic slavery serves to confirm these general points. Between 1699 and 1807 more than 12,000 ships cleared British (or British colonial) ports bound for the slave coast. Bare statistics convey the point. London dispatched 3351 slave ships, Bristol 2105 and Liverpool 5199 in the eighteenth century.[13] Other ports joined in, Lancaster, Whitehaven – even Lyme Regis. As the eighteenth-century slave trade expanded, its local organization followed the initial pattern. Though slave-trading voyages were not as costly (or risky) as ventures to Asia the costs of slaving voyages rose steadily throughout the century, from £3000 to £8000 – a reflection of the growing size of the ships and the rise in slave prices on the African coast. Since a slave voyage took between 12 and 18 months (with the associated risks of the Middle Passage), slave-traders tried to spread their risks. In the major slave ports, a slave ship was normally financed by a core of local investors (their money spread across a number of other slave ships), with a larger number of local investors sinking smaller amounts in the venture. The eighteenth-century slave trade depended on 'the resources of a large number of investors brought together by a small body of regular managing-owners'.[14]

In the course of the eighteenth century the centre of gravity of British slaving shifted from its pioneering centre in London to Bristol and then, most spectacularly, to Liverpool. There were advantages in trading from Liverpool: its labour was cheaper, it was close to an embryonic textile industry, and its vessels were safer in wartime (when the English Channel was dangerous). But even then, London's merchants continued to invest in Liverpool's trade. To pay for goods shipped to Africa and exchanged for African slaves, Liverpool slave-traders used bills of credit and exchange drawn on London merchants. London finance and commerce remained embedded in, and a beneficiary of, the Atlantic slave trade long after the bulk of the slave ships had shifted to Liverpool. Moreover, London merchants also provided many of the goods (British or transshipped Asian goods) which Liverpool slave-traders shipped onward to Africa. Slave-traders from Bristol and Liverpool needed London merchants and the capital's financial system. It is easy to lose sight of the centrality of London throughout the history of the British slave trade, and it is wrong to imagine that the slave trade's importance to London diminished. The basic fact remained; the Atlantic slave trade was an integral element in the financial make-up and material advancement of Britain throughout the eighteenth century – wherever the locus of maritime activity might be found.

One aspect of the history of Atlantic slavery is that the slave experience is often reduced to elaborate accountancy. Logged and documented on arrival on the slave ships, valued and accounted for when sold in the Americas, tabulated and calibrated to the finest degree by slave-owners everywhere on the plantations, even their labour was registered in statistical and financial terms. They were people reduced not merely to the level of property, but to ciphers and figures in the account books of the shippers, planters and merchants. Similarly, we can measure the slaves' labours by the volumes of slave-grown produce arriving at British quaysides.

Some £900,000 worth of goods arrived in London by 1686 – 80 per cent from the West Indies. It was sugar, above all else, which dominated these figures and which filled the holds of the returning ships. The 150,000 hundredweight of the 1660s had more than doubled by the end of that century. Inevitably, it brought about a sharp drop in the price to British consumers; sugar now became hugely popular among all social groups.[15] Originally restricted to the rich, by the end of the seventeenth century sugar was the accompaniment to the poor family's cup of tea. Though imports were to rise still further throughout the eighteenth and nineteenth centuries (and popular consumption rose accordingly), the social trajectory was already clear; what had once been luxurious and expensive was now commonplace and cheap. It was a path followed by other slave-grown produce, notably tobacco.

The 173,000 pounds of tobacco imported in 1620 had risen to 1.25 million pounds in 1640; by 1676 it was 11 million. Costing a mere one penny a pound, tobacco consumption was widespread – an inescapable feature of social life in Britain (and Europe as a whole). Much of the imported tobacco (perhaps two-thirds), like a third of the sugar imported, was re-exported in return for yet more imported goods – with the consequent growth in shipping and maritime prosperity. Refineries, necessary to process the part-refined imported sugar, were built in all the sugar ports (where they were a notorious fire risk). As the eighteenth century advanced, the finished product found its way to the multitude of shops which spread throughout urban and rural Britain. Cheap sugar, available in packages of a few ounces, could be bought by the poor on a daily basis, at their local shop.[16] Tobacco too was bought across the counter, but it was also available in coffee-shops, alehouses and apothecaries. Indeed, both sugar and tobacco – in common with a host of new, exotic imports – entered the pharmacology of contemporary medicine and were used for a range of ailments.

These two simple colonial commodities, in common with others, quickly established themselves as standard items on the shelves of the growing number of British shopkeepers. For many of those shopkeepers, tropical produce formed the single most popular item on their shelves, accounting for a substantial proportion of their livelihood. A simple glance at the world of the early eighteenth-century British shopkeeper confirms that the enthusiasm, first displayed a century earlier, for the benefits of empire had been amply justified.

Another economic argument promoting colonial settlement had been the belief that it would stimulate manufacture and employment through the export trades. As we have seen, the African slaves shipped across the Atlantic were bought on the African coast largely in exchange for British goods. Again, here was a trade which brought material benefit to the British. Equally, British manufacturers benefited from the plantations themselves. Plantations devoured imported goods from Britain; food from Ireland and Scotland, textiles from Lancashire, ironware from the Black Country, artefacts and implements of all kinds were needed in the plantation fields, factories and homes. In 1686 London exported some £111,326 worth of goods to the main slave islands; whites in the islands consumed a much greater value of imported goods than settlers in the northern colonies.[17]

These bare statistics mask a fundamental shift in the nature of England's export trade. Wool had dominated the export trade since the Middle Ages; as late as 1640 wool formed 90 per cent of London's exports. But the American colonies created a much more varied and diverse trade, ranging from re-exported Indian textiles through to axes wielded by the slaves in the sugar fields. Planters and settlers required almost every conceivable item of daily life (and death – they even imported tombstones). Ships cleared London, and later other ports, loaded with an amazing variety of manufactured goods destined for the plantations.

Since so many of those exported goods were ordered in bulk, British manufacturers moved towards the mass manufacture of goods in a standard format. The market demands from the American colonies clearly affected the nature and processes of British manufacture, aiding the move towards a more modernized process of production and sale.[18] A growing proportion of this trade passed through the hands of small numbers of merchant capitalists – men of growing substance able to raise the necessary capital for large-scale and costly projects, but who spread the actual work out among a large number of smaller manufacturers and tradesmen. Thus colonial demand was diffused across a large spectrum of financial and manufacturing England. In the words of Nuala Zahedieh, the colonial needs 'of the 250,000 Englishmen living in what were effectively detached counties west of Cornwall, with little industry of their own, and a protected market, offered an important stimulus to English industry'.[19] The hopes and ambitions of the early-seventeenth-century proponents of overseas settlement – that here lay prosperity for the Mother Country – had been amply confirmed by the end of that century.

It is hard to disentangle the consequences of American developments from the broader emergence of Britain's global trading empire, especially in India. But the sum total of this growing involvement with the wider world was a massive boost to Britain's financial and commercial position. Foreign merchants – especially Jews, following their admission to the colonies in the mid-seventeenth century – flocked to the opportunities afforded by this expansive global trade. Jewish communities thrived in the West Indies, especially in Barbados and Jamaica, and had strong links to London's merchant community. The whole global structure, with its enormous time lapses between voyages, involved a refinement in the way bills of exchange and global debts and payments were made. Bills of exchange became, in effect, a form of international currency, perhaps paving the way for the wider acceptance of paper currency; receipts, merchants' notes and the like formed a 'valuable addition to the money supply'. Behind all this lay the necessity of imposing a tighter, bureaucratic, accountancy system on the way trade was conducted in London. Largely to handle this explosion in global trade, London's world of commerce, insurance and banking had, by the end of the seventeenth century, taken on many aspects of a recognizably modern financial centre.[20]

This financial and mercantile substructure was in place *before* the massive expansion of the slave empire in the eighteenth century, the years when Britain became the pre-eminent Atlantic slave-trader and when her slave colonies (augmented in the course of various wars) disgorged such material well-being into the Mother Country. The eighteenth century saw an explosion in trade generally. The population in British colonies in the Americas increased sevenfold between 1700 and 1775, with huge consequences for trade and manufacture. The proportion of British trade bound up with the Atlantic slaving system increased, thereby prompting an expansion of Britain's maritime fleet. And to protect the whole Atlantic edifice, the Royal Navy itself gradually expanded to ensure that Britain's trading system remained intact and unbreached by hostile outsiders. Both forms of seaborne life – commercial and military – stimulated in turn major growth in the shipping industries (materials for which were drawn increasingly from North America and not from the older, Baltic suppliers). What lay behind much of this remarkable expansion was the knowledge on the part of merchants that the goods they sought to import from abroad would yield an appropriate profit at home. This seemed especially true of slave-grown produce: sugar, tobacco and rice, and a few other tropical staples.[21]

Far and away the most valuable of colonial imports was sugar from the Caribbean. Between 1750 and 1825 (when it was replaced by cotton), sugar was *the* most valuable of all Britain's imports. In 1710 Britain imported 25,000 tons of it; by 1775 it had risen to 97,000 tons. Most of it was consumed in Britain, with only a proportion being re-exported. By then, the British were consuming something like 11 pounds of sugar per head each year (more than five times the French figure). Parallel, and closely linked to this rise in sugar imports, was the remarkable rise in the importation of tea from China, the value of which increased one-hundredfold in the years 1701 to 1774. There were other commodities, of course, which flowed from the slave fields into Britain; indigo (for dye) and rice (used for starch) both came from South Carolina though most of the latter was re-exported to Europe. By the last quarter of the eighteenth century coffee from the West Indies greatly outstripped imports from Asia, though, again, most of it was re-exported to Europe.

Tobacco poured into Britain in the eighteenth century, despite an early stagnation in Chesapeake exports. The volumes were so enormous that a very large percentage of the tobacco imported into Britain was clearly re-exported to Europe. Though it appears that, in strictly fiscal terms, this massive re-export trade of major commodities (notably tobacco, rice and coffee) proved costly to the State, it was directly responsible for the creation of work, at sea and in port, for tens of thousands of British labourers.[22]

The goods imported from colonial America into Britain (and thence to Europe) formed the currency with which colonists bought goods from Britain. The system, first established in the seventeenth century, was again refined and brought to an advanced state of development in the eighteenth. The flow of British goods across the Atlantic to sustain the colonies was enormous. The Atlantic colonies and Africa, for example, consumed huge amounts of exported woollens and linen. Similarly metal goods from the Midlands were exported in growing volume, and were second only to woollens to America by 1772–74. Yet behind these major export commodities there lay a multitude of other items, from the fashionable and luxurious to the utilitarian, which found their way to the colonies and onto the slave plantations.

Thomas Thistlewood was a young Englishman looking around for work, or for opportunities of making money, in western Jamaica in 1751. Local whites told him he could make money by importing books, saddles, boots and greatcoats. He might profitably import shoe-blacks and razor grinders. In the event, Thistlewood imported his own library of books, though he lent them out to friends and neighbours. In 1758, for example, Thistlewood's London agent sent out 18 publications, ranging from agricultural texts to French poetry. At the end of 1763 the *Neptune* arrived, carrying a case for Thistlewood (marked TT, Savanna la Mar), packed with many yards of textiles: linen, oznaburgs and 'Russian drab' (for the slaves), along with Thistlewood's annual supply of new books. Each year's deliveries to Thistlewood repeated the pattern.

When the *Earl of Effingham* docked at Savanna la Mar in January 1784, it contained a great variety of goods ordered by Thistlewood: crates of clothing, books, food, and trees for planting. All had been ordered via his agent in London, who received a flow of sugar and rum in return. A year later a similar cargo arrived, including six barrels of porter. Another delivery, in December 1785, contained a new silk purse, a black hat and a new walking stick.[23] Thistlewood, like all the whites around him, was sustained by the imports of necessities and luxuries from Britain: hardware and foodstuffs, trees and seeds for planting, books for instruction and entertainment, luxury goods to wear and to consume – quite in addition to the huge volumes of materials needed to clothe and sustain their slaves.

These simple examples need to be multiplied by *all* the plantations in the Americas, especially those in the West Indies. Although the transatlantic flow of trade was the most obvious and important, the trading patterns which developed *between* the American colonies were also critical for the profitable conduct of the Atlantic empire. Trade moved north and south between the Caribbean and the northern colonies. Sugar and rum were shipped northwards and foodstuffs (bread, flour and dried fish) were moved south to feed the slaves. Timber from North America went to the islands to be used as roofing and for barrels. This trade was more complex than it seems, but it was just one element in a much broader global, imperial trade. Moreover, it was a trade which was organized and financed by a remarkably complex financial system centred on the financiers, merchants and insurers in London.

As the eighteenth century advanced, the British merchant houses importing slave-grown produce grew larger. However we approach the history of trade to and from the slave colonies (and the colonies in general), the simple fact remains indisputable; colonies in the Americas had massive economic implications for Britain. Most obviously, they sponsored the massive growth in British shipping. It was no accident that 'Rule Britannia', a hymn of praise to British maritime power, was composed and became popular in the mid-eighteenth century.[24] This vast fleet of ships was the instrument which, in bringing exotic produce to the British consumer, served to transform the very fabric of British life itself – in the sprouting of urban and port facilities and (less visibly but still critically) in the evolution of the complex financial and commercial structures centred on London. Manufacturers too were transformed by the colonial settlements. Iron-masters and textile manufacturers in particular were greatly affected by demands from the far-flung imperial settlements. In both iron and textiles, it now seems clear that demand from the plantation economies encouraged or speeded up technological transformations. The slave colonies thus created the economic demand which encouraged the drift towards industrial and technological change in Britain.[25]

To interpret the slave empire simply, or even largely, in terms of profit or loss is to miss the intrusive and all-pervasive influence of the Atlantic slave system on Britain. Even the example of the slave trade can mislead. At first sight it seems clear enough that this specialized branch of Britain's maritime trade was profitable. Why, after all, did so many people, from so many ports, over so long a period, scurry to invest their money in local slaving ventures if not to make money? There were, of course, enormous risks and dangers: slaves might be hard to find on the African coast and disease could make terrible inroads among them, all quite apart from the normal risks of long-range maritime trade. Historians are now generally agreed that, in the last half-century of British slave-trading, the profits on a slave voyage ran at something like 8 to 10 per cent, a good but not excessively high level of return. Moreover, even when the campaign against the slave trade had begun in Britain (after 1787), there was little reluctance by investors to sink their money into slave ships. All the evidence suggests that British slave-traders made a reasonable profit – and harboured the prospects of continuing profits – up to the very eve of abolition. This of course raises the complex question why, in the teeth of such continuing profitability, the British turned their backs against so lucrative a form of trade.

What is clear is that the profits from slaving and the slave trade – the hard cash profits available to sink into other, new ventures – were a relatively small part of investment in Britain. It has been calculated that slave-trade profits by the late eighteenth century formed only 1 per cent of the 'total domestic investment in Britain'.[26] But, as this chapter has been at pains to suggest, the impact of the slave system *transcended* the arithmetical accumulation of profit and loss for the slave-traders. The growth of maritime trade, of imports and exports across the Atlantic, to and from West Africa, between North America and the West Indies, and the linkages to and from the trading systems of Asia, much of this and more hinged on the Atlantic slave system. The tropical staples produced on the plantations were the engine which drove forward much of the growth in the British Atlantic system. And all was made possible by the slaves. In 1750 something like 85 per cent of the population of the West Indies was black. More blacks than whites landed in North America in the years 1700 to 1775. It was clear to contemporaries (and has become clearer thanks to the researches of modern scholars) that 'Britain's trading Empire in America rested on an African foundation'.[27]

When we draw up a balance-sheet of Atlantic profits and loss, there is no doubt who were the losers. Again, it seems callous, brutal even, to seek a balance-sheet of loss for Africa. The haemorrhage of millions of Africans from so vast a region over so long a period was the cause of social and human dislocation on a monumental scale. Even those historians of Africa who have tried to document this process have often fallen short of the task, not least because it was a process of such massive and pervasive destructiveness that tabulations, statistical studies and economic computations can scarcely convey its full enormity. Ultimately it may be impossible to calculate the cost to Africa of the Atlantic slave system. It is surely worth reminding ourselves that in the process of constructing this Atlantic slaving empire, the British were pre-eminent. They were the leading slave-shippers, and British merchants were the 'major agents in inflicting widespread suffering on the peoples of West and central Africa in the century-and-a-half after 1660'.[28] Such damage was, in general, invisible to the British. It took place thousands of miles away, hidden behind those impenetrable coastal and riverine barriers of West Africa which kept Europeans restricted to their precarious coastal posts. Even in the slave colonies themselves, the damage done to imported Africans – though witnessed by tens of thousands of sailors, settlers, traders and visitors – was far removed from the metropolitan homelands. It was out of sight and out of mind.

More tangible, obvious and immediate were the *benefits* of slavery. Those benefits could often be measured in pounds, shillings and pence, in profits (and sometimes losses). They went far beyond the simplicities of contemporary accountancy. The Atlantic slave system helped to transform Britain into a major mercantile and military power. It helped to reshape the face and fabric of waterside Britain. It transformed key areas of domestic life itself (where would British domestic life have been without its sugary tastes?). In the course of the eighteenth century, it helped to confirm the British awareness of their own unique status and identity. Britannia ruled the waves, and she did so in the Atlantic to maintain the security of the sea-lanes between Europe, Africa and the Americas. It is an unremarked irony that the song which affirmed the British determination never to be slaves was penned effectively (though unconsciously) in praise of Britain's slaving role. Whatever historians have been able to discover subsequently, few doubted that here was a system which brought the British enormous material well-being, and it was a critical factor in the British rise to global power in the eighteenth century.

Notes

1 John Peter Demarin, *A Treatise upon the Trade from Great Britain to Africa, by an African Merchant* (London, 1772), pp. 4–5.
2 G. V. Scammell, *The First Imperial Age: European Overseas Expansion c.1400–1715* (London, 1992 edn), pp. 226–8.
3 Jonathan Israel, *The Dutch Republic: Its Rise, Greatness, and Fall, 1477–1806* (Oxford, 1998 edn), pp. 315–27.
4 Simon Shama, *Embarrassment of Riches: An Interpretation of Dutch Culture in the Golden Age* (London, 1988 edn).
5 Jonathan Israel, *Republic*, pp. 325–7.
6 Nuala Zahedieh, 'Overseas expansion and trade in the 17th century', in Nicholas Canny (ed.), *The Oxford History of the British Empire*, Vol. 1, *Origins* (Oxford, 1998), p. 400.
7 *Ibid.*, pp. 403–4.
8 James Walvin, *Quakers: Money and Morals* (London, 1997), Chapter 5.
9 Paul Langford, *A Polite and Commercial People: England 1727–1783* (Oxford, 1992), pp. 640–7.
10 Michael Craton, 'Caribbean Vice Admiralty Courts and British Imperialism', in Michael Craton, *Empire, Enslavement and Freedom in the Caribbean* (Kingston, 1997), Chapter 5.
11 Nuala Zahedieh, 'Overseas expansion', pp. 406–7.
12 *Ibid.*, pp. 408–9.
13 David Richardson, 'Slave trade', in P. J. Marshall (ed.), *The Oxford History of the British Empire*, Vol. 2, *The Eighteenth Century* (Oxford, 1998), p. 446.
14 *Ibid.*, pp. 447–8.
15 James Walvin, *Fruits of Empire* (London, 1997), Chapter 8.
16 *Ibid.*, Chapter 10.
17 Nuala Zahedieh, 'Overseas expansion', pp. 414–15.
18 *Ibid.*, pp. 416–17.
19 *Ibid.*, p. 418.
20 *Ibid.*, pp. 419–20.

21 Jacob M. Price, 'The Imperial economy, 1700–1776', in P. J. Marshall (ed.), *Eighteenth Century*, pp. 78–81.

22 *Ibid.*, p. 86.

23 Douglas Hall (ed.), *In Miserable Slavery: Thomas Thistlewood in Jamaica, 1750–1786* (London, 1989), pp. 19, 85–7, 115, 297, 303, 305.

24 James Walvin, 'Freedom and slavery in the shaping of Victorian Britain', in Paul Lovejoy and Nicholas Roger (eds), *Unfree Labour in the Development of the Atlantic World* (London, 1994), p. 255.

25 Jacob M. Price, 'The Imperial economy', pp. 97–9.

26 David Richardson, 'Slave trade', p. 461.

27 *Ibid.*, p. 462.

28 *Ibid.*, pp. 463–4.

= 7 =

BLACK BRITAIN

In the winter of 1814, something like 6000 American troops were imprisoned in Dartmoor Prison, on England's bleak Devonshire moorlands. They were prisoners of war from the recent Anglo-American conflict. About 1000 of them were black, one of whom, Richard Crafus, stood a towering 6' 3" (in an age when the average height was 5' 6"). He was a massive figure of remarkable strength, 'far greater than both height and proportions together' and became the most prominent man in the prison. Known appropriately as King Dick, he dominated the black prisoners, organizing the men, maintaining discipline and arranging entertainment. White prisoners visited the black quarter where, in the words of one white sailor,

> they have reading whiting Fenceing, Boxing Danceing & many other schools which is very diverting to a young Person, indeed their is more amusement in this Prisson than in all the rest of them.[1]

At first sight this seems a curiosity: large numbers of men, the descendants of African slaves (maybe even slaves themselves earlier in their lives), languishing in the cold embrace of that terrible prison. It is, however, perfectly understandable, for communities of black people were to be found in all corners of the Atlantic world in the era of British slavery. Wherever we look, black faces leap from the evidence – individual and collective reminders of the British role in the deliberate (and accidental) movement of African humanity, back and forth across the Atlantic. They were scattered far and wide, wherever Europeans settled or traded, from

Lima to Liverpool and even, by the end of the eighteenth century, among the criminal flotsam and jetsam of early colonial Australia.

There had been a noticeable black presence in Europe since the early days of European maritime exploration to West Africa. But the massive expansion of slavery and the slave trade between c.1600 and 1800 inevitably led to a massive diaspora of African peoples. In an age of global maritime trade and restless movements of population, it was understandable that more Africans – unwilling pawns in European hands – would find their way to Europe, initially to the major slave ports, and thence quickly into the social and geographic hinterland of Europe's slave-trading nations. Black communities developed in all Europe's major slave-trading nations, made up of Africans who were shipped to Europe, initially direct from Africa, for a variety of economic (and even fashionable) purposes. Those same European societies had, by and large, shed their earlier attachment to domestic slavery, and the arrival and settlement of African slaves inevitably raised the complex issue of the institution's legality.

The black community in Britain (concentrated overwhelmingly in the nation's major port and capital, London) really developed from the mid-seventeenth century onwards, on the back of the rapid development of British slave colonies in the Caribbean and North America, and the growth of British slave-trading in the Atlantic. An entrée to the process, to see how the black community developed, is to look at individual cases.

In 1766 the Rev. Laurence Sterne, vicar of Coxwold in North Yorkshire, received a letter from an admirer in London, declaring the letter-writer's pleasure in Sterne's published sermons and his novel, *Tristram Shandy*. The correspondent was also delighted with Sterne's severe words about slavery, declaring himself to be 'one of those people whom the vulgar and illiberal call "*Negurs*"'. The writer was Ignatius Sancho, an African who had been born in 1729 on board a slave ship bound for the Americas. His mother died soon afterwards, and Sancho was brought to England as a child, where he joined the world of black domestics. He was lucky to be spotted and patronized by a sympathetic employer, who encouraged the boy's interest in books and self-improvement. After a host of set-backs and disappointments, Sancho gradually established himself as a figure in London, and by the 1760s he was making a modest living from a small shop in Westminster. There he was visited by a number of prominent men and women, and was able to catch the eye and ear of the well-placed. From his modest shop, Sancho and his wife Anne raised six children, his much-loved 'Sanchonettas'. While Anne went about the chores of house and shop, Sancho loved to talk to customers over the counter, and in his spare time began a correspondence with the good and the great – starting with Laurence Sterne. Those letters, published in 1782, two years after Sancho's death, have secured his reputation (along with fragments of his surviving music). Although much of the substance of his letters seems common-place, they stand out as a testimony to a remarkable man.[2] Who else had been born in the squalor of a slave ship, and yet was thought worthy of a posthumous literary memorial?

In fact Sancho was not alone, and within a few years of his death another African, Olaudah Equiano, established his reputation as the most famous African in Britain in the last years of the eighteenth century. In the decade before his death in 1797, Equiano emerged as an important figure in the campaign against the slave trade. The autobiography which he published in 1789 (which told the story of his rise from African slave to man of refined sensibility), and which he assiduously promoted for the rest of his life, provided Equiano with a source of income. It also confirmed his name as a man of standing and considerable attainment. Here, in Sancho and Equiano, were two extraordinary men, men of refinement, but ex-slaves, who became familiar to the British reading public and moved comfortably in polite metropolitan circles. Moreover, this took place in the years which saw the apogee of British slavery.

In the troubled years of the 1790s, when war, revolutionary ideals and hunger strained the very fabric of British life, Equiano criss-crossed Britain visiting friends from one town to another, staying with abolitionists wherever he went, moving with ease among local people from Scotland to the West Country and Ireland. Yet these were also the years when the message Equiano promoted – the ending of the slave trade – had lost its early political appeal, driven from political and social respectability by the fears of French revolutionary turmoil, by news of the latest violence from the slave revolt in Haiti and, after February 1793, by the war against France. Equiano was known to be a friend of British radicals in and around the corresponding societies, and though the radicals were driven underground by the mid-1790s, or scattered by the government-inspired forces of loyalism and reaction, Equiano seemed unharmed by it. His energies remained undimmed, his determination to promote his abolitionist book resolute, and his ability to find sympathizers wherever he travelled unaffected.[3]

Equiano's networks throughout Britain were extraordinary. Even more remarkable, however, were his international contacts with Africans in all corners of Britain's Atlantic empire. Equiano was a much-travelled man, not surprisingly – much of his life was spent at sea in the Royal Navy and on merchant ships. It was a career which, inevitably, spawned a host of contacts with other Africans. There were, for a start, large numbers of Africans serving on British and North American vessels, and Equiano worked alongside a number of other blacks on British ships.[4] But Equiano's contacts were more than the mere haphazard shipboard or dockside friendships with fellow Africans (though he recorded plenty of those). He clearly had close friends on both sides of the Atlantic. On a trip to Savannah Georgia in 1767, Equiano 'went to a friend's house to lodge, whose name was Mosa, a black man'.[5] Likewise he had friends in the various places he worked and lived, other slaves in Savannah, on Montserrat and St Kitts. A friend in St Kitts, John Annis 'a very clever black man', had been kidnapped and removed against his will from London to St Kitts, despite Equiano's best efforts. Later, Equiano reported that 'I had two very moving letters from him'.[6] Later, Equiano made contact with the local black community in Philadelphia.[7] By then, in the mid-1780s, he had established himself as a key figure in London's black community, and was at the heart of the initial moves to work with local Quakers in the campaign against the slave trade. By 1787 his prominence in the black community persuaded the government to employ him as an agent in the campaign to recruit the black poor for a 'repatriation' scheme to Sierra Leone.[7] Thereafter Equiano's contemporary political prominence was secured.

Here surely is a remarkable fact: an African – and ex-slave – recruited and paid by the British government to rally other London-based blacks to relocate to Africa. Even more striking perhaps is Equiano's centrality, not simply among that (relatively small) community in London, but in a web of personal links with blacks on both sides of the Atlantic. Able to move with ease among friends in London, Philadelphia, Savannah, Montserrat, St Kitts (and other islands), Equiano provides a single example of the international network which formed the British black Atlantic by the late eighteenth century.

Equiano was, quite clearly, no typical slave. But what precisely *was* a typical slave? There is a temptation to think of slaves as mere beasts of burden for their white owners and employers. And there were, of course, millions of Africans and their descendants who simply laboured throughout their (often too short) lives, sweating in the sugar, tobacco, rice and cotton fields, their lives little more than an infernal drudgery, their meagre rewards whatever they could scrape together for themselves. Yet there are slave stories which, like Equiano's, stand out from the crowd. Those slaves, most of them long-forgotten, provide glimpses of another world – of slave attainment in the most unpromising of conditions. From one corner of the Black Atlantic to another, slaves infiltrated every area of the local economy and social life. From plantation midwives to carpenters, from Atlantic sailors to cowboys on the American frontier, from the fishermen of the West Indies to Billy Waters, the one-legged black fiddler in London, blacks could be found in all walks of life in the era of slavery. And a fair number of them, like Sancho and Equiano, had made a home in London.

In 1787 Equiano was recruited by the British government to act as an intermediary in the complicated process of persuading poor blacks living in London to volunteer for a 'repatriation' scheme to Sierra Leone. But how had those people – Equiano and the black poor – ended up in London in the first place? What brought them from their varied homelands to the poor quarters of the capital? How did black British life come into being?

Britain's American empire depended on migration. It could only thrive, initially at least, through the movement of alien peoples, keen to leave their native land and to secure a different life on the far side of the Atlantic. For the majority of people who migrated to the Americas – i.e., the Africans – choice played no part in the matter. They were unwilling partners in the European settlement and development of the Americas. Nonetheless everyone who settled in the Americas had moved great distances from their homeland. Whatever else bound together the diverse settlers in the Americas, all had endured the terrors of an oceanic crossing. In the wake of such massive, and increasing, flows of people back and forth, there was bound to be human flotsam and jetsam, individuals and groups cast ashore (often they knew not where) by the quirks of maritime expansion and population movement. Thus it was with that growing band of blacks, Africans and local-born, who found themselves in Britain.

We have seen that the black community had roots in Britain which went back centuries, but it was the development of maritime links between southern Europe and West Africa which had shaped the earliest black communities in Europe. It was from those maritime connections (with their onward links to northern Europe) that Africans came to Britain in noticeable numbers in the sixteenth century. They were, from the first, objects of curiosity, people whose skin colour seemed so at odds with prevailing English-speaking concepts of beauty, virtue and purity. The vernacular of colours – of black and white – was steeped in deep-rooted cultural values. Blackness invoked images of dirt, of sin, of evil and of vice. White and the language of paleness, on the other hand, conveyed the opposing ideas: cleanliness and purity, virtue and goodness.[8]

What shaped the treatment of blacks in Britain, however, was the development of the slave empires and the Atlantic slave trade. There is a circularity involved here. Did Europeans come to view Africans as unalterably different – inferior – *because* of the deep-seated European cultural traditions about colour, or were those traditions merely invoked to lend justification and strength to an economic phenomenon? Did Europeans cast around for justifications for enslaving Africans (at a time when Europe was cutting itself loose from centuries-old traditions of enslavement at home), and find in this culture of colour an ideal and widely accepted rationale for their ventures in the Atlantic? In time, the formula changed. Certainly by the time the slave systems had reached their apogee, in the mid- and late-eighteenth century (the very years when Britain's domestic black community had become a 'problem'), the racial justification of slavery was widespread.

The Americas effectively racialized slavery, laying the mark of Cain on the African and his descendants. It was a process greatly assisted by a variety of other factors and by what Europeans learned about Africa and Africans (their 'savagery', their lack of religion – excepting Islam – the alleged crudeness of their social structures). They were, in a word, thought of as barbaric. Above all else, Africans were most easily distinguished, categorized and remembered by their colour. They were quite unlike anything Europeans were familiar with. By the later years of Elizabeth I's reign, Africans were beginning to appear on the streets of London. There were mere handfuls at first (though efforts were made to prevent more arriving); it was the development of the slave colonies which ensured that more Africans would find their way to Britain.

As ever more ships embarked on the Africa trade (the so-called triangular trade linking the three continents), more Africans stepped ashore in Britain. They were used initially as fashionable items, whose exotic presence in the homes of the wealthy would add social cachet to their owners. Like all other exotic items, they were commodities, personal possessions and items of trade acquired through the burgeoning Atlantic trades. Africans were employed as servants, but their status was, on the whole, enslaved. They were imported as slaves direct from Africa or, more likely, via the Americas where they had already been used as slaves. They landed as trained domestics in the service of returning Britons, or as the possession of a sailor (normally a captain) who may have used them on board as a personal servant, and was now keen to sell them as a bonus from the voyage. For the best part of a century, from the late-seventeenth to the late-eighteenth century (when the law and abolitionists began to harry and prevent sailors trying to sell or buy slaves in Britain), sailors were responsible for buying and selling many slaves in Britain.

Blacks arrived in England, then, as a consequence of the expansion of the slave trade and of American slavery. They were used in a variety of positions, but as far as we can tell many, perhaps even most of them, started life in Britain as enslaved domestics. There was no real *need* for black domestics. After all, there was no shortage of labouring people willing and able to be trained up in the skills of domestic service. But black servants/slaves offered much more than mere labouring or social skills. They provided their employers with a way of impressing outsiders, of reaffirming their own exalted and rarefied position. Here was a person or a family at the very height of social fashion, whose wealth and status could be conveyed to others in a number of ways, most notably through lavish displays of material possessions. The latest, costly artefacts from around the world were added to their prominent displays of material consumption. Few were more eye-catching than black humanity, often dressed in regalia and finery which was itself exotic and eye-catching: Africans were dressed in turbans and other Indian clothing, or bedecked in jewellery and silverwear. At times, this mix of exotic people and fashion presented a confusing image but the purpose was to impress: to leave visitors and others in no doubt that the owners/employers of such colourful domestics were people to be reckoned with.

As with all forms of conspicuous display, it did not take long for people lower down the social scale to ape their superiors. What had begun as royal and aristocratic quickly became middle-class, as men of money sought to confirm their economic position by comparable displays of social style. Among such people, returning planters and nabobs were to the fore. West Indian planters were conscious of competing in displays of colonial-based wealth with returning nabobs from India.[9] Lord Shelbourne in 1778 declared that 'there were scarcely ten miles together throughout the country where the house and estate of a rich West Indian was not to be seen'. Ever more West Indians felt the need to shine 'at home', nowhere better of course than in the fashionable watering-holes, especially that of Bath.[10] Men who had made their wealth in the colonies promoted their status in Britain by competing in displays of public extravagance, from stately homes and their elaborate contents to armies of retainers, footmen and the like. Thus did black servants permeate propertied society by the late-eighteenth century. They could be found engaged in the most elaborate of rituals in the grandest of houses, and performing the simplest of tasks in humbler surroundings. Francis Barber, Dr Johnson's black servant, had little to do for that most eccentric of employers.[11]

It was inevitable, in the movement of thousands of ships, back and forth from London, Bristol and Liverpool to Africa and the slave colonies, that Africans would be landed in Britain. Local newspapers regularly carried advertisements for slave sales, or for the return of runaway slaves. Bristol's mid-eighteenth-century newspaper regularly carried such advertisements, and slaves were sometimes offered for sale, in both Bristol and Liverpool, at auctions in a local tavern or coffee shop. Prospective buyers could inspect the slave at a specified time.

Such advertisements have been reprinted many times, but they bear repeating for they often capture the physical image of the long-forgotten slave and they provide an entrée into the contemporary British outlook. Here, after all, were British people advertising other humans for sale alongside the most commonplace items of trade and business. Joseph Daltera, a flour merchant, offered for sale '10 pipes of raisin wine, a parcel of bottle cyder, and a negro boy'. An advert of 1769 offered for sale a job lot in Holborn: a horse and cart, a chestnut gelding, a grey mare and a 'well made, good-tempered Black Boy'. Newspapers in all the slave ports carried similar advertisements in the eighteenth century. But such advertisements faded away in the last two decades of the century when slavery was under attack both in the courts and from the early abolition campaign.

Sometimes the slaves' physical characteristics and personal qualities were described in the hope of catching the reader's eye: 'well limb'd', 'fit to serve a gentleman', 'capable of waiting at table', 'extremely well grown', 'a very serviceable hand'. The slaves' physical condition (especially the smallpox scars that told buyers that the slave was effectively safe against that terrible scourge of the slave quarters), strength, gentility (necessary in domestic service), special skills – 'can Dress Hair in a tolerable way' – all, and more, spoke of the slaves' physical condition and their working experience and prospects. In 1769 an advertisement offered for sale a 10- or 11-year-old who was 'very good-natured and tractable, and would be very useful in a Family, or a Lady's Foot-boy'. The child was offered for a trial period, but the cost was £50. An advertisement for a young black girl at much the same time told that she was 'extremely handy, works at her Needle tolerably, and speaks English well: is of an excellent Temper, and willing Disposition'. Slaves' prices varied (in sterling or colonial currency), depending on their age, health, physique and skills. Slaves were similarly *sought* through the columns of local newspapers.[12]

Slave advertisements have been thoroughly researched in the major American slave colonies, and have yielded a great deal of useful information.[13] By and large, however, slave advertisements in Britain have remained items of curiosity, and are generally not related to broader historical questions. Yet they surely have an importance *beyond* the confines of slave history. Britain, which prided itself on the political freedoms secured for its people in the course of the seventeenth century, and which trumpeted its love of freedom in various forms, not merely orchestrated a major global involvement with slavery, but played host to slavery in the most domestic of circumstances. Slavery existed in Britain, and prospered until the last years of the eighteenth century.

Slaves everywhere sought to escape from their bondage. It was, of course, much harder to hide in Britain, a society where black people remained, in general, isolated individuals who stood out from the crowd. Even in London, with its distinctive but small black community, it was difficult for runaway slaves to disappear completely from the view of slave-owners in pursuit of their human quarry. Nonetheless, slaves in Britain *did* escape from their bondage, and their owners sought their return through newspaper advertisements which were to be found in port newspapers. In an exhaustive study of newspapers in the period 1665 to 1795, a recent scholar has unearthed 35 such 'Hue and Cry' advertisements – 12 of the slaves belonged to sea captains. Slaves ran away from the early days of black settlement in Britain, though by the mid-eighteenth century there was a discernible black group in London willing to aid and abet potential runaways. However, as the life of Equiano testifies (he was kidnapped – as was a friend – in London), blacks were often powerless to resist the arbitrary power of ruthless captains who, on the point of departure, were willing to buy or snatch blacks, free or enslaved. Though the law gradually swung behind the abolitionist lobby, granting writs of *habeas corpus*, and later outlawing forcible removal against their will, there is evidence (from baptismal records, for example) that sailors continued to hold blacks as slaves/servants into the nineteenth century.[14]

The runaway advertisements provide an all-too-rare glimpse of these forgotten people. A number of late-seventeenth-century runaways wore metal collars. Captain Foye's slave in Bristol, Scipio, was 'somewhat Splayfooted'. The facial markings of Africans were described as a means of identifying a runaway. Another Bristol slave, belonging to Captain Courtney, had '3 or 4 marks on each Temple, and the same on each Cheek'. When Mingo ran away from Captain Eaton in Bristol in 1746 (after eight years' service), his owner offered a guinea's reward for his return, but warned 'All persons are hereby forbid entertaining the said Black at their peril.' Threats to prosecute anyone who sheltered a runaway (in 1757) hint that some people were willing to do just that. Clothing, colour and physical characteristics were described: 'having a piece of her left Ear bit off by a Dog', 'a Scar on the Top of the upper Joint of his Arm', 'a scar on his face', 'full of pock holes', 'remarkably bad legg'd and stoops much'. Slaves with pierced ears, filed teeth, with scurvy and a pot belly, tall slaves and small slaves, young and mature (rarely old), mainly men but, occasionally, women – all and more passed through the runaway columns of eighteenth-century newspapers. Their names too are revealing: Scipio, Scipio Africanus, Mingo, Somerset, Starling, Thomas, Jack, Chelsea, Torrie, Liverpool, York, Lewis.[15] None were known by their African names, though we do not know whether slaves called each other by their native names. Like slaves across the Americas, those who ran away in Britain had been given new names: anglicized, classical or ridiculous ones. It was part of that terrible process of deracination, of wrenching Africans loose from their cultural habitat and imposing on them a *persona* that was of their owners' making. Of course it rarely worked as whites intended. The fact that slaves ran away, in so unlikely a setting as a British seaport, speaks of their resistance to their lot.

Such advertisements for slaves are, of course, limited evidence; they are few, spread over a very long period, and relate overwhelmingly to a small number of major ports. But, like other historical evidence, they are important in themselves, they are remarkably rich in detail, and form one piece of a broader historical jigsaw. Most crucially, they confirm the existence of slavery in Britain. Though many of the runaways seem to have belonged to sailors (and were doubtless as transient as their masters) and their bondage was more maritime than land-based, their bondage and escapes raise fundamental issues for our study. Britain's involvement with slavery was not simply colonial or maritime. Slaves landed in Britain, escaped in Britain, were bought and sold in Britain, were advertised, auctioned and examined in Britain. Clearly, this was far removed from the terrifying auctions experienced by Equiano in Barbados. Yet for the individuals concerned, it was a frightening, dangerous and brutal experience, normally at the hands of sailors accustomed to the physical violation of Africans and none too careful about how they manhandled runaways back on board ship.[16] Moreover, this miniature aspect of slavery was in keeping with the overall system. The slave system was pervasive, creeping into most corners of the Atlantic world, and taking root, however precariously, in the most unlikely of places. Yet this was the very nature of the beast. Slavery was a dynamic, global system carried on the back of maritime and colonial movement and settlement. To put the matter simply, it was hard to persuade a captain of a slaver that the slave he had acquired or bought, in Africa or in the Americas, and whom he had employed (often for years) on board ship and in their various ports of call around the rim of Atlantic trading, was different – was a free person – simply by stepping ashore in Bristol or London.

We do not know how many runaways managed to secure their freedom. But it is clear by the mid-eighteenth century that a noticeable black community had evolved from these varied and haphazard landings and settlements of blacks in London. Indeed, by the 1770s a debate erupted about the size, nature and future of that black community. It was a debate prompted by discussions about the legality or otherwise of slavery in Britain and followed a number of specific incidents, in which slaves tried to secure their freedom from masters who insisted on their legal right to hold on to slaves in Britain. The buying and selling of slaves in England had long gone unchallenged. In the words of the Admiralty Judge Lord Stowell in 1827:

> The personal traffic in slaves resident in *England* had been as public and as authorised in *London* as in any of our *West India* islands. They were sold on the Exchange and other places of public resort by parties themselves resident in *London,* and with as little reserve as they would have been in any of our *West India* possessions.[17]

The question which a small band of interested people, black and white alike, began to raise from the 1760s onwards was simple: was such a practice legal?

A number of legal cases had already confronted the question of slavery in Britain. They arose, again, as an inevitable consequence of the burgeoning Atlantic trade and the movement of enslaved peoples, on British ships, to various points in the Atlantic. Moreover, the British slave system, on the high seas and in the American colonies, had, from the first, been shaped by the law – by Acts of Parliament (notably in relation to the slave trade), by colonial legislation (supervised, altered and approved by London), and by a host of common law decisions and judgments. In all this, the legal fine-tuning of the colonial slave system and the maritime industry which served it, London played a critical role. We need to recognize that in the *legal* moulding of Atlantic slavery, the metropolis was a critical player just as it was in the financing and organizing of the whole slave structure. Most of this legal involvement with slavery was, of course, directed at Atlantic slave-trading and slavery in the Americas. But just as surely as slaves found their way to Britain, so too did the legal complexities about slavery in the metropolis.

The most obvious legal question was simple: was slavery legal in England (or in Scotland)? Though a number of cases confronted that question directly, most came to it indirectly. Most slave cases in English courts involved other legal issues which, in their turn, revealed the problem of slavery. Were slaves freed simply by stepping ashore? Were they freed by baptism? Could slaves be used as mere merchandise (for the purposes, for example, of inheritance, bequeathing or the payment of debts)? West Indians, worried about the status of their human property in England, pressed for a legal support of their property rights over slaves in England. Though they secured some legal approval for their claims (in 1729 and 1749), decisions began to go against them, especially from the 1760s when Granville Sharp began his persistent and ultimately effective legal defence of black people in England. Through a string of (often distressing) personal cases, Sharp pressed the argument that *habeas corpus* guaranteed blacks protection against forcible repatriation from England against their wishes. Sharp's growing reputation as defender of the black cause inevitably attracted a string of black supplicants (and the antipathy of the West India lobby who, in Sharp's words, proved themselves 'so tenacious of this kind of property'[18]). There followed a series of slave cases, culminating in the famous Somerset case of 1772, which concerned a master's right to remove a slave from England against his wishes.

The Lord Chief Justice, Lord Mansfield, prevaricated before and throughout that case, but ultimately resolved that *habeas corpus* was applicable to aggrieved blacks, and that they should *not* be removed from England against their will. The end result, though the precise consequences have remained unclear until recent years, was a serious blow to the slave lobby and a major triumph for Sharp and for the black community. The blacks who crowded the public galleries were in no doubt about what they had just witnessed. They

> bowed with profound respect to the Judges, and shaking each other by the hand, congratulated themselves upon the recovery of the rights of human nature.[19]

We know of examples of slavery continuing in England thereafter, but after 1772 it was a rarity, and in any case was always likely to attract legal (and, increasingly, social) hostility.[20] This victory for black freedom might seem a mere token; the English were conceding freedom where it mattered least – at home in England. Outrages continued on the slave ships, none more stunning than the butchery of 132 Africans on the Liverpool ship, the *Zong*, in 1781. Incredibly, the only legal consequence of that mass-murder in Britain was an abortive effort to claim the death of the murdered slaves *as an insurance loss*. It is also true that ubiquitous and persistent violence against slaves continued to oil the slave systems throughout the British colonies, never more bloody and cruel than in the wake of (or under the suspicion of) black resistance and rebellion. Despite all this we ought not to forget or minimize the significance of the legal and social changes in Britain after 1772. The Somerset case formed the beginning, small, partial and limited though it was, of a much broader campaign against slavery *tout court*. The law had been shown to be malleable; it could be bent to the black cause, and was not always or necessarily pitched against black interests. But the law would bend only under pressure from informed and persistent argument and lobbying. That, in turn, could only come from persuasive friends. And those friends were white and liberal, radical or humanitarian – sometimes egalitarian even. Black freedom emerged after 1772 from a potent mix of black agitation and white pressure.

As the Somerset case unfolded it prompted a fierce social and political debate which rumbled on for many years, not merely about the legalities of slavery, but also about the nature and social contours of the black community in Britain, and especially in London. During and after 1772, contemporaries argued about the whys and wherefores of black settlement in Britain. The argument reached new levels of urgency and aggravation a decade later when, in the wake of the British defeat in North America, hundreds of loyalist blacks were resettled in Britain with their fleeing masters. Thus, in the years 1772 to 1788 the issue of blacks in Britain became a source of social and political friction. What were the pros and cons of allowing a black community to grow in Britain? More immediately, what were the numbers involved? And what were the social consequences for the British of permitting a British black community to take root in Britain itself?

Most estimates of the number of blacks living in Britain have, until recently, been little more than 'speculative guesses'. The figures bandied around, from 1772 onwards, came from two sides with particular interests in the size of the black population. Both planters and the philanthropists led by Granville Sharp had reasons to inflate the figures for their own political ends. Edward Long, the West Indian planter and scribe for the West Indian interest in London, thought initially that the figure might have been 3000. But when, in the course of the Somerset case, the figure of 15,000 was mentioned, Long rapidly revised his estimate upwards. Others, writing at the same time, thought it might have been as high as 30,000. The most recent evidence based on detailed archival researches opts for a more conservative estimate of perhaps 5000 in London in the last years of the eighteenth century (out of a total population of 780,000).[21]

The question of numbers became more troublesome still when, defeated in North America in 1783, loyalists and military men returned home, bringing with them a large number of black soldiers, servants and ex-slaves who had been attached to the losing British side. It was from the ranks of this particular group that there emerged the 'black poor', to form so noticeable a contingent of indigent people on the streets of London in the mid-1780s. Private and government-backed philanthropy was organized to help them. This, in turn, led directly to the scheme for black re-settlement to Sierra Leone.

From the first, the Sierra Leone scheme of 1786 to 1788 was contentious. It was also unlikely to attract large numbers of black volunteers even with the assistance of Equiano. Who wanted to risk the physical dangers of pioneering settlement, *and* in an area still plagued by slave-traders? Equiano quit the scheme in some anger and confusion (largely because of the corruption he alleged against another official). The scheme led to fiery arguments and letters in the press, with opponents flinging racist barbs at Equiano. The whole unhappy episode did, however, serve to establish Equiano's name and position as the most prominent black in London, a position he capitalized on in 1789 with the publication of his autobiography. But for the first black settlers in Sierra Leone the story was disastrous. Within four years, only 60 of the original 364 were still alive.[22]

It had been a voluntary scheme, though pressure was applied to the black poor to join. Yet it is surely significant that a range of interested parties (including some of the philanthropists) were keen to see the emergence of a model community of free blacks in Africa, but not in London. The Sierra Leone scheme touched a number of sensitive nerves in Britain, about black settlement, about questions of 'race' and about relations between black and white. Whatever the numerical size of the black community, however keen a number of contemporary parties might have been to prevent its further growth (and even to diminish it), it had become a *fact* of metropolitan life in the last quarter of the eighteenth century. The simple existence of a black community in London, reflected in a range of contemporary literature and graphic material, was also an indication of the remarkable span of the Black Atlantic. It reached from the slave barracoons of West Africa to the very edge of the American frontier, to street corners of London, and into the remotest corners of rural Britain (where the wealthy were occasionally attended by black servants). When the first convict ships made tentative landfall in Australia, the scattering of African peoples had even reached the Antipodes, in the form of a handful of transported black criminals.

What was it all *for*? What lay behind this revolutionary diaspora of Africans to all corners of the Atlantic world and, in 1788, even further afield? This whole global edifice had been brought into existence to bring to western tables new exotic produce, and to satisfy western tastes for that produce. However, it brought much else besides. We need now to turn to the consequences, the fruits, of slave labours, to study the material and social produce of the labour of those transported Africans, and to consider its broader impact on the western world.

Notes

1 W. Jeffrey Bolster, *Black Jacks: African American Seamen in the Age of Sail* (Cambridge, MA, 1997), pp. 102–3.
2 *Letters of the Late Ignatius Sancho, an African* (1782) (Penguin edition, edited by Vincent Carretta, London, 1998); Reyahn King (ed.), *Ignatius Sancho, an African Man of Letters* (London, 1997).
3 James Walvin, *An African's Life: The Life and Times of Olaudah Equiano, 1745–1797* (London, 1998).
4 W. Jeffrey Bolster, *Black Jacks*, Chapter 1.
5 Olaudah Equiano, *The Interesting Narrative* (1794). Edited by Vincent Carretta (Penguin, 1995 edn), p. 158.
6 *Ibid.*, pp. 101–2.
7 *Ibid.*, pp. 137–49.

8 Winthrop D. Jordan, *White over Black: American Attitudes Toward the Negro, 1550–1812* (Baltimore, 1968 edn), Chapter 1.

9 Richard S. Sheridan, 'Caribbean plantation society, 1689–1748', in P. J. Marshall (ed.), *The Oxford History of the British Empire*, vol. 2, *The Eighteenth Century* (Oxford, 1998), p. 414.

10 Richard S. Sheridan, *Sugar and Slavery* (Kingston, 1994 edn), p. 473.

11 Peter Fryer, *Staying Power: The History of Black People in Britain* (London, 1984), pp. 424–6.

12 *Ibid.*, pp. 58–61.

13 Gad Heuman (ed.), *Out of the House of Bondage* (London, 1986); Billy G. Smith and Richard Wojtowicz, *Blacks Who Stole Themselves* (Philadelphia, 1989).

14 Norma Myers, *Reconstructing the Black Past: Blacks in Britain, 1780–1830* (London, 1996), Chapter 4.

15 Peter Fryer, *Staying Power*, pp. 62–4.

16 See the experience of Equiano in James Walvin, *Equiano*, Chapter 3.

17 Quoted in Peter Fryer, *Staying Power*, p. 60.

18 Quoted in *ibid.*, p. 119.

19 Quoted in J. J. Hecht, *Continental and Colonial Servants in 18th Century England* (Northampton, MA, 1954), p. 48.

20 For a recent discussion of this and the broader legal issues, see James Walvin, *Equiano*, Chapter 4. Though these cases were *English*, they had important consequences for Scottish practice.

21 Stephen J. Braidwood, *Black Poor and White Philanthropists* (Liverpool, 1994), pp. 22–3; Norma Myers, *Reconstructing*, pp. 27–36.

22 James Walvin, *Equiano*, Chapter 11.

= 8 =

THE FRUITS OF
SLAVE LABOUR

It is a historical truism that, by the late eighteenth century, Britain had become a nation of shopkeepers. Tens of thousands of shops catered for the buying and consuming habits of the British people. Most eye-catching were those in London's Oxford Street, where fashionable society could buy 'the whim-whams and fribble-frabble of fashion'. Others were perhaps even more impressive as the purveyors of basic goods and commodities to people across the country. Even in the most remote and isolated of communities, far from the faddish pressures of taste and contemporary style, in small Welsh villages and remote Highland communities, and in the poorest of plebeian districts in the British urban heartland, the local shop (often no more than a counter in the front room) made available the goods which the British had come to demand. Those goods were basic to the way the great majority of British people led their mundane domestic and social lives. Foremost among them were the fruits of slave labour, notably tobacco and sugar. Even the commodity which united all social classes – tea – was linked to slave labour: the British drank their tea sweetened by lashings of West Indian sugar. (The West India lobby encouraged tea consumption because they knew it was good for the sugar business; the more tea the British drank, the more sugar they added to it.[1])

All of these commodities – tea, sugar and tobacco – were sold in small portions to poorer customers. In the words of Adam Smith, shopkeepers were responsible for 'breaking and dividing . . . rude and manufactured produce into such small parcels as suited the occasional demands of those who wanted them'. It was the ideal way of selling goods to poor customers. Adam Smith, again, made the point that shopkeepers enabled the working man 'to purchase his subsistence from day to day, or even from hour to hour, as he wants it'.[2]

One such shopkeeper was Ignatius Sancho, the African man of letters, whose shop was in George Street, Westminster. As Sancho talked over the counter with his various customers, drinking tea with special visitors, his wife Anne worked in the background, breaking down the sugar into smaller packages. Sancho's trade card, advertising his shop and his wares, portrayed slaves gathering tobacco in the tobacco fields. Here was a perfect reminder of the way colonial slavery came full circle: slave-grown produce advertised and sold – by an ex-slave – in the heart of London. And all for the comfort and pleasure of the British consumer.

Slave produce had very quickly passed from the luxurious to the essential, in a complex, but relatively swift, process. Much, of course, had to do with purchasing power – the ability of people to set aside money for items which, only a few years before, had seemed beyond their reach and more the preserve of their betters. But as Africans were poured into the colonies, and as the volume of slave produce increased dramatically, the cost of tobacco and sugar (and of all the other related items) plummeted. Though it sometimes irritated outsiders (especially those investigating the roots of British poverty), the poor (like everyone else) were able to buy sugar, tea and tobacco.[3] The precise origins of these mass tastes are difficult to ascertain, but once a taste had emerged as a major economic force, local men of enterprise turned their energies and resources to satisfying it. It was from such origins that there thus emerged the nation of shopkeepers, men (and women) who secured imported slave-grown produce from London, Bristol or Liverpool (and later from Glasgow). Bulky goods were broken down, in the local shop, and repackaged into smaller volumes, or sold in the particular amount demanded by customers. Promoted by word of mouth, and later (with the rise of cheap and popular print in the eighteenth century) via handbills, trade cards (Sancho's, for example) and local newspapers, tropical staples flooded the British market in the course of the late seventeenth and eighteenth centuries. By the end of the eighteenth century, the British imported 322 million pounds of sugar, 16 million pounds of tea and 15.3 million pounds of tobacco.[4] Substantial amounts were re-exported, but much went to satisfying the national craving for slave-grown produce, and most was sold over the counters of the 33,000 or so shops scattered across Britain.[5]

Britain's shops formed a remarkable system which had emerged in tandem with the rise of British global power and colonial domination. It may seem odd at first to link the two – the humble corner shop and the world of overseas empire. They were, however, intimately linked, not least because it was the prime produce of that empire (especially its slave-grown produce) which filled the shelves of the shops. This was particularly true for humbler shops whose main source of income was the sale of sugar, tea and tobacco. Produce from the very edge of colonial settlement and trade (tea from China, tobacco and sugar from the slave-fields of the Americas) found their way into the hands of British consumers via tens of thousands of small shopkeepers. These were the people who ensured that, whatever the vicissitudes of warfare, changing taxation policies or accidents of weather, the pleasures and comfort of sweet tea or coffee, and a pipe of tobacco, were always to hand for British consumers, wherever they might live or travel. At home (high or low), in public places, when travelling or when at work, the fruits of slave labours were accessible and within the budget of even the poorer people. One mid-eighteenth-century account caught the process perfectly. Charles Deering told how,

> being the other day at a Grocers, I could not forbear looking with some Degree of Indignation at a ragged and greasy Creature, who came into the Shop with two ragged Children following her in a dismal Plight as the Mother, asking for a Pennyworth of Tea and a Half penny-worth of Sugar.

The customer, explaining herself to the shopkeeper, said, 'I do not know how it is with me, but I can assure you that I would not desire to live, if I was to be debarred from drinking every Day a little Tea'[6] (mixed – of course – with sugar). But how had this extraordinary state of affairs come about? How did these fruits of slave labour manage to establish themselves as the necessities of everyday life for even the very poorest of British people?

The sweetening of food with honey had been basic to the British diet long before the development of the sugar colonies, but cane sugar had enormous advantages over the old sweetener. It was easily preserved, and so was a suitable ingredient to keep on the kitchen shelves. Moreover, it was ideally suited to the varied processes of mixing and blending with other foods and ingredients. It could be dissolved in liquids or mixed with other foodstuffs. When mixed with ground almonds to make marzipan, it could be moulded into a variety of shapes. Men on the make, anxious to confirm their social status as well as their rising material prosperity, might well announce that status through elaborate culinary displays, the centrepiece of which was often sugary confections. As sugar production switched from the Mediterranean, first to the Atlantic islands and then to the New World, and as prices fell, sugar crept into a host of dishes, added as a condiment, mixed with other spices and additives – often to the culinary disapproval of purists who disliked the mixing of sweet and savoury tastes. One clear indication of the growing popularity of sugar was the way it secured a place in the growing number of cookery books of the sixteenth and seventeenth centuries. Sugar became ever more accessible by the mid-seventeenth century, because it was produced in ever-increasing volumes by slaves in Brazil and the West Indies. In the process sugar was transformed from its early status as a luxury, restricted to the wealthy, into a commodity which even the humblest of people aspired to, and which they could afford.

Like so many exotic substances (including tobacco), sugar also arrived as a medicine. A number of exotic substances passed into European medical culture from the East, the Mediterranean and North Africa, and later from the Americas, encouraged (and sometimes discouraged) by a range of contemporary advocates.[7] Tobacco, for example, was once regarded as remarkably effective for a host of ailments and it continued to be used as medicine long after it became popular for smoking. It is hard to know precisely what caused the initial transfer of tobacco from its native American Indian habitat to Europe (and thence to the wider world), but it happened quickly, most probably via sailors and adventurers who picked up Indian habits from their time in the Americas. By the time the British established their own American colonies, and long before the Chesapeake began to produce tobacco for export, tobacco-smoking had become a major habit in Europe. Indeed the hostility of the newly arrived James I to smoking in England in 1603 has become the stuff of historical legends. His opposition was fruitless, however, not least because the market for tobacco was so obviously lucrative; it generated profits for importers, distributors and for the state itself, which was able to tax imported tobacco. Like sugar, tobacco quickly established itself as a major source of income for a state ever keen to expand its base of income in the teeth of mounting expenses.

Tobacco could be bought in the alehouse, from the apothecary and, later, from specialist tobacconists (sporting the trade symbol of the North American Indian above the door), and from the all-purpose corner shop.

In its early days in Britain, tobacco was vigorously promoted by landlords of taverns and alehouses, quickly establishing the links between the public world of masculine drinking and smoking. Much the same happened in coffee houses, which also became infamous for the clouds of tobacco smoke clogging the atmosphere at the height of the day's activities. In the 1620s, only 65,000 pounds of tobacco were exported from the Chesapeake, but 50 years later the volume had grown to 20 million pounds. This was made possible by the armies, first of indentured servants, and later of Africans, deposited in Virginia and Maryland. By the late seventeenth century, African slaves had begun to replace white indentured servants as the labouring force on the tobacco plantations.[8] The result of their labours was that Europeans, by the mid-seventeenth century, smoked huge volumes of Chesapeake tobacco. Tobacco was enjoyed by both men and women in its early years, but habits changed and tobacco became primarily a masculine pleasure (though snuff-taking remained a fashionable female habit). Not until the development of the modern cigarette were women expected to smoke tobacco. Tobacco consumption (normally through clay pipes, the manufacture of which became an important industry in itself), generally in the company of other men over ale or coffee, became a defining characteristic of masculinity in the late seventeenth and early eighteenth centuries. Despite a polite drive against smoking in the late eighteenth century, smoking had securely anchored itself as a major social habit in British (and European) life.

Tobacco provided the state with a lucrative source of income. Indeed, tobacco duties became so high, with the associated expense to the consumer, that smuggling of non-taxed tobacco actually provided British smokers with most of their tobacco. Smugglers brought their goods ashore in remote places, relying on local suspicion of authority to keep the prying eye of government officers at bay. Tobacco also took root via the fashionable world of watering places, through provincial capitals (from Newcastle to Exeter) and in the immediate hinterland of the tobacco ports. There, the fashion of smoking took root among men of substance before permeating the lower social orders. The process was assisted by the emergence of the 'outports' – the smaller ports across Britain which also involved themselves in the lucrative Atlantic trade from the late seventeenth century onwards. Whitehaven emerged as a major entrepôt for the import and transshipment of tobacco from America; from the mid-eighteenth century onwards the role was taken over by Glasgow. Thereafter Glasgow was transformed from a poor city into a major international port. Wherever tobacco was imported, it was also sold and distributed onwards, throughout the immediate hinterland of the ports.

Alongside other exotic goods, tobacco had a role in the development of contemporary society and its mores. Men smoked – normally in the company of other men – women did not. Tobacco-smoking came to be one of life's rites of passage, the moment when a boy became a man. If an artist wished to convey an impression of an old crone, he would often put a pipe in her fist: a sure sign of a woman beyond the pale of ladylike behaviour. By the early eighteenth century, only the most eccentric (or lewd) of women would be seen smoking. However, the smell, the smoke, the stains of tobacco-smoking were everywhere. Tobacco stained domestic and public furnishings, it prompted coughing and spitting, and clearly had a harmful effect on smokers' health.

Then as now, tobacco was an essential feature of military life. The miseries of life below decks for sailors (as well as slaves) were eased by tobacco. The sight of a lighted pipe often provided a clue to a hidden enemy in close combat. Men fighting Indians in early colonial America often gave away their position by the fires used to satisfy their 'Epidemical plague of lust after Tobacco'.[9] Soldiers and sailors were notorious for their smoking habits – these were of course the people who travelled to the very edge of European settlement, conflict and trade, and who took with them the habits popular at home and on the ships. Millions of men smoked in the massive conflicts of the Revolutionary and Napoleonic Wars. Kept at their tasks by ample supplies of alcohol and tobacco, survivors returned home in 1815 firmly addicted to the habits they had picked up during the wars.

Military life alone, however, could not explain the ubiquitous spread of tobacco-smoking. There were, for example, special smoking rooms in fashionable homes as early as 1690, with more adopting the pattern in the early eighteenth century. Indeed, there was a clear drive to segregate (sometimes even to ban) the smoker from polite society. It proved an uphill battle, but even the formidable Duke of Wellington had to concede, outlawing smokers in his own house to the servants' quarters.

Tobacco, then, moved out from its American homelands to permeate thoroughly European social life. It dominated life on board the thousands of ships which linked the Atlantic economies of Europe, Africa and the Americas. Similarly, it moved onwards, to all corners of European maritime contact. After all, the sheer volume of tobacco imported to Britain from the Chesapeake was far too much for domestic British consumption, and the British had to re-export the bulk of it. The commercial importance of tobacco was not restricted to Britain. Tobacco from Brazil (Bahia) was a key item in the burgeoning trade between West Africa and Brazil from the mid-seventeenth century onwards. Brazilian tobacco was in great demand in West Africa, notably on the Mina Coast, but also in Angola, São Tomé, Príncipe and Benguela. Lisbon dominated the Bahian tobacco trade, and the Lisbon markets ensured that the tobacco was re-exported to other parts of Europe: to Italy, Spain, France and Hamburg. Inevitably, Brazilian tobacco also found its way into Portugal's vast global trading empire – to Goa, Macao and Timor, and also to China. Even more curiously, Brazilian tobacco was popular with Indian peoples of the Americas, who sometimes preferred it to the Chesapeake varieties. Here then, the story had come full circle. The very people who had first introduced Europeans to tobacco – the indigenous peoples of the Americas – had seen their taste transformed by a particular form of slave-grown tobacco. Now the Indians preferred to smoke tobacco in clay pipes made in England.[10]

Tobacco was consumed throughout the slave system, and there was demand for tobacco on both sides of the Atlantic. It was popular in West Africa; it was used to pacify slaves in the squalor of the slave decks; and it was often distributed to them on arrival in the Americas. When the slave ship the *James* reached Barbados in 1626, the captain recorded 'gave my slaves tobacco and pipes'. When the slaves were later prepared for sale, they were again given tobacco.[11] Tobacco was also burned to fumigate the vacated slave quarters on board the slave ships. In the sugar colonies, planters supplied slaves with pipes and tobacco. In 1790 William Beckford wrote how slaves could be seen throughout Jamaica smoking pipes. Archaeological evidence (pipes in slave graves and middens) confirms what we know from other sources, that smoking was widespread among West Indian slaves.[12] Here was a remarkable irony; a slave-grown product was being used to facilitate the slave system, in the Americas, on the slave ships and in West Africa itself.

Tobacco-smoking and other tastes rooted in slavery had thoroughly permeated British life by the mid-eighteenth century. Moreover, wherever around the world the British travelled, settled, migrated or fought, there they transplanted the cultural habits forged courtesy of the slave colonies of the Americas. The British at home became infamous for their sweet tooth, and for their addiction to tea, and they ensured that those tastes (and the produce which underpinned them) were transplanted to the most distant points of settlement or trading. There was, in effect, a globalization of taste for slave produce. Along with their languages and institutions, the imperial and global powers of the eighteenth and nineteenth centuries introduced their cultural habits to all corners of the globe. With time, in those new settings, those habits became so normal, so much a part of the cultural fittings, that it is easy to forget that they were shaped by specific historical circumstances. Moreover, we need to remind ourselves that much of this cultural environment traced its origins back to the world of Atlantic slavery. Social life for the British (and for other Europeans) around the world had become unthinkable without the pleasures from home. But many of those pleasures were shaped by the Atlantic slave economy.

In India, Asia, Africa, in North America and (in the last years of the eighteenth century) in the penal colony of Australia, the British turned for comfort and pleasure to slave-based produce. In India, where the range of local foodstuffs was enormous, the British transplanted habits from home, most notably a sweetened cuisine. A feature of British life in India was the attachment to the pudding, with its various ingredients augmented by the luxury of cane sugar. More noticeable perhaps, the British introduced the coffee house into India, the first one thought to have been in Calcutta in 1780. The Exchange Coffee Tavern at Madras, modelled on the one at Lloyd's in London, similarly offered details of the arrival and departure of ships and made available British newspapers for customers. Other coffee shops provided billiard tables.[13] Businessmen and soldiers had their own coffee shops in Calcutta, and the habit spread 'up country' to brighten the social life of military men and civilian alike, long before the institution of 'the club' took root in British India. When tea-drinking in India became widespread, following the introduction of tea cultivation into the sub-continent from the 1840s onwards, it was drunk (as in Britain), with the addition of cane sugar. (Some, however, served it Mogul-style, with spices.)[14]

The British needed sugar and tobacco wherever they travelled or settled, ensuring that supplies were ferried to them by sea or overland. In British North America, sugar consumption paralleled the domestic British taste, the two sides of the British Atlantic vying with each other as the most avid consumer of sugar after 1750.[15] But the conscious movement *away* from tea-drinking by Americans, fashioned by the urge to independence, ensured that coffee, not tea, became the main beverage to which the sugar was added in North America. In the early settlements of Australia, sugar, tea and tobacco were high on the list of demands by settlers. The First Fleet carried five tons of sugar from England to Botany Bay – a sure sign of its importance to that collection of prisoners, crew and military. By 1790 the initial sugar supplies had run out and were not replenished until the arrival of a ship from Calcutta in 1792. Even more remarkably, the Australian appetite for sugar rapidly outstripped even that of the British. Within a century of settlement, Australians were consuming an average of 88 pounds of sugar *per head* each year.[16] One of the first female convicts wrote of the initial years of settlement:

> We are comforted with the hopes of a supply of tea from China . . . Something like ground ivy is used for tea: but a scarcity of salt and sugar makes our best meals insipid.

Some years later, itinerant Australian workers were paid in weekly rations – the famous 'Ten, Ten, Two and a Quarter', i.e., 10 lbs of flour; 10 lbs of meat; 2 lbs of sugar and $1/4$ lb of tea, and some salt. At sea or when safely arrived in Australia, it was assumed that tea and sugar would be among the basic food supplies of the early settlers.[17] Not surprisingly perhaps, when the white settlers sought to bring local Aboriginal people to heel – to woo them to European habits, 'good behaviour' and industriousness (i.e., mainly working for local pastoralists) – they distributed rations as bait. It was hoped that European foods and clothing would persuade Aboriginals to work for the Europeans, and prevent them from stealing settlers' foodstuffs and animals. The rations were based on the white working-man's rations. Thus, the Aboriginal peoples of Australia quickly became addicted to tea and sugar (and flour). In times of illness, the sugar ration was doubled. Later, tobacco was added to the supplies, normally as a reward for good behaviour or service.[18]

What does all this prove – such random examples of social habits from different corners of the globe? They are, after all, familiar because so widespread and current to this day. But they are also creations of a particular set of historical circumstances, notably the rapid scattering to the wider world of habits and customs shaped within the world of Atlantic slavery. What becomes clear is the degree to which the Atlantic slave system had *global* consequences. Goods and social habits fashioned for Europe were spread around the world in the wake of European migration, trade and settlement. At one level this was simply another aspect of the rise of modern material consumption. On the very rim of European settlement, where colonists and settlers clung to insecure local roots, in unfriendly environments and often confronted by hostile indigenous peoples, they naturally turned to familiar habits. Foremost among them were exotic commodities produced by slaves.

Europeans, understandably, carried their cultural habits with them. This had the effect, inevitably, of persuading native peoples to adopt those European/settler habits. Indeed the Atlantic slave system itself actively won over vast stretches of the Atlantic rim to the consumption of European goods. This was most striking in West Africa. Goods flowed into Africa in profusion in return for the millions of slaves, goods which served to transform local economies and to whet the local appetite for imported goods and luxuries. Metalware and hardware, from Birmingham and Sheffield, pots and pans from Bristol, metal bars which were used as a means of exchange, and – above all – firearms poured in. At the height of the slave trade something in the region of between 283,000 and 394,000 firearms were imported into West Africa *each year*. In 1802 alone, firearms to the value of £145,661 were landed.[19] Whatever the military shortcomings of the weapons themselves, they helped to transform a range of local societies by empowering those who traded in arms and those who commanded them.

West Africans devoured imported goods. Textiles from India, Ireland, Scotland and England were especially important. By the end of the slave trade, the British were shipping something like a third of a million pieces of textiles to West Africa. A similar story could be told of other European slaving nations. Indeed, every conceivable artefact was exported to West Africa as part of the slave trade: knives and pans, clocks and wines, rum and sugar, tobacco and pipes. African merchants and traders became ever more choosy about which imported goods they wanted and found acceptable in barter for their slaves, rejecting those which fell below their expectations. But whatever their particular likes and dislikes, Africans clearly expected to be fed a regular and varied diet of imported goods, in return for their slaves.

A similar story unfolded, in a different format, across the enslaved Americas. From Brazil to Virginia and throughout the Caribbean, as we have seen, colonial life could only function effectively thanks to imported goods. And those goods had a massive impact among the native peoples of the Americas. Indians now smoked tobacco in European pipes (they had happily consumed it previously without such equipment). Wines and rum, guns, knives, axes and mirrors – all passed into Indian hands in return for an apparently endless supply of skins, pelts and furs (with devastating consequences for American wildlife). Indians acquired goods from China, from Venice and Germany. Above everything else, however, and like the

African slave-traders on the other side of the Atlantic, they wanted firearms and alcohol, with all the well-known, devastating consequences. The impact of European goods on North American Indian life was profound. Archaeological evidence suggests that, by the mid-seventeenth century, upwards of three-quarters of all Indian artefacts were of European origin.[20]

The British empire of the eighteenth century was designed to foster such consumption of British goods, and to provide raw materials and produce for British use and consumption. Among those North Americans who began to challenge British control, resentment at the way they were locked into the British economy created a grievance which exacerbated political disagreements from the mid-century onwards. Americans bridled at the fact that they were required to consume the 'baubles of Empire', primarily for the benefit of the metropolis.[21]

The Atlantic economy was a complicated, interlinked set of smaller distinct economies. The whole edifice was held together by consumers, on both sides of the Atlantic, devouring goods which, only a few years earlier, had been unknown, utterly alien or beyond their financial reach. What underpinned much of this social structure was the world of African slavery. Obviously, it is difficult to highlight just one element from within a major social and economic structure; all were locked together in a mutually interdependent system. But contemporaries were agreed that slavery and the slave trade were the engine which drove the whole system. Moreover, it was accepted that this trade in humanity was vital. It was 'so beneficial to Great Britain, so essentially necessary to the very being of her colonies, that without it neither could we flourish, not they long subsist'.[22]

The Black Atlantic, then, was much more than the enforced movement of millions of Africans from their homelands, and their re-settlement in the Americas. It was a major international economic system which transformed separate (but related) regions of the world, with links onwards to even more remote regions. It had massive social and economic consequences right around the world. From what seems, at first sight, a relatively simple story (an account of slave-grown produce in the Americas), there flowed lines of trade, patterns of social change and the development of new cultural habits which had, by the late eighteenth century, become truly global. It is often difficult to remember the slaves behind all this.

Who even thought of slavery when the first Australian settlers complained of the lack of sugar? Who remembered, when Aboriginal peoples eagerly acquired a taste for sugar, that the product was cultivated by Africans in the West Indies? Which person, in far-flung European outposts, settlements or barracks, gave so much as a passing thought to the slaves who cultivated the tobacco and sugar taken for granted as part of daily life? The fruits of slave labour were everywhere, but the slaves remained out of sight and out of mind.

Notes

1 James Walvin, *Fruits of Empire: Exotic Produce and British Taste* (London, 1987), Chapter 10.

2 Quoted in *ibid.*, pp. 165–6.

3 Sir Frederick Eden, *The State of the Poor*, 3 vols (London, 1797), Vol. I, pp. 496, 535.

4 Hoh-Cheun Mui and Lorna H. Mui, *Shops and Shopping in Eighteenth Century England* (London, 1989), pp. 13–14; John E. Willis Jnr, 'European consumption and Asian production in the seventeenth and eighteenth centuries', in John Brewer and Roy Porter (eds), *Consumption and the World of Goods* (London, 1993).

5 James Walvin, *Fruits*, p. 169.

6 Quoted in Dorothy Marshall, *English People in the Eighteenth Century* (London, 1956), p. 172.

7 Roy Porter, *The Greatest Benefit to Mankind: A Medical History of Humanity from Antiquity to the Present* (London, 1997), pp. 190–4.

8 James Walvin, *Fruits*, pp. 74–5.

9 *Ibid.*, p. 66.

10 Jordan Goodman, *Tobacco in History: The Cultures of Dependence* (London, 1993), pp. 162–5.

11 Elizabeth Donnan, *Documents Illustrative of the Slave Trade to America* (Washington, DC, 1930–35), 4 vols, Vol. I, pp. 204–5.

12 B. W. Higman, *Montpelier, Jamaica: A Plantation Community in Slavery and Freedom, 1739–1912* (Kingston, Jamaica, 1998), pp. 241–2.

13 David Burton, *The Raj at Table: A Culinary History of the British in India* (London, 1993), pp. 176–7; Chapter 15.

14 *Ibid.*, Chapter 15.

15 Harvey Levenstein, *Revolution at Table: The Transformation of the American Diet* (New York, 1988), p. 6.

16 Alan Frost, *Botany Bay Mirages* (Melbourne, 1994). I am grateful to Dr Peter Griggs for this information, given in his paper 'Sugar in Australia, 1788–1900', University of Adelaide, July 1998.

17 Michael Symons, *One Continuous Picnic: A History of Eating in Australia* (Adelaide, 1982), pp. 16, 27, 28.

18 Robert Foster, 'Rations, co-existence, and the colonisation of Aboriginal labour in the South Australian pastoral industry, 1860–1911', Workshop on Sugar, University of Adelaide, July 1998.

19 J. K. Inikori, 'The import of firearms into West Africa', in J. E. Inikori (ed.), *Forced Labour* (London, 1982).

20 James Axtell, 'The first consumer revolution', in *Beyond 1492* (New York, 1992).

21 T. H. Breen, '"Baubles of Britain": the American and consumer revolutions of the eighteenth century', *Past and Present*, No. 119, 1988.

22 Jon Peter Demarin, *A Treatise upon the Trade from Great Britain to Africa* (London, 1772), pp. 4–5.

= 9 =

QUAKERS AND OTHER FRIENDS

Did slaves have any friends outside their own circles and communities? Certainly, when looking at Atlantic slavery at its peak, it is hard to see any who were the Africans' friends. They had enemies in abundance, of course, people on either side of the Atlantic, ranging from those other Africans who enslaved them initially through to the planters and other slave-owners who controlled their lives from their final landing point in the Americas. In between these two extremes – African enslavers on the one hand, American slave-owners on the other – slaves faced a host of tormentors, all of whom played a part in their continuing misery: agents and dealers on the African coast, European sailors on the high seas, agents and others on landfall in the Americas, men (black and white) charged with moving newly arrived Africans onwards from the quayside and barracoons to distant plantations and settlements in the Americas.

Once settled into a local 'home', Africans faced a motley collection of plantation-based whites who, operating beneath the planters' overall control, could dole out daily, often unknown and invisible (to outsiders) indignities and pains to the slaves in their care – or indeed to any black who might simply cross their path. There was a litany of gratuitous and capricious hurts which whites of all sorts administered with impunity to blacks throughout the slave colonies. More vigilant and sensitive slave-owners guarded against the common outrages inflicted on their slaves, but they were often powerless, certainly on larger properties, to prevent the slaves' sufferings. Those slave-owners whose prosperity enabled them to distance themselves from the centre of slave-owning, who used their slave-based wealth to return to Britain or to the more congenial environment of the nearest American city (Charleston, for example), were dependent on their overseers for slave management. Owners could only hope that such men would treat the slaves tolerably. Too often they were disappointed, and local control of slaves fell to men whose fears and inadequacies were transformed into a regime of brutalized misery. There was no single pattern to this slave experience, but there were common denominators – the reality, or threat, of white violence and humiliation at all turns.

All of this was in addition to the pains of the formal slave system itself. From first to last, slavery (in Africa, at sea and in the Americas) evolved as a draconian institution. Europeans equipped their slave systems with a legal structure which hinged on punishments of the most violent kind. Laws governing trade and navigation, colonial laws governing local slave society, all enshrined violence against the slaves, in addition to the informal, violent conventions of plantocratic slave management. From the midst of this welter of violence, the question recurs: who were the slaves' friends?

There had been critics of the worst excesses of slavery from an early date. Some had even disputed the validity of and justification for slavery itself. But the early objections, led by Las Casas, the friar who was 'protector of the Indians' in Spanish America, were simply swept aside by the rising tide of material bounty which surged from the slave colonies. Moral scruples seemed a luxury in the teeth of the slave-based well-being disgorged from the returning slave ships. It would be wrong, however, to deny the existence of a critical voice which doubted the morality or utility of Atlantic slavery. Though generally drowned out by the pro-slavery clamour, it was a voice which asserted itself with ever-greater stridency in the last quarter of the eighteenth century. There is a confusing paradox here: at the very time the British slave trade reached its peak, opposition to the system began to assert itself as never before. In that process, in the 1780s, the Quakers proved critical.

If slaves had friends at all, they were to be found among the Society of Friends. From their earliest days as a persecuted sect (one of many among the myriad groups spawned by the upheavals of the English Civil War), Quakers spoke up for the persecuted and defenceless. Similarly, they spoke against slavery. This was an institution which offended the Quaker attachment to the equality of mankind. The founder of the Quakers, George Fox, spoke out against slavery on his travels in America and the West

Indies. Visiting Barbados in 1671, he was keen to see slaves converted to Christianity and reared 'in the fear of God'. Quakers in the West Indies preached to the slaves, but urged them 'to be subject to their masters and governors'.

These early Quaker strictures against slavery did not prevent some Quakers from owning slaves, or from involving themselves in the slave system. Anyone involved in trade to and from the slave islands would, inevitably, be tainted by slavery. Olaudah Equiano's own master in Montserrat was a Quaker (though he eventually allowed Equiano to buy his freedom). Major British Quaker merchants developed a profitable livelihood from trade to the slave colonies. Thomas Corbyn, London's greatest pharmaceutical manufacturer in the eighteenth century, did a lively trade with Quakers in Jamaica and Antigua, sending boxes of his goods to be distributed to 'the Doctors and considerable Planters'.[1] The London Yearly Meeting of the Quakers (effectively their governing body) periodically urged Friends to steer clear of slavery, but that was no easy matter; slavery had become so pervasive, its consequences so thoroughly permeating British life, that it was hard for men in trade and business to avoid it completely. Quakers were formidable businessmen and traders, and large numbers of them operated in the retail trades. There, in their shops and warehouses, they inevitably dealt in slave-grown produce, notably sugar and tobacco. The metal industry, 75 per cent owned by Quakers by the mid-eighteenth century, manufactured a range of goods for the slave trade of course, to say nothing of armaments (which offended another Quaker tenet – opposition to warfare).

There were, then, a series of ethical and personal problems for Quakers in their dealings with the slave economies. But the Yearly Meeting remained steadfast in its opposition to slavery. In 1758 (repeating a statement of 1727), all Quakers were warned against involving themselves in the slave trade, which was so 'evidently destructive of the natural rights of mankind'.[2] It was understandable, therefore, when abolition emerged as an issue in the 1780s, that Quakers would form the driving force and the core support behind the initial campaign. The fiercest denunciation of slavery, however, came from the other side of the Atlantic, from the American centre of Quakerism, in Philadelphia. As early as 1758 the Philadelphia Yearly Meeting had resolved to exclude all Friends who continued to buy and sell slaves, urging them instead to free any slave that they might own. In 1776 they resolved to exclude anyone who persisted in owning slaves. Three years later, they urged that compensation be paid to freed slaves. Unlike their British associates, American Quakers lived cheek-by-jowl with slavery; they saw and experienced its daily realities and yet (possibly for that very reason) they took a firmer line against slavery, and from an earlier date, than British Friends.

Two American Quakers in particular, Anthony Benezet and John Woolman, brought abolitionist pressure to bear on British Quakers in the 1760s and 1770s.[3] Quakers regularly criss-crossed the Atlantic, normally in their varied business capacities, and were always keen to press their current ideas on Friends on the other side of the Atlantic. There was a clear transatlantic community of Friends in the second half of the eighteenth century, linked not merely by business interests, but also (and partly in the wake of business) by theological and ethical concerns, each side prodding the other to adopt this or that latest stand. Americans often spoke in London and in the major centres of Quaker life. Publications from Philadelphia were republished in Britain, and British Quakers in general were kept aware from the 1760s onwards of the problems posed by slavery.

In 1782 British Quakers formed a committee to investigate the slave trade, and by June of the following year the London Yearly Meeting was ready to discuss the issue. A number of London's prominent Quaker businessmen were anxious to move more quickly, though the structure of Quaker governance dictated a slow pace as issues moved through the formal Quaker system. A group of six businessmen (some of whom had seen slavery at first hand in the Americas) gathered in 1783, with the idea of enlightening the British people about the slave trade. They initiated a series of articles in newspapers across the country. They assumed, of course, that slavery was morally and ethically flawed, but they also argued a case (recently promoted by Adam Smith in *The Wealth of Nations* (1776)) that slavery was uneconomic. Slavery's greatest strength – the one factor which had enabled it to overcome or deflect any criticisms – was its unquestioned economic importance. The slave system brought economic bounty to all concerned – or so it seemed. By the end of 1783, this Quaker group had distributed ten batches of articles to twelve newspapers in London and the provinces. Thereafter Quaker anti-slavery literature began to flood the country, the material easily distributed through existing Quaker networks. Quaker money enabled the material to be placed in the provincial press.[4] The Quakers used a range of arguments against the slave trade, urging the British people to take a stand against the whole system by refusing to buy slave-grown produce. It was the beginning of a remarkable campaign which was to bring an end to the British slave trade within 20 years. Moreover, it seems clear that abolition would have come sooner had it not been for the convulsions of the French Revolution after 1789. Even so, few of those Quakers who formed the first abolition campaign in 1783 could have dreamt that their activities would lead to such a swift and sudden end to the slave trade.

There were other, earlier strands of opposition, which converged in the 1780s to strengthen Quaker arguments. There was, for example, Granville Sharp's long-running campaign to have slavery *in England* declared illegal. It was, as we have seen, an uphill struggle, but he was not to be deflected by legal disappointments, nor by political and social opposition (notably from the West India lobby). Distressing news – of blacks consigned to outward-bound ships, of grotesque treatment on the slave ships – merely spurred him on. He campaigned among the good and the great, published what were, in effect, abolitionist tracts (long before any formal abolition campaign had been launched), and orchestrated arguments in court. More than that, Sharp's activities proved to blacks in Britain that they had a friend, a man who would defend their interests to the utmost and provide them with practical assistance, and hope, in a world which afforded them little of either.

Granville Sharp's great achievement was the Somerset case of 1772, which, for all its subsequent confusions, effectively put paid to slavery in England. There were examples of slaves held in England after 1772, but thereafter slavery was rare and could survive only when it remained hidden. In 15 cases between 1772 and 1784, the rights of owners to assert their hold over slaves in England were refused. Of course blacks were threatened by arbitrary arrest and mistreatment, and sometimes they failed to gain the legal protection which would have secured their freedom, but after 1772 the legal situation had undoubtedly changed. Henceforth, English law could *not* be used by slave-owners to secure their ownership over slaves in England. It was not just the law that had changed either. There was a transformed social atmosphere which encouraged a different view of slavery, and especially of the slave trade. More and more people seemed prepared to accept a critical judgement of the slave system, *despite* the prosperity which continued to flow from the slave islands. It is easy to overstate this process and to imagine that change was the order of the day. Initially, as we might expect, this change in sensibility was a small, minority concern. But by the late 1780s it began to break out of those restricted circles and to make important inroads among British people of all sorts and conditions. Abolition began to take on a popular dimension.

Why was this so? Why should the question of slavery – its moral, religious and fundamental economic consequences – begin to attract growing opposition, in all social corners, at the very time when the slave system continued to deliver material bounty to Britain? The first and obvious point to make is that abolition in the 1780s became a stunningly effective political campaign, swiftly grabbing the high moral ground and able from the first (thanks to Quaker networks) to operate as a national campaign. Abolition became so popular, so quickly, because it was in the beginning an off-shoot of Quakerism itself.

The structure of Quaker government was unique, with local meetings (themselves remarkably democratic and responsive to local opinion) reporting regularly to regional meetings, and thence to the central, Yearly Meetings in London. It was, moreover, a highly literate society, which maintained close scrutiny of its own proceedings and monitored its members' behaviour with a close eye. Furthermore, Quakers were formidably successful business people (those who failed at business were simply excluded), with ventures ranging from Quaker shops (some of which spawned major companies, notably the Quaker chocolate magnates such as the Frys) through to major international bankers, traders and manufacturers. Quakers had national and international connections and access to remarkable wealth (much of it put to a range of 'good causes'). In brief, Quaker networks, buttressed by wealth, oiled by a finely tuned sense of moral purpose, and informed by highly literate social and religious discussion, formed an instant, ready made structure for the abolition campaign. Initially at least, abolition was an alien growth on the Quaker body politic, but it thrived because it was sustained in its critical, formative years by the strength of Quakerism. It is easy to misunderstand the Quakers; behind their gentleness and quietism there lay a steely resolve and an often ruthless pursuit of self-interest – qualities forged in the formative years of their own sufferings in the seventeenth century. Indeed, the word 'sufferings' had become part of Quaker vernacular. And who suffered more, in the Atlantic world, than the slaves?

What provided a focus for these early abolitionist complaints in the press and pamphlets in the mid-1780s was the condition of one particular group of ex-slaves: the black poor in London. Once again, the Quakers were at the centre of the debate. This and the earlier black presence (though the numbers were so small it scarcely amounted to a community) aroused fierce passion, especially among the planters and the West Indian interests in Britain. The West Indian lobby had every reason to dislike London's black community (notwithstanding the fact that West Indians continued to import their own black servants and slaves). The legal issues which arose from this enslaved black presence brought unwanted attention to slavery in general, often in ways which cast slavery in a poor light; maltreatment, deprivation, brutality, inhumanity, all and more seeped from the slave cases like a bad smell from the plantocratic corner.

The more grotesque forms of treatment of slaves in England, publicity about how they were kidnapped and transported on the Thames, the general disregard for black humanity – all served to draw attention to what was wrong with the world of Atlantic slavery. It was a world turned upside-down, where only acts of outrageous inhumanity and a culture of fearful, repressive violence could keep the system in place. Moreover, it was perfectly clear that London's black community was not an aberration. It was a direct and inevitable consequence of the slave system itself. As we have seen earlier, Africans and their descendants were cast to the far edges of European expansion by that complex system of maritime trade and settlement. London's small black community was, then, just one more outpost of the Black Atlantic, brought into being and sustained in the seventeenth and eighteenth centuries by the same forces which had populated the slave islands and the settlements in the Chesapeake. Moreover, as long as the slave trade continued, England's black community was bound to increase.

In the aftermath of Lord Mansfield's 1772 judgment, the number of free blacks in London seemed to rise, though this may have been more because of the changing social climate than the legal judgment. The overall number of blacks remains vague, but the numbers themselves cannot explain the fierce political and social controversy which erupted in the mid-1780s about this black presence. The arguments bore witness to a complexity of attitudes and spoke to cultural values about black and white, all of which found a focus in the debate about Atlantic slavery.

Black slavery was not designed for Britain. It had been shaped for the Americas yet had, in however small a way, taken root in Britain. It could be sustained there with little controversy as long as most slaves remained under the roofs of their masters or owners. The growth of an independent black community in London, however, created tensions of an entirely different order. To make matters more complex, the black population was expanded, after 1783, by the arrival of loyalist refugees and ex-slaves from

North America. There quickly emerged the 'black poor' – a phrase which contemporaries *assumed* referred to black refugees from America. As such, it was a problem which needed addressing.

The experiences of such small-scale free black communities were quite unlike the slaves' experience on the American plantations, but they illustrate, indirectly, some important features of plantation slavery. The basic purpose behind the Atlantic diaspora was to provide enslaved labour for capital and ownership in the Americas. When slaves, or their descendants, were removed, willingly or unwillingly, to societies where slave labour had no place, blacks found themselves in limbo – denied any meaningful economic role and yet vilified; the object of that complex of racial antipathies generated by slavery itself. Free blacks in slave societies, blacks shipped to London after 1783, the loyalist blacks moved to Canada after 1783 (and thence to Sierra Leone),[5] all faced enormous practical difficulties. They had no obvious role, no clear work or society to fit into. In a world shaped and determined by slavery, theirs was a miserable lot, scratching for a livelihood and a role in a hostile world which, though formally allowing them freedom, saw them increasingly as a 'problem'. Their political masters in London (and in colonial capitals) wondered what to do with them.

It is indicative of the mentality of Britain's governing classes that solutions to these human and social problems were devised in terms of migration. To move large groups of people – by force or with their co-operation – became a stock response of men whose fate was to govern the British empire, either from the metropolitan heart or on the colonial periphery. In some respects it is easy to see why this was the case. The late-eighteenth-century Americas had been brought into being by the migration of peoples – Europeans through various patterns of migration, both free and unfree, and, of course, African Atlantic slaves. It seemed merely an extension of the same process to devise schemes for the removal of 'problem' peoples to other regions of the world: blacks 'back' to Africa from Canada and from London, criminals from Britain to whichever land beckoned (after casting around, Australia seemed ideal), the Mosquito coast for intractable West Indian slaves. The British official urge to expel, to remove and transport its human 'problems' extended well beyond its dealings with poor blacks and can be traced back to those seventeenth-century schemes to remove groups of poor and criminals (notably the Irish and Scots) across the Atlantic. But this must have been of little comfort to blacks caught up in the schemes of the 1780s.

By the mid-1780s many of London's black community were poor. Discussions among government officials and men of philanthropic instincts about how to deal with black poverty soon turned to repatriation. The outcome was influenced by Quaker ideas. Anxious to devise a way to end the slave trade, a group of London Quakers, led by Dr John Fothergill, had begun to toy with the idea of developing a colony in West Africa, where free labour would produce the very staples cultivated by slaves in the Americas. Fothergill was a prominent botanist and had the best experimental garden in England; he was also a close friend of Benjamin Franklin. Along with other Quakers, Fothergill backed an experimental visit to West Africa by the maverick Henry Smeathman, who returned with fanciful claims for the benefits and potential of Sierra Leone, both for trade and colonial settlement. His Quaker backers were sceptical of his ideas, but Granville Sharp, the long-time activist for blacks in London, proved more gullible.

The rising number of black poor in London had persuaded a group of city businessmen and merchants to form a 'Committee for the Relief of the Black Poor', their coffers augmented by Quaker contributions. Black supplicants quickly emptied the funds. Discussion strayed, among the blacks and their patrons, to repatriation. But to where? Nova Scotia and the Bahamas were mentioned (this while the First Fleet was being prepared for Botany Bay).[6] At this point, Smeathman dangled before the committee his tantalizing ideas about Sierra Leone (without mentioning the problems of disease and of continued slave-trading in the region). Philanthropists and government officials were won over, and in the summer of 1786 the government began to organize a state-funded settlement of volunteer blacks, willing to 'repatriate' to Sierra Leone. They would be transported in Royal Navy ships, clothed, fed and settled at government expense – but they would be expected to be self-sufficient within three months. For the scheme to be successful it needed the confidence and support of London's black community, and that was never forthcoming. Despite official reassurances, the blacks knew the problems involved, not least the threat of re-enslavement. More than that even, here was another risky oceanic venture. Africans in their midst had *already* crossed the Atlantic twice (once under dire conditions). It was also obvious that the scheme was, at best, a risky, speculative venture. Smeathman's fantasies may have persuaded the backers, but they failed to impress the blacks.[7]

The scheme began in confusion and ended in disaster: 350 black passengers were marshalled onto three Royal Navy vessels; Equiano acted as intermediary, but he quit before departure. The expedition departed from Plymouth, arriving at Sierra Leone a month later. Within four years only 60 of the original settlers remained alive.[8] Whatever consequences the scheme had on the future story of Sierra Leone, or for London's black community, the episode was important for the course of abolition. Arguments about the scheme as it evolved, and as it collapsed into bickering feuds centred on Equiano, surfaced in the press. This prompted a wider discussion about the slave trade and abolition. The condition of the black community, schemes for maritime transportation, the role of prominent black spokesmen – all of these topics were hotly disputed in the British press at the very time abolitionists were making their first major inroads into British life.

The Sierra Leone scheme received wide press coverage and much of the commentary was not designed to inspire confidence among blacks. Fears of again falling victim to slave-traders may have weighed most heavily in their general resistance to join the scheme.[9] There was talk in the press of outlawing black organizations and even, following the French example, of banning further black settlement in Britain.[10] Equiano, abroad when the scheme had first been broached, was initially enthusiastic. He was the obvious choice as the black spokesman for the scheme (formally 'Commissary of Provisions and Stores for the Black Poor to Sierra Leone'), for he was familiar with a number of the philanthropists, Quakers and evangelicals backing the scheme.[11] He was a bright, educated, competent man, literate, numerate and alert to the needs and interests of black emigrants. By the time the Africa-bound convoy reached Plymouth, however, on the initial leg from London, Equiano had lost all patience with the scheme and with the men in charge, and he published his complaints in the press.

Already denounced in official circles as the cause and occasion of the black unrest on board the ships, Equiano wrote to the press (and friends), partly to salvage his own reputation. He was all too familiar with the tricks and deceptions whites were accustomed to play on blacks (and had been victim of many). His dismissal was inevitable, and the black settlers were shipped on without him, to their ghastly fate in West Africa. In the subsequent press debate about his role in the Sierra Leone scheme, Equiano found himself the object of fierce racist attack; letters spoke of Equiano's 'cloven hoof', he was accused of lies 'as deeply black as his jetty face' – indeed the word *black* became the vernacular of denunciation.[12]

But by the early summer of 1787, the abolitionist campaign had taken off, and the two sides, abolitionists and the slave lobby, were ranged against each other – each firing critical publications at the other. It was a debate marked on the West Indians' side by a growing emphasis on racist stereotypes and denunciations of blacks as people who could only be trusted, forced to work and kept in place by the constraints of slavery itself. One of the many problems facing the West India lobby, however, was that there was powerful and obvious evidence to the contrary, not least in the persons of blacks living in England. If what this lobby claimed was true – if blacks were so feckless, so indisciplined, so beyond the pale of civilization that only slavery could secure their disciplined civility – why had so many West Indians and others returned to Britain accompanied by black domestic servants? And how could they explain away the likes of Equiano and others, men of civility, refinement and attainment? By a curious twist, the example of British-based blacks served to reveal plantocratic arguments for what they were: self-serving ideological assertions designed solely to maintain their supplies of and control over enslaved labour.

In the wake of his dismissal from the Sierra Leone scheme, and faced by a litany of racist denunciations in the press, Equiano decided to write a book – an autobiography – which would, at once, be a contribution to the swelling tide of abolition and a personal statement of an African's life in the era of Atlantic slavery. It was a timely (and ultimately profitable) venture, which secured Equiano's historical reputation. In the short term it added a new strand to the evolving abolitionist argument.

From 1783 to 1785, abolition had effectively been a Quaker campaign: Quaker tracts, Quaker money and Quaker publishers showered readers with anti-slave-trade literature. In 1785 Anglicans began to join their ranks, led by William Wilberforce and Thomas Clarkson, whose Cambridge prize-winning student essay *An Essay on the Slavery and Commerce of the Human Species, Particularly the Africans* was the cause of his own seminal conversion to abolition. These two very different men transformed the history of the abolition campaign. Wilberforce adopted the slave trade as his prime parliamentary campaign, while Clarkson resolved to spread the abolition message across the country, at the same time urging people to think of the economic potential offered by free trade to Africa. The Abolition Society was founded in May 1787, with a large Quaker presence, both within the committee and in the network of sympathizers they rallied across the country. Abolitionists launched a broadside of words against the slave trade, their first tract coming from Equiano's friend, the Rev. James Ramsay (a cleric who had served 19 years in the West Indies and who had been active among London's black poor).[13] The outcome surprised even the most optimistic of abolitionists. The anti-slave-trade issue clearly struck a chord among certain sectors of the British people, who rallied to the cause in numbers, and at a rate and from quarters that no one might have predicted. Within a matter of months it was clear that abolition had an army of friends.

Since the early days of British slavery in the late seventeenth century, the slave trade had effectively gone unchallenged. Earlier arguments about slave-trading tended to be about the best methods of securing Africans – was it best done by monopoly or by open, free trade? For all the obvious and well-known barbarities, the morality of Atlantic slaving went almost undisputed. Criticism was the preserve of a small minority of people of sensibility. Yet in 1787 it soon became apparent that something had changed. Large numbers of British people were revealed to have strong negative feelings about an institution which, nonetheless, continued to bring prosperity to their door. Abolition burst out of its initial Quaker cocoon and was revealed as a popular phenomenon.

Notes

1 Quoted in James Walvin, *Quakers: Money and Morals* (London, 1997), p. 84.
2 *Ibid.*, p. 127.
3 D. B. Davis, *The Problem of Slavery in Western Culture* (Ithaca, NY, 1966).
4 James Walvin, *An African's Life: The Life and Times of Olaudah Equiano, 1745–1797* (London, 1998), Chapter 12; Judith Jennings, *The Business of Abolishing the British Slave Trade, 1783–1807* (London, 1997), pp. 22–8; J. R. Oldfield, *Popular Politics and British Anti-Slavery* (Manchester, 1995), Chapter 1.
5 James W. St. G. Walker, *The Loyalist Blacks* (London, 1976); Robin W. Winks, *Blacks in Canada: A History* (New Haven, 1971).
6 Alan Frost, *Botany Bay Mirages: Illusions of Australia's Convict Beginnings* (Melbourne, 1994).
7 Stephen J. Braidwood, *Black Poor and White Philanthropists* (Liverpool, 1994), Chapters 2–3.
8 James Walvin, *Equiano*, Chapter 11.
9 Ottobah Cugoano, *Thoughts and Sentiments on the Evil and Wicked Traffic of Slavery and Commerce of the Human Species* (London, 1787).
10 Peter Fryer, *Staying Power* (London, 1984), p. 200.
11 Olaudah Equiano, *The Interesting Narrative* (1794). Edited by Vincent Carretta (Penguin, 1995 edn), pp. 226–7.
12 James Walvin, *Equiano*, Chapter 11.
13 *Minute Book of the London Abolition Society*, Vol. 1, MS 21, 254, 22 May 1787 (British Library); Roger Anstey, *The Atlantic Slave Trade and British Abolition, 1760–1810* (London, 1975), pp. 248–9.

= 10 =

ATTACKING SLAVERY

Given the importance of Atlantic slavery to Britain, it is unremarkable that criticism of slavery was limited and largely ignored. Serious criticism began to surface only in the last quarter of the eighteenth century, in the very years when the trade was yielding its greatest material bounty. (From the 1760s the British were especially active in the Bight of Benin and record numbers of Africans were loaded onto British ships there, for the Atlantic crossing.[1]) At first sight, it seems strange that the people who seemed to benefit most from the late-eighteenth-century Atlantic system began to express a widespread (and later a genuinely *popular*) outrage against slavery *at the very height* of its economic importance. It is an historical curiosity that when, after 1787, abolition petitions flowed into Parliament in record numbers, they came from people who were conscious of the importance and value of the slave trade, *not* from people convinced of its irrelevance or redundancy.

The initial Quaker push for abolition was able to make use of Quaker networks on both sides of the Atlantic. These networks brought to abolition Quaker money, a metropolitan core of well-organized and motivated Friends, and an ethic of efficiently run businesses. Anti-slavery was, from the first, the best-organized campaign of all contemporary reforming groups. From 1787 to 1838 it was the *efficiency* of abolition – the management of anti-slavery as a highly efficient business – which was one of its most striking features. This derived directly from its Quaker roots.

Quakers were the most business-minded of all contemporary Christian groups. They exercised extraordinary economic power, out of all proportion to their numbers. Quakers scrutinized each other's personal and economic conduct, with an intrusive eye for wrong-doing and errors, and expected each other to accord to their communal high standards; backsliders were excluded, accounts were scrutinized, financial advice and practical help were offered and Quaker networks scoured for self-help and mutual benefit. The end result was that Quaker life spawned a distinct business mentality which flowered amidst the commercial opportunities of the eighteenth century. Quakers were, quite simply, remarkably good business people, a veritable eighteenth-century caricature of the Protestant work ethic. They applied that business acumen to everything they tackled: to social reform, to the conduct of the local Meeting House, to family life and to the management of the local Quaker schools. It was these same qualities which became the hallmark of the anti-slavery campaign in the half century after 1787.

Quakers had from an early date a root-and-branch opposition to slavery. The origins of their dislike lay, not in a recently discovered awareness that the slave system was uneconomic (much of the evidence pointed in the other direction), but in a deep-seated moral and theological dislike of slavery itself. There was little in its immediate origins to suggest that Quakers' opposition was inspired by economics, but they quickly came to attach an economic critique of slavery to their fundamentally religious objections. And as the abolition campaign developed, and as more and more people criticized slavery, the slave system came under ever fiercer economic attack.

The abolition campaign launched in 1787 emerged from a reforming sensibility which reached back to traditional British roots, but it was nurtured by Quaker pressure from Philadelphia. What no one predicted (and what clearly surprised the early band of abolitionists) was the reaction they provoked. Abolition immediately tapped into popular support across the country. Towns and cities saw hundreds of abolitionist organizations and contacts established among local people of a reforming bent. There were groups of people across Britain who had already demanded political change (with opposition to the American War, parliamentary reform and economic change in the 1780s). Indeed, a whole raft of reforming measures and campaigns had brought together local men of reforming interests, helping to focus local radical concerns and generally whet the appetite for political change. Even so, the national reaction to the first abolitionist invitations to organize petitions or to speak out for abolition was remarkable. Though the initial prompting came from London, the response was provincial. This relationship between the capital (where all political activity had to deliver its message, if only to persuade Parliament) and the rest of the country was critical to the entire history of the campaign against the slave trade and slavery.

London was the formal centre of British anti-slavery. How could it be otherwise? But there were powerful provincial centres of abolition sentiment, notably in Manchester and Liverpool. This, again, raises the issue of the economics of abolition. Much of the initial campaign to broaden the base for abolition came from Manchester, whose abolitionists pioneered a massive anti-slave-trade petition (with 10,639 signatures) in 1787. Later, anti-slavery was developed in England's greatest slaving port, Liverpool, by local Quakers (led by William Roscoe). There and elsewhere, abolition emerged quickly with major support among the propertied and the respectable. Clergy and professionals, the fashionable and the educated, men and women, all quickly rallied to the anti-slavery campaign after 1787, telling Parliament of their fierce opposition to the slave trade, and demanding its abolition. These groups incorporated the artefacts of anti-slavery into their social lives. Campaign pictures and plaques, medallions and jewellery, abstention from sugar consumption – the imagery and practice of anti-slavery quickly entered British domestic and political life. These same people also began to lend their growing political self-confidence and clout to the task of persuading those in power – especially local MPs – that they should vote against the slave trade in Parliament.[2]

Both sides – the abolitionists and the West Indians – were taken aback by the obvious strength of abolitionist feeling, especially in the form of petitions with tens of thousands of names attached, which flowed into Parliament between 1788 and 1792. Thereafter the petition, with all the complex organization required to initiate it and to recruit signatures and support, became a central tactic in the abolition movement. It was later adopted by all subsequent early-nineteenth-century reforming movements. Petitions seemed better able to capture the current mood than any other tactic. They enabled people, both propertied and property-less, to express their views direct to a Parliament which sought, as a rule, to keep public opinion at arm's length. Abolition was, in effect, one step (perhaps the main and the first) towards the democratization of the unreformed British State. And it was set in motion on behalf of Africans in the Atlantic system.

There were a number of distinct phases in the history of anti-slavery (though each phase broke down into narrower episodes). The first campaign, beginning in 1787, was directed against the Atlantic slave trade itself, and ended when Parliament outlawed the slave trade in 1806 (effective from 1807). Success came, initially, in banning slave-trading to foreign settlements or newly acquired colonies (where most British slaves were sold). There was a flurry of anti-slave-trade activity in 1814–15, in the immediate aftermath of the Napoleonic Wars, in an attempt to enforce an international ban on slave-trading, but the next major phase only really began in 1824. Thereafter the campaign was directed to end slavery itself, though using the old tactics, organizations and personnel. By then, the arguments about slavery were twofold. Should emancipation be immediate, and should compensation be paid to the slave-owners? (Why not, some argued, compensate the victims, i.e., the slaves?) This phase continued through to the introduction of 'apprenticeship' – the interim replacement of slavery – in 1834, and the final abolition of British slavery in 1838. Thereafter, the British embarked on that remarkable campaign which persisted throughout the nineteenth century, to ensure that slave-trading and slave systems be abolished globally. Using treaties regulated by the Foreign Office, force of arms (notably the Royal Navy) and economic clout, the British slave poacher of the eighteenth century turned abolitionist gamekeeper in the nineteenth.

The transformation wrought by the ending of slavery was remarkable, so remarkable that, when looking at British anti-slavery policy in the nineteenth century it is hard to recognize that here was the nation which had perfected the very system they now attacked with such self-righteous zeal. It was not simply that the British had turned against slavery (which they had), but that the British had become a very different sort of people. British society in, say, the 1830s was unrecognizably different from its predecessor of a century earlier. The society which master-minded the Atlantic system was hardly the same polity which was now the scourge of slave-traders everywhere. Clearly, this massive transformation operated at a multitude of levels. To understand the British mutation from slave-trader to slave protector, we need to explore the foundations of the anti-slavery campaign itself.

The anti-slavery movement (though initially more narrowly based than this term suggests) took root across the face of urban Britain, and within Parliament. They were, of course, intimately linked, and the key achievement of the various public anti-slavery campaigns and organizations was to persuade Parliament of the powerful feelings held by the British people about slavery. The Abolition Society was an amazingly effective pressure group, able to tap into and then to manipulate public anti-slavery feeling (through lectures, the printed word and a host of campaigns). For this it needed organization, money, leadership – and moral fervour. It had all in abundance.

From 1787 through to 1838, and notwithstanding recurring conflicts about tactics, personalities and aims, anti-slavery was an unusually well-organized campaign. In its early years it was better-organized in the country at large than it was in Parliament. The parliamentary spokesman, William Wilberforce – who devoted much of his considerable efforts to anti-slavery and who came to personify the campaign – was a poor parliamentary manager. With better organization the slave trade might even have been ended *before* 1807. Nonetheless, what happened in the early phase of abolition set the tone for much of what followed.

Anti-slavery campaigners quickly seized the moral high ground from a West India lobby which, like everyone else, was caught unawares by the speed and strength of anti-slavery feeling. By 1792 a series of anti-slave-trade debates had opened up a broad abolitionist front in Parliament. The campaign was national, it secured massive publicity (in a press which proved largely sympathetic) and clearly captured the popular mood. In 1791–92 the early popular radical societies (Corresponding Societies) also adopted abolition, though expressing their views in plebeian tones and with a roughness of expression which, to propertied ears, sounded too much like Tom Paine for their liking. However, when the French Revolution turned violent, and when St Domingue exploded into revolutionary slave revolt, it seemed that everything the West Indian lobby had predicted was coming true: remove the restraints of slavery – drop the plantocratic guard against the ever-resistant slaves – and catastrophe would inevitably follow.

The ideals of 1789 – of liberty, equality and fraternity – had seismic consequences for slave society. And no slave society was better-primed for those ideas than St Domingue (Haiti). Africans had been thrown into that island in unprecedented numbers and with unseemly speed. The end result was a booming tropical society, but one which harboured deep and pervasive enslaved African grievances. The unfolding of the political drama in the island, spawned by events in France, ignited a slave uprising which consumed everything in its path, and which sent people fleeing for their lives throughout the Americas. The shock waves from this slave uprising reverberated throughout the Caribbean, North America and Europe. Haiti became a major strategic and economic test for all Europe's slaving nations, an example of what could be gained, and lost.

The British initially hoped to be able to wrest St Domingue from the French, disabled both by the Revolution and by the slave uprising in 1791, and expected to add that rich colony to their own string of slave-based islands. They hoped to destroy French naval strength and thus to enhance their own, and to seize French West Indian possessions – of which St Domingue was the most tempting (its foreign trade in the 1780s outstripped that of the USA). The value of the French West Indies to France was enormous. The islands generated two-fifths of France's foreign trade, two-thirds of the country's ocean-going tonnage, and employed one-third of its seamen. To seize the most lucrative of those French islands would deal the French a grievous fiscal and strategic blow.[3] The British had, however, calculated without the slaves, and without the reverses of war in Europe.

As the war with France developed after 1793, the West Indies proved critical. William Pitt the Younger, who had been attracted to slave abolition in the 1780s, promised the West Indian planters that Britain would cling to the islands when the war was over. In effect, Pitt's government had sided with the planters against the slaves. In the process Pitt helped to disperse that mood of sympathy for the slaves so assiduously cultivated by the Abolition Society in the previous years. Events in the islands had the same effect. The slave rebellion in Haiti was followed by slave uprisings in British islands, in Grenada, St Vincent and Jamaica. The British dispatched an army of 32,000 men to the West Indies in 1795 and though control was restored, half the expedition died (mainly from disease).

It was vital for British interests that the West Indian islands be held. This simply meant that the grip over slaves should be tightened everywhere. There was an irony here for, on the eve of 1789, many British ministers were sympathetic to abolition. Now, in the heat of war against revolutionary France and a brooding slave population, the same men found themselves forced to clamp down on the slaves. The alternatives were too fearsome to contemplate; they had only to look to Haiti (and there were plenty of horror stories circulated in the press and Parliament about events there) to see what might easily happen in their own slave colonies. There had been nothing like the upheavals in Haiti before. The British army on the island, sent there to bring the island into the British imperial fold, found itself destroyed by a lethal mix of conventional attack, guerrilla warfare and an island-wide convulsion of racial upheaval – in addition to deadly diseases.

The cost – and the losses – to the British were enormous. More than 40,000 Britons died and the cost ran to millions of pounds. Indeed, the peak year of military spending was in the effort, in 1795, to secure Haiti.[4] Inevitably perhaps, the blame for such sufferings was placed firmly on the slaves. Lurid tales of violence and savagery circulated in Britain. The image of black violence was everywhere by the mid-1790s. Before 1789, abolitionists had promoted the idea that slavery itself was the source and cause of violence in the region, but by the mid-1790s there was a reversion to type. Slaves and ex-slaves were now commonly portrayed in terms which planters had commonly used: primitive peoples whose natural African 'barbarisms' would surface if the restraints of slavery were removed. Put simply, the events in Haiti (the British losses and the black victories) served to harden opinion against slaves everywhere. By the late 1790s it was hard to find signs of anything but serious setbacks for the abolitionists. Paradoxically, however, in the midst of the terrible sufferings and losses, some progress was made, though it was hard to detect at the time. Ever more people – especially those in high office who saw the figures – asked the question: was it worth it? Were the West Indies *so* valuable that they warranted such investment in men and money?

Thus, by a curious twist of fate, the issue of the importance and value of slave colonies (and hence of slavery) became a political issue. Similar questions had already been raised in the 1780s, first by Quakers and later by other abolitionist writers (most notably Equiano). Might there be *other* ways of conducting trade to and from Africa which would yield continuing prosperity to Britain, whilst avoiding entanglement with slavery itself? Though the war inevitably meant that the politics of dissent and critical opposition were effectively silenced, events had begun to raise new critical questions about slavery. Was it *really* worth the terrible suffering involved? Ironically, the question was prompted by the degree and level of *white* suffering by the mid-1790s. In the previous decade abolitionists had struggled to publicize the ubiquity and severity of *African* suffering. However, it was possible by the late 1790s to stand back and see slavery for what it was – a system which could only be sustained and kept in place by levels of inhumanity which ensnared both black and white. (Of course, weighed in the balance, there was no doubt where the preponderance of misery lay.)

The immediate and direct threats facing Britain in the mid- and late-1790s came from French arms poised at the security of mainland Britain itself. The preoccupations of that war swept aside those other political considerations (parliamentary reform, abolition) which had begun to make an impact in the 1780s. The ending of the slave trade had to wait the coming of peace (temporarily in the event) and the demise of Pitt. Even so, when the slave trade was outlawed by 1807 (led by the Danes and joined by the Americans), it constituted a leap in the dark. Abolitionists hoped that an end to the trade would bring about not only an end to the inhumanities of trading on the African coast and the high seas, but would persuade West Indian planters to rethink their treatment of the slaves in the islands. They hoped that planters, now starved of fresh supplies of Africans, would realize that their future prosperity lay in treating their existing slaves better. Once plantation management moved into a more benign mode, abolitionists expected slavery to fade away (though they did not describe precisely how). Decent management and humane treatment of slaves – an overall amelioration of conditions – would simply encourage slavery to wither away, and planters would come to accept that free labour was better for all concerned. The outcome was to be quite different.

At its simplest, the ending of the slave trade meant that it was no longer legal for British ships to transport Africans across the Atlantic (or anywhere else for that matter). But the aim of abolition was more complex than that. It was hoped that improved plantocratic treatment would encourage slave reproduction. It had, in general, been one of the failings of the West Indian islands that slave populations had not grown as their overall numbers might suggest, though this now seems to have been more the result of a peculiar demographic structure and illness (with regular infusions of sick Africans) than plantocratic neglect or maltreatment.

How could anyone predict the consequences of abolition? It was imperative that the slave societies should be monitored to reveal any changes brought about by the ending of the slave trade. There thus followed the establishment of a period of registration – a census of all slaves in the islands – to monitor the demographic and social progress (or otherwise) of the slave communities. It was a complicated process which took time to develop, and it was years before the raw data were available for analysis. Moreover, the abolitionists' efforts to outlaw slave-trading everywhere had run into the sands of diplomacy, and often clashed with the national interests of other slave-trading nations. At the Congress of Vienna (in 1814) the French, for example, were allowed to renew their own slave trade, an agreement which revived the British abolitionist movement and prompted unprecedented numbers of abolitionist petitions. This public outburst, organized and driven forward by the same methods and personnel of a generation earlier, established abolition as an international and diplomatic issue. It gave slave registration an important new impetus, and made clear that the relationship which West Indian planters had always regarded as sacrosanct (i.e. the one between themselves and their slaves), was now a legitimate matter of concern and investigation by people on the other side of the Atlantic.

Slave-owners could no longer expect to conduct their business of managing their slaves out of sight of public scrutiny. The public gaze fell across their every action, and abolitionists saw to it that slave management took place in the full glare of an increasingly hostile British public and political scrutiny. The institution of West Indian slavery was slowly prised apart by abolitionist pressure; it was criticized and called to account as never before. The old days had clearly gone when planters could do whatever they wanted with their human property. How the slaves were worked, housed, fed, treated – their freedoms and miseries (and even the intimacies of family life) – were all now exposed to the public gaze. In Britain there emerged a growing (and vociferous) readership for ever-more detailed news from the islands. Slavery made its presence felt everywhere in early-nineteenth-century British life; perhaps most critically of all, abolition was taken up by men in the pulpit, especially in the dissenting chapels whose organizations had begun to make such inroads among West Indian slaves. Chapels, missionaries, cheap print – all conspired to bring home the realities of West Indian slavery to the British reading and worshipping public. They did not like what they saw and heard.

British unease about slavery in the 1820s was exacerbated by news of slave unrest. Contrary to abolitionist expectations (that abolition of the slave trade would lead to improvements in slavery), there was accumulating evidence that West Indian slaves remained deeply unhappy with their lot. Whatever objective evidence the slave registrations might reveal (that slave populations were, at last, beginning to increase from the mid-1820s onwards), there were periodic rumblings of slave unrest. Worse still, the major slave revolts of the period (Barbados in 1816, Demerera in 1823 and, most violent of all, Jamaica in 1831–32) brought home the starker realities of slavery. The violence endemic to the system, never more blatant than in Jamaica, was shocking even by the standards of that island. Slave discontent, upheavals, plantocratic punishments and retribution on an almost medieval scale deeply shocked British observers. To compound the growing British sense of outrage, many of the slaves involved were Christian. The early efforts of the missionaries to the islands had yielded a good harvest of slave converts (the Jamaican revolt was known, significantly, as the 'Baptist War'), and the plantocratic attacks on black Christians, on their ministers (missionaries and local black preachers), the destruction of slave chapels and the subsequent restrictions on slave worship, all served to outrage British religious feelings. British Nonconformists simply saw their enslaved co-religionists being persecuted. If the slave system could be kept in place only at such a cost, the question arose again: was it worth it?

The British abolition organizations, revived from 1824 onwards, and bigger and better-organized than ever, took up the issue of full black freedom. Abolitionists had differences of opinion of course (should they aim for gradual or immediate emancipation?), and they had to battle for attention against other political campaigns (notably parliamentary reform). There were gaps in the abolitionist campaigns, but two major issues transformed the anti-slavery movement in the years before the granting of full black freedom in 1838. First, women involved themselves in the politics of abolition to a degree which historians have only recently recognized.[5] Secondly, slavery and slave-grown produce came under fierce *economic* attack. There was a small economic critique of the slave trade from the early days of abolition campaigning in 1787, but by the 1820s the economic denunciation of slavery came centre-stage.

In the 1780s the economic critique of the slave trade was not the core argument. It was hard to argue that the Atlantic slave system was unprofitable; on the contrary, most were agreed that it was a lucrative system. Moreover, it was hard, if not impossible, to draw up a balance-sheet for the Atlantic system. No single person or organization had available all the data which might be rendered into an overall account of profit or loss. Clearly, individual sectors of the system understood their own economic transactions. Planters, shippers, merchants and the like, each knew the state of their own economic involvement in the broader system. But these were the very people most wedded to the perpetuation of the slave system. Those most intimately involved – shippers, backers, planters – were, on the whole, the most vociferous in arguing for the continuation of slavery.

The initial economic critique of slavery had emerged at a tangent, not so much a frontal economic attack on the slave system itself as a suggestion that Africa might offer alternative forms of trade and business based, not on slavery, but on free trade. There had been earlier economic grumblings against the slave trade, notably from Malachy Postlethwayt as early as 1757, who asked whether Europeans might not find their economic interests better served by free trade with Africa, not slaving. The slave trade, he argued, was 'the greatest hindrance and obstruction to the Europeans cultivating a humane and Christian-like commerce with those populous countries'.[6] Quakers were always alert to economic prospects, and were among the first to suggest that the slave trade might be replaced by a more profitable free trade with Africa. Indeed the origins of the Sierra Leone scheme were rooted in this Quaker idea.[7] But it was the assertion of rights – human rights – promoted initially by the American Revolution, and later by France after 1789, which established a political framework within which all else followed. As early as 1776 an MP had denounced the slave trade as contrary to 'the Rights of Man', a form of attack which became basic to the abolitionist campaign after 1787.[8]

It was, however, the Quaker Anthony Benezet's ideas which proved most influential, if only because his tracts were reprinted and distributed in very large numbers throughout Britain in the 1780s and 1790s.[9] They were even distributed to all the major public schools. His basic proposition, that Africa's incalculable resources and markets beckoned, quickly embedded itself in abolitionist thought. The initial attack on the slave trade assumed that an end to the trade would lead to an expansion, not a contraction, of British overseas trade.

> Were Africa civilized, and could we preoccupy the affections of the natives, and introduce our religion, manners, and language among them, we should open a market that would fully employ our manufacturers and seamen, morally speaking, till the end of time. And while we enriched ourselves, we should contribute to their happiness.[10]

This argument became key. Thomas Clarkson, for example, whose nationwide lecture tours provided the impetus to abolition, carried with him a collection of African artefacts and produce, displaying them wherever he spoke as proof of what gains could be had from open trade with Africa. Gums, cotton, indigo, musk, peppers, mahogany, textiles and more were readily available to the imaginative trader. And this was quite apart from the industries and enterprise which such trade might unleash among the African peoples who were currently engaged in providing slaves for European slave-traders. Abolitionists also hoped that Christianity would seep into the continent on the back of open trade. Clarkson and others genuinely believed both that the slave trade would be outflanked by the development of normal trade to and from Africa and that this would pave the way for the Christian conversion of the region.

In the early years of the abolition campaign, the most influential African of the period was Equiano. His thoughts, expressed in his autobiography, inevitably reflected this early economic critique of the slave trade. He sought to silence critics who claimed that abolition meant economic disaster.

> I doubt not, if a system of commerce was established in Africa, the demand for manufactures would most rapidly augment, as the natives would insensibly adopt the British fashions, manners, customs, etc. In proportion to the civilizations, so will be the consumption of British manufactures.

African markets were, Equiano claimed, so enormous that Europeans could scarcely grasp their importance. African peoples would consume British goods on a scale which would dwarf any economic benefits derived from the slave system.

> A commercial intercourse with Africa opens an inexhaustible source of wealth to the manufacturing interests of Great Britain, and to all which the slave trade is an objection.

In brief, Equiano thought that trade to Africa 'lays open an endless field of commerce to the British manufacturers and merchant adventurers'. In effect, Equiano turned the slave-trade lobby's argument on its head. Far from damaging Britain's economic system, abolition would enhance it. 'The abolition of slavery would be in reality a universal good.'[11]

What is striking, however, is that Equiano, an African, was discussing the ending of slavery itself. At the time (1789), the abolition movement was concerned simply with the ending of the slave trade (though with the ultimate aim of bringing down slavery). The focus for this early economic critique was Africa itself. The proposed aim was to tap into the wealth of the continent, to cultivate consumer tastes among Africans for British manufacturers and, generally, to woo over Africa to forms of trade other than slavery.

There were many obstacles to this economic argument, notably that abolitionists spoke only (or at least primarily) about trade to and from *Africa*. Yet the British Atlantic system involved much more than trade to Africa, and *much* more than the simple acquisition of African slaves. The American slave colonies were sustained by British (and British colonial) trade and manufacture. Defenders of the slave trade were thus defending not merely the continuation of vital supplies of African slaves; they also wanted – needed – the myriad manufactured goods and produce ferried to the colonies in British ships. The slave lobby also needed *markets* for their slave-grown produce. In short, the slave islands needed to maintain their presence within the broader Atlantic system, to enjoy the material benefits of being part of the British Atlantic system. The slave societies had to have guaranteed markets for their produce and, of course, they also required protection by British military power. This last point was graphically illustrated in the 1790s when slave unrest threatened to spread from Haiti throughout the Caribbean, and when British military power was jeopardized by a potent mix of French revolutionary aggression and slave insurrection.

In the last years of the eighteenth century, slave-owners felt increasingly vulnerable to the dangers posed by slave resistance, and by the corrosive talk of equality. But they were no less at risk from the long-term threats to the markets for their produce. Here, again, an economic critique of the slave system proved important. Slave-owners sold their produce, basically sugar and rum, to Britain (and thence to other parts of the world) courtesy of the special relationship they had always enjoyed with the metropolis. Theirs was, in effect, a subsidized concern with competing produce kept out, and duties levied, to the benefit of West Indian producers. There was, however, a fundamental issue at stake. Did the British consumers actually *need* these tropical staples? If the British people could be persuaded to overcome their passion for sugar, perhaps the slave system which underpinned it might collapse? A sugar boycott might damage the slave system. At this point female abolitionists proved their importance.

Women had been active in the abolition campaigns from their early days, but their sphere of activity had been restricted by the power of social conventions. Denied access or a central role in more open abolitionist activities, female abolitionists initially involved themselves in 'womanly' roles. Now, they were central in the sugar boycott because here was a campaign which went to the heart of domesticity – ordering foodstuffs for the family kitchen. The refusal to buy and to use slave-grown sugar spread quickly. By 1792 Clarkson calculated that 300,000 people had pledged not to use it. The West Indians were alarmed by the way women had effectively domesticated abolition. Overall, however, the markets for sugar especially in Europe (where much British sugar was re-exported to) remained buoyant, especially after the collapse of French sugar production in Haiti.[12]

The sugar boycott was taken up again from the mid-1820s with the revival of anti-slavery campaigns, with women again to the fore. Women's anti-slavery groups, women's publications, female door-to-door anti-slavery canvassing, pressure on local shopkeepers (and the promptings to use East, not West, Indian sugar), all attracted large numbers of women to the abolition campaign. Tens of thousands of women signed the abolitionist petitions in the great surges of petitioning between 1830 and 1838; previously petition-signing had been thought to be a male preserve. Now, prompted by a new urgency to end slavery itself, women began to sign. The critical move seems to have come from within nonconformist chapels, and from female outrage at the persecution of their enslaved fellow worshippers in the islands.

By the mid-1820s the key argument was about *when* black freedom should be granted – sooner or later? The women's campaign was for immediate freedom, and here abstention from sugar consumption was thought important. Moreover, the abolitionist case began to focus on the privileged status of West Indian sugar at the expense of the British consumer. Why should British people (and especially the poor who, despite their poverty, were addicted to sugar) effectively subsidize the West Indian planters by paying the sugar duties? An argument thus developed that duties should be equalized on all sugars, or be removed entirely. At a broader level, a more critical approach was emerging towards sugar's role in British society. In effect, the economic assumptions which underpinned the entire slave system were being challenged. Why consume this unnecessary commodity at all? Why should its trade be so heavily weighted in favour of the West Indians – the very people who maintained the slave system? Why should British consumers not be able to buy their sugar in a more open market, i.e., from other regions, freed from the restrictions which had characterized the Atlantic system for a century?

The West India lobby *needed* these restrictions. They depended on the privileges which their position had secured over the years, of being sugar monopolists (defended by the British state). The market for sugar had changed dramatically, however. Sugar was now cultivated around the world – often (or so it seemed) by non-slave labour. Abolitionists were greatly attracted to non-slave sugar, for here was a product which blended personal and economic freedom. The labourers were free and, in an ideal free market, the consumer benefited by not having to pay unnecessary duties and taxes. This had an even greater appeal in the 1830s to those activists who were anxious to improve the material lot of impoverished working people. Poor British consumers could square the circle if they were allowed access to non-slave sugar; their money would go further and they would be avoiding the fruits of slave labour.

By the late 1820s the slave system was seen to belong to a different world order. The emergent economic strength of Britain was rooted in a very different set of economic relationships, of manufacturing industries (located in different parts of the country) and of management and capital operating freely, generally untrammelled by restrictions and controls. Of course, this ideal of free trade is deceptive. It was slow to emerge, and was never as perfectly formed as its proponents would have liked. But the world of *laisser-faire* economics formed a sharp contrast to the highly controlled and regulated system which had moulded the Atlantic slave system. At its apogee the slave system *needed* the British State for its very survival. British law regulated the slave trade and its thousands of ships; law dictated the administration and enforcement of the slaving system (courtesy of the power of the Royal Navy) and produce to British and European consumers through a slate of duties and taxes. Indeed, the State itself needed that money to help with its own burden of expense.

For their part the West Indians appreciated their dependence on Britain. Indeed, the initial sympathies in some of the islands with the American break-away from Britain in 1776 were quickly stifled when they pondered their economic and strategic exposure. The most critical factor was the slaves. The people who ran the slave systems in the islands – planters on the plantations, merchants and shippers in the towns – were isolated in a sea of black humanity. Always exposed to local slave resistance, they also faced external threats, especially after 1789, from the French and from the corrosion of egalitarian ideas. Only the Royal Navy and the British merchant marine could defend them effectively, ferrying men and materials around and between the islands in times of trouble. Throughout the late eighteenth and early nineteenth centuries, those troubles came thick and fast.

The British and the West Indians were locked into mutual dependence, each clinging to the other for vital support. The West Indies could not have survived (in their slave-based form) without the British State and its economic and military power. On the other hand, the British State derived economic sustenance from the slave system. The British people for their part had become so wedded to slave-grown produce that it was hard to imagine social and domestic life without it. But what would happen if the whole edifice of the transatlantic relationship began to change? What if tropical staples could be had more cheaply elsewhere? What if the British

State might finance itself from other, more profitable ventures? And what if British capital, having enjoyed such bounty from the sweat of slaves, found other ways (perhaps closer to home) of securing profits?

This is precisely what began to happen in the years after the French wars (though the process had origins which went back further). A new economic order – and its social and political spokesmen – was emerging which increasingly looked askance at the old slave system. Slavery itself had been conceived in, and nurtured by, an economic mentality which looked increasingly alien. Was this an example of capitalism turning its back on an outdated system? At the point British slavery seemed most buoyant, capital and mercantile interests in the metropolis were faced with new, utterly different (and more tempting) economic prospects. The British slave system was not so much rendered unprofitable, but by-passed by the changing economic and social order in Britain.

Notes

1 David Eltis and David Richardson (eds), *Routes to Slavery* (London, 1997), Chapter 1.
2 J. R. Oldfield, *Popular Politics and British Anti-Slavery* (Manchester, 1995).
3 Michael Duffy, 'World-wide war and British expansion, 1793–1815', in P. J. Marshall (ed.), *The Oxford History of the British Empire*, Vol. 2, *The Eighteenth Century* (Oxford, 1998), Chapter 9.
4 Robin Blackburn, *The Overthrow of Colonial Slavery, 1776–1848* (London, 1988), p. 563.
5 Clare Midgley, *Women Against Slavery* (London, 1992).
6 Quoted in James Walvin, *An African's Life: The Life and Times of Olaudah Equiano, 1745–1797* (London, 1998), p. 179.
7 *Ibid.*, Chapter 11.
8 *Ibid.*, pp. 176–7.
9 Judith Jennings, *The Business of Abolishing the British Slave Trade, 1783–1807* (London, 1997), p. 42.
10 James Walvin, *Equiano*, p. 180.
11 *Ibid.*, pp. 180–1.
12 Clare Midgley, *Women*, Chapter 2.

= 11 =

CONSEQUENCES

The consequences of the British slave system were profound and varied. They went far beyond mere profit and loss. Indeed, slavery so influenced British life that it is hard to disentangle it from the warp and weft of British social life in the seventeenth and eighteenth centuries. The slave system was central to the rising power of Britain in the eighteenth century, most notably in consolidating British maritime power in the Atlantic. But the *most* obvious of all its consequences was the scattering of African peoples across the face of the Americas. It brought about a human revolution in the Atlantic world. Yet what lay behind that revolution was a simple economic imperative.

From its inception through to its death, the British Atlantic slave system was designed to make money. It was established by capital invested by European backers in search of profitable returns. It was based on cheap labour, and marshalled that labour into a proto-industrial system. Some of the enslaved labour force – at least in sugar production – worked in 'factories' long before the introduction of industrial factories in Britain itself. The profits from this slave system were, in their turn, dispersed throughout Europe, reinvested in other commercial ventures, used to secure status (land, grand homes and their furnishings) or put to work in the development of new areas of trade and commerce.

It is difficult to describe the precise *accountancy* of the slave system, though until the last years of the eighteenth century very few people doubted that here was a commercially profitable world. For all the risk and dangers – the gamble of long-distance global trade, the threat of war and foreign enemies, the perils of the oceans, nature and disease (to say nothing of the

permanent worry about slave upheavals) – there is no sign that contemporaries fought shy of the slave system. Quite the contrary. British people, of
all sorts and conditions, were only too keen to stake a claim in the Atlantic
slave system, hoping that with luck, their efforts or investments would yield
a living or a profit. In the event, rewards for investors tended to be moderate
rather than lavish, though there are plenty of examples of planters and
traders returning 'home' with wealth 'beyond the dreams of avarice'.

The British dominated the slave Atlantic for the best part of two
centuries. The loss of the North American colonies in 1776 scarcely dented
Britain's profitable involvement with the Atlantic slave system. The French
(Britain's enemies throughout the eighteenth century), tried to reduce
British power by military action and by diplomatic manoeuvres; they later
sought to strangle British economic activities by boycotting British goods
and trade. Yet the British emerged from a generation of war in 1815 not
merely as the lynchpin of a victorious military alliance against the French,
but as the dominant force, still, in the Atlantic. All was to change with the
rise of the USA but, in the short term, Britain remained pre-eminent.
Moreover, her burgeoning industrial growth seemed to promise more of
the same.

In the emergence of the slave-based Atlantic system, a number of
features had been critical to British success, and were to be vital in her
subsequent economic development. There was, first, a stable financial
system with a national bank (the Bank of England) and firm parliamentary
control over State finances (to which duties on slave-grown staples made
a major contribution). Merchants in London (and the provinces) funnelled
monies and profits from their business in the slave colonies into London's
coffers, adding further financial strength to that city's ability to make
important investment decisions wherever seemed appropriate. Behind
this whole commercial and trading edifice there hovered the British State
itself, recast after the seventeenth-century revolution and keen to afford
protection and encouragement to the commercial and trading interests of
its expanding mercantile communities.

The strength of these British political and financial foundations secured
the massive expansion of British trade to and from the slave colonies. That
trade had to be maintained and safeguarded. The economic prospects of
Britain's Atlantic slave system were hugely attractive to other European
maritime nations, as each one tried to secure advantage over its nearest
rivals. The British themselves had risen to slaving pre-eminence by
attacking the Spanish system in the Caribbean. In their turn, the British

were anxious to keep the French away from their colonial honey-pot in the Americas (and elsewhere, of course – notably in India) throughout this period. To achieve this, British merchants, traders and colonists needed State power, especially the military strength of the Royal Navy. It was in these years that the reputation and image of the Royal Navy was created; many of its heroes were forged in the protracted eighteenth-century conflicts with the French (and Dutch) for primacy in the Atlantic, and thence the world at large.[1]

Put at its simplest, the British developed a telling combination of a powerful State, based on secure financial institutions and practices, and domestic political stability, alongside a thriving mercantile class which was able to enhance and profit from their dealings in the Atlantic slave system. In all this the Royal Navy was critical. The mid- and late-eighteenth-century lauding of the Navy's achievements was well founded. Hidden from view, however, never praised, and rarely sung about, was another force, often described in military terms – the army of slaves whose enforced labour was the foundation on which much of the Atlantic system rested.[2] These two key elements were more closely linked than we might imagine. Without the strength and reach of the Royal Navy, the British maritime trade could never have fed ever more Africans into the maws of American slavery. The trade would have been eroded by the predatory attacks of other nations and other slave-traders. Moreover, the stability of the slave colonies themselves was secured (or as secured as any slave society could be) by the ability of the Navy to keep out interlopers, to maintain local defences and generally to guarantee the supplies, defence and exports of plantation society. West Indian planters ought to have raised a nightly toast to the Royal Navy.

The French were Britain's major rivals, but comparisons of their respective trades with the Americas reveals the extent of the British advantage. It has been calculated, for example, that whereas 19 per cent of French exports went to their colonial markets, the British sent 38 per cent. By the mid-1790s about two-thirds of all British exports went to the Americas. There was a cloud on the Caribbean horizon, however, in the form of the remarkable rise of the French sugar island of St Domingue, which threatened to displace the British system by a French variant, in the time-honoured process of one European nation leap-frogging over another in the drive towards slave-based power and prosperity. The French Revolution put paid to that threat and by the late eighteenth century the British stood pre-eminent.

Britain's pre-eminence as a slaving nation was quickly followed by the rise of British industrial power; the one seemed to follow the other in natural succession. What was the exact connection (if any) between the two? Today the question seems obvious. Curiously, however, no one really asked it before the pioneering work of two Trinidadian scholars, C.L.R. James and Eric Williams.[3] Their work has prompted a deluge of research, especially in the past generation. From the welter of detail and the ebb and flow of historical argument over the past generation, one thing has become clear: we need to move beyond a historical analysis which deals merely in profits and loss. The impact of slavery on British life transcended this simple analysis. Nonetheless, the economic ramifications of slavery on Britain were enormous.

Take the matter of manufacture, for example. British manufacture increased hugely in the course of the eighteenth century. Initially the great bulk of exported manufactures went to Europe, but by the end of the century just as much was heading for Africa and the Americas as to Europe. As we have already seen from plantation ledgers, the slave colonies absorbed every conceivable type of British goods, though they were especially keen on goods from newer industries, i.e., from the very industries which were undergoing technical change and modernization. In particular, the slave colonies wanted textiles to clothe the slaves and the metal goods used in the operation of basic plantation life. Thus the engine which was substantially responsible for driving forward the export of British manufactured goods was the Atlantic system.[4] This was especially true in the metal industry, where demand from the Americas more than made up for slack periods of domestic demand. Moreover, foreign trade helped to persuade iron-masters to modernize, to the extent that by the end of the eighteenth century the British metal industry (dominated by Quakers) was the most advanced in Europe.

The same process was even more striking in textiles. At critical periods from 1760 onwards, demand from Africa and the West Indies was crucial in shaping the new cotton industry. Exports to the Americas increased enormously year on year throughout the eighteenth century, so that the cotton export boom was *itself* a major factor in the broader growth of Britain's export trade. Moreover, it was a booming export trade which continued right through the years of 'illegal' slave-trading in the nineteenth century. As long as slaves were bought on the African coast (destined in the nineteenth century for the plantations in Cuba and Brazil), Lancastrian textiles provided a major means of exchange.

The importance of the slave system to this expanding British economy is all the more striking when we recall that the level of direct exports to the plantations was especially high, despite the regular interruptions of war. Here again we need to acknowledge the role of the Royal Navy, which maintained the trade routes despite the efforts of the French to strangle British trade. Whatever the ups and downs of strategic fortunes in the second half of the eighteenth century, British exports to the Americas remained buoyant and strong, providing a major stimulus to British industry as a whole, and especially in critical *new* areas of growth. There is little doubt that the Atlantic slave system served to expand Britain's industrial output.

The most contentious arguments about the impact of the slave system on Britain have been those prompted by Eric Williams about the levels of profitability, and the impact of those profits on the subsequent rise of British industry. For more than 50 years historians and economists have reworked the slave system data (and have found new data to which earlier scholars had no access). The question seems simple: how much profit flowed back to Britain from the slave system? Robin Blackburn's recent reformulation of the data has suggested that substantial profit flows returned to Britain.[5] Needless to say, the precise computation of the figures is controversial and remains an area of dispute. However, the most recent calculation of the attendant *overall* profits – direct and indirect – from the slave trade is in the order of £4,336,000 by 1770.[6] It has been claimed that something in the region of 20 to 30 per cent of slave-trade profits were reinvested in British capital. Of course, money flowed into Britain in the late eighteenth century from a variety of places, from Ireland, from India, but, above all, from the slave colonies. It was in these same years that the physical transformation of Britain became noticeable, with massive expansions of, and investments in, the merchant marine, in docks and canals, in agriculture and industry.

Profits from empire (enslaved and free) were ploughed back into a great variety of domestic British enterprises. Money accumulated in the Atlantic trades was transmuted into loans for other investments. Profits were re-invested in yet more business in the Atlantic trades. Returning nabobs became improving landlords and landowners. West Indians were to be found among the improving landlords who were central to the modernization of late-eighteenth-century British agriculture. Similarly, merchants from Bristol and Liverpool invested money in the development of late-century canals. There were also close links between the Atlantic trades and the initial growth of the Lancashire textile industry. Indeed, a range of northern industries were nurtured by their dealings with slave-traders in Liverpool.

Behind this whole mercantile structure lay that 'web of credit' which enabled merchants and slave-traders to thrive *despite* the protracted periods involved in trading from Liverpool to Africa, then to the Americas and thence back home.[7] Critical to everything was that remarkable network of merchants which stretched from Liverpool and Bristol to London, men who had accumulated experience in the tortuous and protracted dealings of the Atlantic trade over the course of the eighteenth century.[8] Their resources, networks and experience were put to good use in the subsequent periods of economic change in Britain.

Some of the most notable men to emerge from this ruck of financiers, businessmen and manufacturers to form the core of early 'modern' industrialists were men of capital, or men who had access to credit accumulated through earlier textile business. As we have seen, much of that textile business (and the profits from it) was in the export trade. A great deal of the British textile trade was with the slave colonies. By the late eighteenth century, plantation slaves were clothed in simple textiles shipped from Britain. There were other areas of British domestic industry which were closely and obviously linked to slavery. The sugar refineries of London, Bristol and Liverpool were one example. Tobacco similarly generated the growth of industries in and around Glasgow. And, to repeat, the metal industries thrived on the supplies demanded by Africa and the American plantations. There are, then, a host of readily identifiable industries which profited from the Atlantic slave system.

What distinguished the British system from its European rivals was its size and its efficiency. Moreover, it drew confidence from British naval power in the course of the eighteenth century and was able, in the second half of that century, to pour ever more capital back into Britain. No less striking was the amount of raw materials which the slave colonies produced for early British industry. Three-quarters of Britain's cotton imports came from slave plantations in the late eighteenth century. The 3.3 million pounds imported annually between 1761 and 1765 rose to almost 16 million pounds between 1801 and 1805. This link between slave cotton and Lancashire textile mills became even more marked with the dramatic rise of the US cotton slave plantations in the early nineteenth century. By the 1820s three-quarters of Britain's cotton came from the USA (i.e., it was grown by slaves).[9] It was more than merely symbolic when the city of Manchester, adopting a new civic coat of arms, incorporated a sailing ship onto its crest – a ship bringing cotton from the slave plantations of the American South. This link between British industrial power (in this case textiles) and slave-grown produce was merely the latest in a series of connections between British well-being and the efforts of slaves on the far side of the Atlantic.[10]

Britain finally turned its back on slavery in 1838. It is hard to deny that the black slavery which the British now rejected had been instrumental in the shaping of modern Britain. Britain would have been an utterly different place, and a poorer place, without that scattering of African peoples which underpinned the whole process. But who among the British (even in 1838 when they were flooded with images of slavery and freedom) could fully recognize that indebtedness? The British had brought into being enormous black communities in the Americas, but they were separated from them by the vastness of the Atlantic.

There is one calculation about slavery we need not make. Whatever historical doubts remain about the levels of profit to Britain, and who benefited from the Atlantic slave system, there can be no doubt who were the losers – the peoples of the African diaspora.

But what was it all *for*? What was the aim of this remarkable transformation of the Atlantic world by so brutal, so protracted, a diaspora of millions of Africans?

Despite the complexity of the Atlantic slave system, its basic purpose was simple enough. It was created and was kept in place by the desire to cultivate tropical and semi-tropical produce, as conveniently and as profitably as possible. This aim was designed and sustained by Europeans and by European settlers in the Americas. Two other constituencies intimately involved – the Indian peoples of the Americas and the peoples of Africa – had no say in the matter. In time, groups of Africans who profited from the slave system on the coast and in the African interior developed their own distinctive attachment to the Atlantic system. Nonetheless, the purpose of Atlantic slavery was to benefit, to profit and to pleasure Europeans and American settlers. What made that aim attainable were the peoples of the African diaspora.

This has been a central theme of this book. I have been keen to stress that the British, though late on the scene, were the key actors in Atlantic slavery at its apogee. There was little doubt in the minds of those most closely involved by, say, the mid-eighteenth century what the Atlantic system was for. It was, in essence, for the benefit of the metropolis. But what would happen if this simple question (what was it for?) provoked a different answer? What if Atlantic slavery's purpose became less clear, less certain, and less clearly answered? In effect, this is what happened in the years after 1787, though of course the question was rarely posed so simply, tending instead to take different, more complex and troubling forms.

By the late eighteenth century there were other ways in which the old purpose of Atlantic slavery could be served. Tropical produce could be had from other regions of the world. Increasingly, those basic crops produced by slaves could be cultivated by non-slave labour. Perhaps the basic principle of the system – that slavery was a profitable way of cultivating staples – was no longer true? At a time when new ideologies of freedom spawned by the Enlightenment, by the American and French Revolutions and by new theorists of economic behaviour, might not free labour, rather than slavery, better serve the old purpose?

In the years between the launching of the abolition campaign (in 1787) and the granting of full black freedom (in 1838), it became clear to more and more people in Britain that the aim of the old slave colonies was no longer self-evident. But the means by which that aim had been achieved, the enslaved labour force, remained in place. Three-quarters of a million people of African descent were, in effect, turned loose in the 1830s, henceforth left to their own devices in the islands. They now had to make their own way as free people, finding work, land, habitation and new economic and social roles in societies which had, up to the moment of emancipation, provided all those things for them. It was a troubled, uneasy transition that took a different course from one colony to another.

The story was different in other parts of the Americas. Some societies clung tenaciously to their slave systems, notably the USA, Cuba and Brazil. There, slavery continued to have a purpose which could be profitably attained on traditional plantations. True, those successful plantations moved on to new crops: coffee and tobacco in Brazil and Cuba, cotton in the USA. In North America after 1800, slavery was revived and utterly transformed by the development of cotton, and the creation of cotton plantations on new frontier lands. North American slaves were moved westwards in an internal slave trade which, though lacking the oceanic horrors of the Atlantic crossing, nonetheless had its own personal and communal miseries for its victims. Here it was clear enough what slavery was for, and slavery continued to reward its owners and backers by delivering produce at a commercially attractive price to consumers on both sides of the Atlantic. However, even though a rationale for slavery survived, it was, from about 1800, under mounting pressure and attack from a new army: abolitionists who (initially inspired by Britain) resolved to end slavery world-wide. Having perfected and benefited from slavery, the British henceforth embarked on a single-minded campaign to ensure that slavery would be ended everywhere.

When the British brought their slave empire to an end, finally (and with loud and self-proclaimed pronouncements of British virtue), they effectively turned their backs on a distinct historical episode which had characterized their history for more than two centuries. Thereafter they opted for other forms of colonial and commercial activities, in an increasingly industrial and urban society, and sought commodities and markets wherever they were available. But they eschewed the old attachment to slavery as the best means of organizing labour for their broad economic interests. More than that, they determined that other nations should *also* reject slavery. Despite these efforts slavery thrived in a number of societies, especially in the USA until the Civil War, and in Brazil and Cuba until the 1880s.

The decision to free its slaves in the 1830s provided Britain with a perfect opportunity to flaunt its virtue and to urge others to follow its lead. Other nations were less impressed. The French, the Americans (in the South at least), Cubans and Brazilians thought slavery continued to make good sense. They saw little reason to follow the promptings of people who, as they all knew, had been the world's leading slave-traders in the eighteenth century. Nonetheless British emancipation had the result of transmuting the British into the most powerful anti-slavery power in the nineteenth century. But the consequences of what they had *already* done – the development of their own slave societies – were profound and were to be felt, however indirectly, down to the present day.

The most obvious legacy of the British involvement in the African diaspora was the existence of a black population scattered across the Americas. Some three-quarters of a million people of African descent now lived as free people across the West Indies. The slave population of North America had been placed there primarily by the British. The development of the independent USA and the distinctive trajectory of slave history in the USA after 1776 has generally obscured the central fact that it was the *British* who had been largely responsible for transporting the slave population into the northern colonies. The 'problem' of slavery in American life had been created in large part by the

British. Both in North America and the British West Indies, local black populations were the descendants of African slaves imported, initially, to serve British interests. It is easy to overlook this fact when we consider slavery as a *North* American issue after 1776. Similarly, the simple passage of time tended to draw a veil over the British historical involvement in shaping the peoples of the West Indies. It was almost as if the British were keen to forget their historical involvement in the Caribbean. They certainly lost interest in the region after slavery. Of course, Britain maintained its colonial grip over its West Indian possessions until the coming of independence in the 1960s, and it continued to have a direct interest in local economic and social affairs. In the immediate wake of 1838, however, the islands – so recently the jewel of the British Empire – lost their attraction. The traditional commodities were now produced more cheaply elsewhere, and not until new commercial opportunities arose (oil, bauxite, new fruits, tourism) did the islands prompt real interest and renewed commitment among their former colonial masters. In slavery, the West Indies had been a prize worth fighting for. In freedom, they drifted into economic marginality; their people were viewed from London as a persistent problem offering no obvious benefit to the mother country. But what of the ex-slaves?

Without land or work, for many freedom seemed a mixed blessing. On the bigger islands, blacks quit the plantations. On smaller islands where the alternatives were fewer, landlords could maintain some kind of control. Planters, still a force, however diminished, demanded labour to fill the void created by the departing ex-slaves. There followed a new form of indentured labour, devised and orchestrated by the British again, in which boatloads of labourers from India were shipped to the islands (and to other areas of imperial economic interest in Africa and the Pacific). It was a scheme which survived until 1919, and was responsible for transporting some 450,000 Indians into the Caribbean. It looked uncomfortably like slavery itself. In fact, the system had come full circle, for the indentured Indian labour schemes of the nineteenth century were more akin to the indentured labour schemes of the seventeenth century, which had seen the shipping of Irish and Scots workers to the colonies in the Chesapeake and the Caribbean. This new scheme was not slavery, of course, but once again the British turned to massive movements of peoples to advance their commercial and imperial schemes. This is not to claim that indentured labour – whether seventeenth-century Irish or nineteenth-century Indian – was the same as African slavery. They were clearly sharply different. But behind it lay a metropolitan mentality which was extravagant with the lives of others.

The British had become the world's leading slave-trader for their own economic advancement. In the process a complex formula of social attitudes had evolved to deal with the consignment of humanity to the level of property and commodity. The enslavement of Africans and their descendants was so out of kilter with contemporary domestic values, especially by the mid-eighteenth century, that slavery required more than its own conventions or economic custom to maintain itself. The law, for example, was crucial. The slave system was intimately shaped by the law, both in the metropolis and in the colonies. Moreover, that law was not simply a process of rubber-stamping what was already in place. Legislators, statesmen and judges played a role in shaping particular aspects of British slave systems. Even then there was much more at work in the development of British slavery than the interplay of legal processes and national economic self-interests. Slavery generated a complexity of *attitudes* towards black humanity which were, again, important to the way the system worked. The slave had been reduced to the level of a thing, an item of trade bartered, sold, bequeathed and inherited, like any other object. It was clear enough, however, that the African was *not* a thing. From the first there was a tension in Atlantic slavery between the slave's chattel status and his or her self-evident humanity. One critical element deflecting that humanity – a distorting prism through which successive generations came to see black humanity – was the racism of the Atlantic system.

The European development of Atlantic slavery had created new societies in the Caribbean and in North and South America. They were new, not simply in the sense that they were created from scratch, in newly settled lands which had been cleared, by and large, of their indigenous inhabitants. They were new in the sense that they were *unique*, utterly different from anything that had gone before. No other societies had been shaped from such massive oceanic importations of enslaved peoples, to cultivate commodities not for local consumption, but for distant (European) markets. Nor had any other society (in the Atlantic world at least) been so stratified by race. Indeed, new concepts of race – and of racial categories and hierarchies – were developed to cope with and justify the slave societies of the Americas.

To use the concept of racism poses a number of serious problems, but it is hard to see which other term will suffice. Here was a system which hinged on the understanding (shared, as time passed, by all the major European slave-trading powers) that the African slave was not merely a slave, but that his or her slavery was determined by colour, by blackness. The development of the tropical plantations, and the squeezing out of white and Indian labour from key areas of tropical production ensured that slaves, and only slaves, were thought suitable and appropriate for that work. From one slave society to another it was the slave's blackness which became a defining characteristic. Slaves were black; only blacks could be slaves. To be black was to be enslaved (at least in the Americas). Free blacks had to prove their freedom in the teeth of the commonly held assumption to the contrary.

Behind such assumptions there lay hugely complex forces of intellectual change and cultural transformation. Nonetheless the problem was reduced to a simple formula. Europeans and European settlers in the Americas needed to view black humanity as natural slaves, consigned to an inferior rank by virtue of their distinguishing colour. When slavery ended, such attitudes did not simply disappear on the stroke of emancipation. How could it be otherwise? Slavery was ended. But the people who had formed the slave communities were still there. So too were many of the attitudes that had ensured they remained locked in place – the natural, unchallenged labour force at the base of all slave societies.

The history of racism has been a fiercely contested area of historical debate, and this book does not try to suggest that what came *after* slavery in the English-speaking world – the racism of the nineteenth and twentieth centuries – was the same as the racism of Atlantic slavery. But one persistent survival of that slave empire was the intrusion into western life of attitudes about black humanity which influenced the emergence of modern forms of racism. The development of scientific racism, and the contribution of early anthropology to that mode of thought, served to create more complex patterns of racial thinking. But there remained a sub-stratum of thought, inherited from the years of slavery, which remained resolutely attached to the idea of black humanity as deeply and unchangeably inferior.

The black populations of the Americas had been created by the massive, enforced oceanic movements of people we know as the slave trade. Travel (and especially the *nature* of that travel) within Africa and more especially on the slave ships, became a defining feature of slave life everywhere throughout the Americas. The Atlantic crossing has, to this day, continued to haunt the public memory in black society in the Americas and, more recently, in Europe. After emancipation, the black population became a defining part of the Americas. It also continued to move, to migrate, within the Americas and even further afield. Peoples of African descent migrated in large numbers, in pursuit of new economic and social opportunities wherever they might present themselves, especially in the second half of the twentieth century. The free populations of the Caribbean proved themselves remarkably mobile. Because the islands often afforded few opportunities for personal improvement, migration gave growing numbers of West Indians an alternative. Caribbean people moved between the islands, from Jamaica to the new plantations in Cuba, for example, or to Central America (most notably to Panama for the construction of the Panama Canal).

It was World War II and its aftermath which saw the most dramatic changes in West Indian migrations. The experience of tens of thousands of West Indian servicemen in Britain and the labour demands of the post-war British economy laid the foundations for large-scale post-war migrations between the Caribbean and Britain. Those population movements at once transformed West Indian life and permanently changed the human face of Britain itself. Within the space of little more than a generation, people whose ancestors had been African slaves came to form a substantial minority of Britain's population. Black Britons have had a complex and often troubled relationship with British society, but it is surely important to know that modern black Britons are in a direct line of descent from a community with old and well-established roots in Britain. Moreover, it is no less important to grasp that Britain needed and greatly benefited from black labour, first in the Americas and then, post-1945, in Britain itself. This, the latest episode in the diaspora of African peoples, was no mere accident or a freak of casual and haphazard circumstance. It was shaped and driven forward in both the eighteenth and twentieth centuries by the economic interests of Britain.

The economic impact of this outflow of peoples on the islands was enormous, even after severe restrictions were placed on further West Indian immigration by Britain and other host countries. Remittances home, for example, became a major economic factor in island life. So too have been the return migrations of West Indians, keen to re-locate in their island home after a lifetime's labour in North America or Britain. Substantial numbers of West Indians also migrated to the USA and to Canada, so that the Caribbean presence in a string of major cities – New York, Toronto, London, Manchester, Bristol and elsewhere – has transformed local life.

These West Indian migrations, back and forth across the Atlantic, are part of a much broader, global movement of peoples in the second half of the twentieth century. Most striking has been the movement of people from countries which were once colonial or imperial settlements inwards to the old imperial metropolis. Migrants have moved to Britain from India and Pakistan, from Africa, and from the West Indies. A similar pattern has unfolded in France and the Netherlands.

The domestic populations of the old European imperial powers have been utterly transformed, since 1945, by settlements of peoples from their former colonies. In the wake of these settlements, social life throughout western Europe, and thence around the world, has been re-shaped. Wherever we look, at food, entertainment, at sports, literature and artistic activity, the impact of post-colonial settlements within Europe has been profound and far-reaching. These transformations in Europe's population have served to raise new questions about the way the histories of the former colonial powers are written. The old unchallenged narratives of national history are hard now to sustain in the face of the transformed populations of Europe. To take a simple example, histories of Britain which pay little or no regard to Britain's dealings with the wider world (say, with Atlantic slavery) are of limited value in modern Britain. Just as the historiography of the USA since 1945 has been forced to come to terms with the complexities of America's slave past, Britain too has needed to revise its sense of its own past and of its dealings with its former subject people. This is one factor behind the current historical attention being paid to the question of British identity, expressed most influentially by Linda Colley,[11] but deriving from a varied set of social and intellectual influences.

This latest, post-1945 aspect of the black diaspora has not simply added a new chapter to the broader story, but has brought in its train a re-evaluation of earlier histories. The history of Britain since the seventeenth century needs to incorporate the British involvement with Atlantic slavery (and with other various global entanglements), not as aspects of imperial or colonial history, but as the warp and the weft of British history itself. This book has tried to describe how the British became key players in the making of the Black Atlantic. In its turn, the Black Atlantic helped to transform Britain. The diaspora, the scattering of African peoples for British advancement, is now evident in Britain itself. It is as if, since 1945, the story of the diaspora has come full circle.

Notes

1 John Brewer, *Sinews of Power* (London, 1989).

2 See James Walvin, 'Freedom and slavery and the shaping of Victorian Britain', in Paul E. Lovejoy and Nicholas Rogers (eds), *Unfree Labour in the Development of the Atlantic World* (London, 1994).

3 C. L. R. James, *Black Jacobins* (London, 1980 edn); Eric Williams, *Capitalism and Slavery* (London, 1944 first edition); B. L. Solow and S. L. Engerman, *British Capitalism and Caribbean Slavery* (Cambridge, 1987).

4 Robin Blackburn, *The Making of New World Slavery: From the Baroque to the Modern, 1492–1800* (London, 1997), pp. 19–27.

5 *Ibid.*, pp. 536–7.

6 *Ibid.*, p. 541.

7 *Ibid.*, p. 548.

8 David Hancock, *Citizens of the World* (Cambridge, 1995).

9 Robin Blackburn, *Making*, pp. 555–6.

10 See Chapter 8 above.

11 Linda Colley, *Britons: Forging the Nation, 1707–1837* (London, 1992).

GUIDE TO FURTHER READING

For a pioneering discussion of the concept of 'The Black Atlantic', see Paul Gilroy, *The Black Atlantic: Modernity and Double Consciousness* (London, 1993). Though I have been influenced by Gilroy's work, my concerns are very different and take a more historical trajectory. There is an expanding literature about the idea of the 'African Diaspora'. The modern pioneering historian of the concept was George Shepperson; see his 'Introduction' to Martin L. Kitson and Robert I. Rotberg (eds), *The African Diaspora: Interpretative Essays* (Cambridge, MA, 1976). For a recent discussion see Stuart B. Schwartz, 'Expansion, diaspora and encounter in early modern South America', *Itinerario*, 19 (2), 1995.

The historiography of slavery continues to expand at an amazing rate. Readers who wish to keep abreast of current work in this field should consult the bibliography, compiled by Joseph Miller and published annually, in the journal *Slavery and Abolition*. The most recent appeared in Vol. 19, Number 3, December 1998, pp. 169–236 (Frank Cass, London).

Among recently published books, the following are outstanding. For a comprehensive account of slavery in its wider setting, see Robin Blackburn, *The Making of New World Slavery: From the Baroque to the Modern, 1492–1800* (London, 1997). The eighteenth-century world of Atlantic trade and commerce is brilliantly described in David Hancock, *Citizens of the World: London Merchants and the Integration of the British Atlantic Community, 1735–1785* (Cambridge, 1995). For the changing historical traditions of West Indian scholarship, see B. W. Higman, *Writing West Indian Histories* (London, 1999). The same author's *Montpelier, Jamaica: A Plantation Community in Slavery and Freedom, 1739–1912* (Kingston, Jamaica, 1998) provides a detailed case study of many of the issues dealt with here in a more general fashion. The most important book for many years on slavery in British North America is by Philip D. Morgan, *Slave Counterpoint: Black Culture in the Eighteenth Century Chesapeake and Low Country* (Chapel Hill, NC, 1998). The early history of slavery in North America is described in Ira Berlin, *Many Thousands Gone: The First Two Centuries of Slavery in North America* (Cambridge, MA, 1998). A recent study of slave religion in the English-speaking colonies is by Sylvia R. Frey and Betty Wood, *Come Shouting to Zion* (Chapel Hill, NC, 1998). See also Michael Gomez, *Exchanging Our Country Marks: The Transformation of African Identities in the Colonial and Antebellum South* (Chapel Hill, NC, 1998).

Though my book has been concerned primarily with the English-speaking world, it is impossible to ignore the wider story of European involvement with Atlantic slavery. The Brazilian story is best approached through Stuart Schwartz, *Sugar Plantations in the Formation of Brazilian Society, Bahia, 1550–1835* (Cambridge, 1985). Readers interested in the Dutch story should begin with Jonathan Israel's massive study, *The Dutch Republic: Its Rise, Greatness and Fall, 1477–1806* (Oxford, 1995). Of the many books offering general accounts of the history of slavery, three of the most recent are: Peter Kolchin, *American Slavery* (London, 1995); James Walvin, *Black Ivory: A History of British Slavery* (London, 1992); and Robert William Fogel, *Without Consent of Contract: The Rise and Fall of American Slavery* (New York, 1989). Hugh Thomas, *The Slave Trade* (London, 1997), is especially good on the Iberian involvement with slavery.

Essays on specific aspects of the history of the slave trade and slavery can be found in three recent encyclopedias: *Macmillan Encyclopedia of World Slavery*, 2 vols, Paul Finkelman and Joseph C. Miller (eds) (New York, 1998); *A Historical Guide to World Slavery*, Seymour Drescher and Stanley L. Engerman (eds) (Oxford, 1998) and *The Historical Encyclopedia of World Slavery*, 2 vols, Julius P. Rodriuez (ed.) (Oxford, 1997). For those interested in Africa, good starting-points are John Illife, *Africans: The History of a Continent* (Cambridge, 1995), and John Thornton, *Africa and Africans in the Making of the Atlantic World, 1400–1680* (Cambridge, 1992).

Readers keen to locate the history of British slavery in its imperial setting should consult the excellent essays in *The Oxford History of the British Empire*, vol. 1, *Origins*, Nicholas Canny (ed.), and vol. 2, *The Eighteenth Century*, P. J. Marshall (ed.) (Oxford, 1998). The decline of slavery is admirably described in Robin Blackburn, *The Overthrow of Colonial Slavery, 1776–1848* (London, 1988).

INDEX